HARVARD HISTORICAL STUDIES

PUBLISHED UNDER THE DIRECTION
OF THE DEPARTMENT OF HISTORY

FROM THE INCOME OF
THE PAUL REVERE FROTHINGHAM BEQUEST

VOLUME LXIV

ROBE AND SWORD

THE REGROUPING OF THE FRENCH ARISTOCRACY AFTER LOUIS XIV

by
Franklin L. Ford
HARVARD UNIVERSITY

HARVARD UNIVERSITY PRESS
Cambridge, Massachusetts
1962

Second Printing

Distributed in Great Britain by
OXFORD UNIVERSITY PRESS
LONDON

LIBRARY OF CONGRESS CATALOG CARD NUMBER 52-12261
PRINTED IN THE UNITED STATES OF AMERICA

To

my Mother and Father

Preface

THERE IS A PASSAGE in La Bruyère which expresses as concisely as any I know the familiar historical impression of the French nobility under Louis XIV: "A nobleman, if he lives at home in his province, lives free but without substance; if he lives at court, he is taken care of, but enslaved."[1] There, in miniature, is the picture of a class of subjects reduced to indigence by economic developments beyond their powers of adaptation or broken to sycophancy by the cardinal and the king who had dominated the Grand Siècle.

But consider the same class a century later, in the 1780's. It had ruined Maupeou and Turgot, reconquered every bishopric in the realm,[2] imposed the rule of four quarterings of nobility for high army appointments, and forced the monarchy into a cowed, ultimately fatal solicitude for privileged interests. To Arthur Young, it is true, even this later nobility seemed ineffectual; and theorists such as Pareto and Sorel have sneered at the humanitarian anemia which had sapped its capacity for violence in its own defense.[3] Nevertheless, the French aristocracy, if it did not have the strength to suppress revolution, had at least recovered enough strength to make revolution inevitable.

The present study thus originated with the posing of a problem, that of the "dynamics of obstruction." It is clearly not enough to say that a revolutionary situation takes shape when the Left produces the power and determination to do something, while the Right refuses to do anything. The difference between an explosive volcano and a harmlessly bubbling crater lies partly in the hardening of the

[1] *Les caractères* (ed. A. Regnier, in *Les grands écrivains de la France*, Paris, 1865-1878), I, 326.

[2] Albert Mathiez, *La Révolution française* (Paris, 1922), I, 4.

[3] Arthur Young, *Travels in France during the Years 1787, 1788 and 1789* (ed. Matilda Betham-Edwards, London, 1889), 152; Vilfredo Pareto, *The Mind and Society* (tr. Arthur Livingston, New York, 1935), IV, 1516 ff.; Georges Sorel, *Réflexions sur la violence* (7th ed., Paris, 1930), 95 ff. and *passim.*

former's crust. Had the French aristocracy before 1789 been a ruling group too weak to block even gradual reform, there would have been no such revolution as in fact occurred. But we are still faced with the discrepancy between a noble class groveling before Louis XIV and the same class intimidating Louis XVI. Just what were the mechanics of the oft-cited "feudal reaction" of the eighteenth century, what was its chronological staging, and in what sense can it be said to have been feudal?

The answers to questions such as these are not to be found in even the closest study of the immediate background of the Revolution. They belong to the history of the *ancien régime* itself, viewed not as a mere prelude but as a period having its own internal suspense. Whoever immerses himself in the public records, the family papers, the memoirs and correspondence of the last hundred years of the old monarchy cannot fail to share some of that suspense, even as he finds his initial curiosity increasingly focussed on what he begins to discern as the critical issues and periods of years.

In examining the general resurgence of the French nobility, I have been steadily forced toward primary concentration on the magistracy of the sovereign courts, the high *noblesse de robe*, as the crucial element. Similarly, it soon became clear that the decisive stage in the aristocratic regrouping lay in the period between 1715 and the middle of the eighteenth century, and that during subsequent decades privileged groups tended rather to exploit their reestablished power than to form new alignments. For reasons which will be discussed in the opening chapter, 1715 represents an obvious starting point. The choice of a terminal date is admittedly more difficult. There is, however, some value in having a specific year to place beside that of Louis XIV's death as a boundary marker for the study as a whole; and 1748, which saw the end of the War of the Austrian Succession and the appearance of Montesquieu's *Spirit of the Laws*, seems to me the strongest candidate. After Aix-la-Chapelle the nobility, especially the nobility of the robe, for the first time revealed the full extent of its obstructive political power, based on less apparent developments of the preceding decades. Simultaneously the former Bordeaux *président à mortier* published the greatest single statement of the aristocratic position, as it had grown out of social fusion and intellectual cross-insemination between parlementary and feudal groups. Thereafter, at both the political and intellectual levels, historical interest inevitably shifts to other forces—the monarchy and the Third Estate—which still offered alternative possibilities of behavior and expression.

I am not inclined to underestimate the appearance of presumption which some may see in this undertaking. What, the critic may ask, can one add to the best of the institutional studies of specific parlements, Egret's for Dauphiné, for example, or Le Moy's for Brittany?[4] What chance of supplementing Mousnier and Göhring on the sale of offices,[5] Leclercq on the narrative of the Regency,[6] or Carré on the nobility's public standing?[7] Further than that, how can a non-French student hope to avoid the pitfalls which await what one formidable authority has called "jugements d'étrangers incapables de recourir à ces notations subtiles, à ces analyses délicates que réclame le caractère de la nation française?"[8]

To treat the last point first, there is so far as I can see no technique which will guarantee success in attaining to those "delicate analyses." All that a twentieth-century American can do is to endeavor honestly to understand men of a past age in a country not his own. Whether or not he succeeds only his readers, ultimately his French readers, can say; but at least he will then not have failed through condescending self-assurance.

The relationship between the present study and the monographs to which it owes so much may best be characterized as non-competition. I have employed some of the same materials as the historians mentioned above, but in different proportions, because with a different aim. Even though one makes use of original sources to a considerable extent, he cannot, in what remains essentially a synthesis, hope to match the detailed coverage supplied by any given work

[4] Jean Egret, *Le Parlement de Dauphiné et les affaires publiques* (Grenoble-Paris, 1942) 2 vols.; A. Le Moy, *Le Parlement de Bretagne et le pouvoir royal au XVIIIe siècle* (Angers 1909).

[5] Roland Mousnier, *La vénalité des offices sous Henri IV et Louis XIII* (Rouen, 1945); Martin Göhring, *Die Ämterkäuflichkeit im Ancien Régime* (Berlin, 1938).

[6] Dom H. Leclercq, *Histoire de la Régence* (Paris, 1921-1922), 3 vols.

[7] Henri Carré, *La noblesse de France et l'opinion publique au XVIIIe siècle* (Paris, 1920).

[8] Leclercq, *Histoire de la Régence*, I, lxv.

devoted entirely to one institution, one individual or one locality. I have benefited greatly from the opportunity to work in the archives and manuscript collections in libraries at Paris, Toulouse, Bordeaux, Dijon, Grenoble and Aix-en-Provence; but I should not for a moment pretend to have superseded any of the best regional or institutional studies. What I do believe is that there is something to be gained from a more general look at the France of Louis XV as a whole, in all its rich variations. I also believe that there is a special value in the effort to get at the interaction of political events, social and economic conditions, and ideas, all placed in their institutional framework and examined within the limits of a manageable historical situation. If one begins with these convictions, he can do full honor to the contributions of Mousnier, Leclercq, Roupnel, Carré, and countless other mature researchers without having to feel that any of them has blocked his path.

The research in France which constituted the *sine qua non* of my investigations I owe to a Sheldon Traveling Fellowship from Harvard University and to a Research Training Fellowship from the Social Science Research Council. It is unfortunately not possible to specify by name all those individuals who have helped me at one stage or another of the project; but I am sincerely grateful to all of them, not least to the dozens of French archivists and *bibliothécaires* who extended cordial and intelligent service to an importunate foreigner—and more than once left him convinced that he should be taking care of the documents and they, writing the book. Among the senior scholars to whom I am indebted I would mention in particular Professor Crane Brinton of Harvard, Professor Georges Lefebvre of Paris, and Professor Edmond Esmonin of Grenoble, the latter two retired. Professors Brinton and Esmonin contributed generously of their time in reading and criticizing the work; to both is due credit for numerous corrections, to neither is due blame for the shortcomings which remain. No list of acknowledgments should omit my wife, who labored over sections of the manuscript and cheerfully shared the headaches of successive revisions.

F. L. F.

Bennington, Vermont
March 1952

Contents

BOOK ONE: 1715

Chapter One
The Legacy of the Great Reign 3

Chapter Two
The Structure of the Noblesse 22

Chapter Three
The Sovereign Courts 35

Chapter Four
The Magistrate as Nobleman 59

BOOK TWO: THE SOURCES OF HIGH ROBE POWER

Chapter Five
The Right to Remonstrate 79

Chapter Six
The Ownership of Office 105

Chapter Seven
The Robe Family 124

Chapter Eight
The Robe Fortune 147

BOOK THREE: LEADERSHIP WITHIN THE NOBILITY

Chapter Nine
The Claims of the Peerage 173

Chapter Ten
The Defense of Privilege 188

Chapter Eleven
Social Aspects of Fusion 202

Chapter Twelve
The Restatement of the *Thèse Nobiliaire* 222

Conclusion 246

An Essay on Bibliography 253

Index 273

Illustrations

A Lit de Justice
Facing page 128

A Pro-Parlementary Print of the 1730's
Facing page 129

A Robe Mansion and A Robe Chateau
Facing page 144

The Magistrate as Social Lion
Facing page 145

The illustrations facing pages 128, 129, and 145 are reproduced by courtesy of the Bibliothèque Nationale, Cabinet des Estampes, Paris.

BOOK ONE

1715

Note on References

In reproducing quotations from seventeenth- and eighteenth-century documents, I have retained the orthographic peculiarities which appear in the original texts, including in many cases the partial or total absence of modern French diacritical markings. Translations are my own, unless otherwise specified. For convenience and brevity, I have employed the following abbreviations in footnotes:

A.N.	Archives Nationales.
B.N.	Bibliothèque Nationale.
A.D.	Archives Départementales de . . .
Bib.	Bibliothèque Publique (or Municipale) de . . .
Ms(s). fr.	Manuscrit(s) français at B.N.
Ms(s) fr. nouv. acq.	Manuscrit(s) français, nouvelles acquisitions at B.N.

Chapter One

The Legacy of the Great Reign

1

On the morning of Sunday, September 1, 1715, in a fetid room at Versailles, the longest reign in modern history came to an end. Within the hour, couriers were pounding over the dusty road to Paris, while behind them in the great palace the halls and reception rooms began to fill with courtiers, brought scurrying from their cramped but precious sleeping quarters by the whispered words of serving men. From Versailles to the capital and thence out across the provinces and the rest of Europe, even to the scattered colonies across the seas, the news spread as swiftly as hoof and sail could carry it. The king was dead.

Difficult as it is today to appreciate the full significance of Louis XIV's passing, it was no simpler to grasp for men still living when he died. Not that it was a surprise. A week earlier, surrendering to the relentless gangrene in his leg, he had received extreme unction; and in any event, his advanced age had made the prospect a matter of constant speculation for several years past. Nor was the reaction one of intense grief, in spite of lavish displays in all the churches. From the noble duke who somewhat prematurely hailed the end of the "reign of the vile bourgeoisie"[1] to the mob which jeered the royal catafalque on its journey through the Faubourg Saint-Denis,[2] the strongest immediate reaction was a surge of relief. Yet a sense of

[1] Louis de Rouvroy, Duc de Saint-Simon, *Mémoires* (ed. A. de Boislisle, Paris, 1879-1928), XXVII, 64.

[2] Most of the memoirs of the period refer to this public demonstration of resentment, which the government had hoped to avoid by not permitting the cortège to pass through Paris itself. See especially Mathieu Marais, *Journal et mémoires* (ed. Lescure, Paris, 1863-1868), I, 192; and Duclos, *Mémoires* (ed. F. Barrière, Paris, 1881), 129-130.

momentary bewilderment also shows through every account of that day and those immediately following. Few Frenchmen then living had ever known another monarch. For almost three-quarters of a century, from the frightened childhood in the cold halls of Saint-Germain, through political reorganization and religious persecution, through great military victories to greater defeats, he had been the living personification of France. Even the totalitarian states of the twentieth century provide no adequate standard for measuring the degree to which Louis XIV's personality had dominated the life of his era. Yet we recognize that domination the moment we touch upon any aspect of the Great Reign; for then we find the figure of the king rising before us—his lust for *gloire*, his conversion from profligacy to bigotry, his conception of social order, his ministers, his generals. Even in the sphere of literature and art, through the active and intelligent interest which was his most attractive quality, he had presided over one of the greatest outbursts of national genius in the history of civilization.

It would, no doubt, be a mistake to stand too long beside the royalists, gazing up at the Sun King's statue, whether it be the warrior in the Place des Victoires or the supreme courtier in rippling white marble at Versailles. Both are idealized and both are apt to result in optical illusions. The king's existence, important as it was, obviously did not give to his long reign the quality of static unity. At the very least, it is essential to recognize the traditional subdivision which treats the 1680's as its watershed. Whether the change be measured by the disappearance of Colbert and Louvois, by the disintegration of old assumptions, described by Paul Hazard in his *Crise de la conscience européenne*,[3] or by the rapid deterioration of France's international position, the end of the seventeenth century unquestionably had already brought substantial departures from what had gone before. In just the last two years of Louis XIV's life, France had emerged from a nearly fatal conflict, had entered a period of religious unrest over Clement XI's attack on the Jansenist-Gallicans, and now found itself immersed in a desperate financial crisis. Regardless of who was on the throne in the second decade of the eighteenth century, it would have been a period of changes. In

[3] (Paris, 1934-1935), 3 vols. including one of notes.

the judgment of Philippe Sagnac, who goes to the opposite pole from the monarchist enthusiasts, "the death of Louis XIV brought with it nothing completely new: the mores of the eighteenth century had already appeared and the Regency had begun before there was a Regent."[4]

Yet it is worth noting that this conclusion is not wholly borne out even by the structure of its author's own work; for Sagnac, though discussing social rather than dynastic history, nevertheless retains 1715 as the most suitable dividing line between his two volumes. There is, of course, no justification for making the change of rulers a sudden horizontal line cutting across all the vertical strands representing gradual changes. At the same time, the end of a long, eventful and singularly personalized reign played its own part in those changes by permitting them to be expressed with an articulateness which they had hitherto lacked. To the observer's view, as Michelet wrote in one of his more measured passages, there is now revealed "a whole world arranged and masked for fifty years."[5]

The merit of Michelet's formulation lies in conveying some sense of Louis' hold on the nation he had ruled. It recalls the matchless showmanship with which this strange, limited, but infinitely painstaking and attentive individual had played his part at the apex of both the governmental and the social hierarchies, never forgetting his own place or that of any of his subjects, seeking to regulate every human relationship from the right of a duchess to remain seated in the presence of a prince of the blood down to religious faith and paternal authority in a peasant home. No one who has turned the pages of Saint-Simon will forget his portrait of the king: "Never a man so naturally polite, nor so measured in his politeness, nor so polite by degrees: never a man who distinguished better [the gradations of] age, merit, rank . . . . These various degrees were indicated meticulously in his manner of greeting and of receiving obeisances."[6]

The arch of Ludovican society had first been reared with the approval of a population which had turned from the anarchy of the Fronde to seek order as an absolute good. Its principle of construc-

[4] *La formation de la société française moderne* (Paris, 1945-1946), II, 1.

[5] *Histoire de France* (Paris, 1835-1867), XV, v.

[6] *Mémoires*, XXVIII, 145-146.

tion had been the king's determination to separate actual power from apparent grandeur in the population beneath him. Its aesthetic appeal lay in a vision of unity, of static symmetry, with every rank and every individual assigned a fixed place in relation to the crown. By 1715 the arch, at no time as perfect as its principle, was obviously crumbling in a number of places; but it had survived as an official concept as long as its original keystone had remained in place.

Now the keystone was gone. Therein lies the real significance of the deathbed at Versailles. Changes in actual power relationships, many of them of some years' standing, were translated into overt demands for recognition with an attendant clamor and confusion which contemporaries felt and which their accounts still transmit to the modern reader. When such demands had been voiced under Louis XIV, they had appeared piecemeal, with relative timidity, in a wholly different atmosphere; for the old king, by insisting at every point on the stability of each group's relationship to himself, had succeeded to a remarkable extent in maintaining the stability of its relationship to all the others. His skill, whether artful or instinctive, in containing the thrust of a variety of forces by keeping them convergent on a center he controlled, was a characteristic of his reign which the Duc d'Orléans, acting for the five-year-old Louis XV and lacking the public sanction with which his predecessor had emerged from the Fronde, could not hope to duplicate. For the great lords, for the nobility in general, for the parlements, for the Gallican enemies of the late ruler's Jesuit advisers, for the increasingly powerful business class, even for the peasantry, hopeful of a lightened tax load and fewer troops swarming over the countryside, long-suppressed ambitions were at last able to emerge onto the surface of public life.

2

Since my study is primarily concerned with subsequent developments affecting the nobility, I must limit this backward look at the Great Reign to two of its features which were destined to have major importance for the history of the Second Estate. The first of these was a general principle to which I have already referred in passing: the policy of seeking to minimize the extent to which any subject could combine in his own person high degrees of both external grandeur and actual power, or, stated in other terms, the effort to exclude individuals enjoying some degree of independent, especially hereditary prestige from the sort of governmental functions which might have made that prestige dangerous to the crown. This was no innovation in royal policy, any more than noble opposition to it was a new development. The Carolingians' *missi*, the medieval Capetians' *baillis* and *sénéchaux*, the intendants of the sixteenth century and even more under Richelieu, all had represented stages in the crown's long effort to retain control over its officialdom by superimposing new administrative layers over previous agents who had succeeded in converting into personal property their respective segments of delegated sovereignty.

In the case of Louis XIV, whose reign had begun amid the chaos of a civil war in which the great families had renewed their bid for power, the determination to exclude them had been a conscious rule of government. The passage from his instructions to the Dauphin which deals with his choice of Colbert, Le Tellier and Lionne is enlightening:

> To make completely clear to you the course of my thinking, I believed that it was not in my interest to seek men of more eminent station because . . . it was important that the public should know, from the rank of those whom I chose to serve me, that I had no intention of sharing my power with them. [It was also important] that they themselves, conscious of what they were, should conceive no higher aspirations than those which I chose to permit.[7]

The conception of two separate hierarchies, one of grandeur, the other of power, has been invoked repeatedly since its emergence in the complaints of noblemen under the *ancien régime*.[8] It is a useful picture; for, at least down to 1715, such a distinction did exist to the full extent of the crown's ability to enforce it. Needless to say, the

[7] *Mémoires de Louis XIV* (ed. Charles Dreyss, Paris, 1860), II, 391. This portion of the memoirs was apparently written by the Dauphin's tutor, Périgny, under the supervision of the king himself.

[8] Most recently by Henri Brocher, *Le rang et l'étiquette sous l'ancien régime* (Paris, 1934), 55 ff.

distinction between the two hierarchies never, even in Louis XIV's high period, achieved mathematical precision. It was inconceivable, given the power of personal ambition and family pride, that it should. Quite aside from the fact that certain members of the old nobility entered the power hierarchy from time to time by displaying personal, especially military, qualifications, the counter-pressure from newly risen families of officials worked to bridge the gap between functions and honors. Before the end of the seventeenth century, the sons of Colbert enjoyed the titles of Marquis de Torcy and Marquis de Seignelay; his brothers were Marquis de Croissy and Comte de Maulevrier; and a grandson was destined to be Duc d'Estouteville. The son of Le Tellier was a marquis, Louvois, as were all his grandsons. Generations of Phélypeaux are hidden beneath a series of titled names: Pontchartrain, La Vrillière, Maurepas. But these, after all, were only the greatest, most favored ministerial families. Public functions below the first rank, while they might confer nobility, scarcely carried great titled prestige. The important point here is that individual exceptions did not seriously alter the prevailing pattern under Louis XIV.

Why should there still have been two hierarchies in 1715? The functioning of government made indispensable an official one. Clear enough. That the crown should seek to keep noblemen with traditions of territorial power out of that structure, nothing more understandable. But what explains the protection and enforcement, even the considerable increase, of ranks, privileges and ceremonial distinctions? If they were no longer a feature of government, why should not the government have sought to minimize their *éclat*?

In the first place, it is important not to forget how tenaciously individuals and families can cling to the vestiges of even long-departed authority, especially when those vestiges still carry certain material advantages. The aristocratic family of the seventeenth century might lament the loss of influence which robbed its honors of their original *raison d'être;* but let the government seek to abolish those honors! Such a government would have had to reckon with resistance at the moment and a continuing fund of resentment, ready to contribute to any more broadly based unrest which might subsequently have taken shape. A Boileau or a La Bruyère might ridicule distinctions unsupported by distinguished virtues;[9] the fact remains that the type of popular resentment necessary to justify a truly anti-aristocratic policy was still decades away.

3

Even if such support had been in prospect, would Louis XIV have sought to level the hierarchy of privilege? The answer, I think, is very definitely that he would not; and here we arrive at the second aspect of his attitude toward the nobility which, with the separation of hierarchies, was to have lasting importance: namely, the fundamental inconsistency of that attitude. Without some recognition of this ambivalence, we should find incomprehensible the posture of privileged groups in 1715.

On one side stood the whole array of royal measures which continued Richelieu's and Mazarin's efforts to limit, to control, even to exploit the nobility. The exclusion from effective offices has already been touched upon. Admission to other positions, lucrative if not influential, could be bought only at the price of adulation. The regime of court favor, under which the king's response, "I never see him," spelled death to any request for a pension or appointment, is one of the most constant features of contemporary accounts. Madame de Sévigné referred to the king in 1685 as a being who was compared to God in such a manner that it was clear that God, not the king, was the copy.[10] And in his curious manual of 1706, the Sieur de

[9] Boileau's "Satire V: Sur la noblesse" begins:

"Sans vertu, pas de vraie noblesse. Qu'est-ce qu'un grand qui fait rougir, par la bassesse de ses actions et de ses moeurs, la longue suite de ses aieux? . . .

Mais je ne puis souffrir qu'un fat, dont la mollesse
N'a rien pour s'appuyer qu'une vaine noblesse,
Se pare insolemment du mérite d'autrui,
Et me vante un honneur qui ne vient pas de lui."

Satires et épitres (ed. Charles Aubertin, Paris, 1886), 45 ff.

Boileau wrote the above in about 1665, and when La Bruyère wrote the following, he undoubtedly had the famous satire in mind: "Si la noblesse est vertu, elle se perd par tout ce qui n'est pas vertueux; et si elle n'est pas vertu, c'est peu de chose." *Les caractères*, II, 169. On this subject see Maurice Lange, *La Bruyère, critique des conditions et des institutions sociales* (Paris, 1909), 240-274.

[10] *Lettres* (ed. Monmerqué, Paris, 1862-1866), VII, 402.

Chevigny sought to improve on Castiglione by offering the following dialogue:

Demande. A quoi sont obligez les personnes qui sont à la Cour?

Réponse. A se conformer à l'esprit & aux manières qui y dominent.

D. Y a-t-il quelque chose de fixe & de reglé à la Cour pour l'esprit & les manières de se mettre & d'agir?

R. Non, tout dépend de la disposition de l'esprit & du coeur du Prince qui règne. S'il se tourne du côté de la dévotion, toute la Cour est dévote, au moins en apparence; s'il s'abandonne aux plaisirs, aux amusemens, toute la Cour embrasse ce parti avec joie, d'autant plus qu'il est conforme au penchant du coeur.

And a little later:

D. Quelles sont les choses les plus nécessaires à un Courtisan?

R. De la patience, de la politesse, point de volonté; tout écouter, ne jamais rien rapporter. Paroître toujours content. Avoir beaucoup d'amis, peu de confidens.[11]

Behind this passive pressure to obey stood the certainty of sufficient force. Richelieu had demonstrated that a rebel lord, if captured by the king's officers, could no longer look forward to being treated as a sovereign enemy worsted in combat but must expect the punishment of a traitor.[12] Even after the Fronde, in itself an affair too widespread and involving too many highly placed conspirators to be susceptible of such harsh counter-measures, there was required only one more application of force, early in Louis XIV's reign, to destroy any revived illusions of aristocratic immunity from the king's writ. After the "Grands Jours" of 1665, no nobleman was inclined to forget those implacable assizes which Louis and Colbert had sent into the remotest highlands of Auvergne to hear public complaints and to jerk the offending barons down from their mountain retreats—often to the headsman's block.

With the Estates General suspended since 1614 and with the remaining provincial estates subordinated to the initiative and the scrutiny of royal commissioners, the seventeenth-century nobility

[11] *La science des personnes de la cour* (Paris, 1706), I, 1-2.

[12] Georges d'Avenel, *La noblesse française sous Richelieu* (Paris, 1901), 13.

was almost completely bereft of any organ of corporate expression. True, one set of nobles, the officers of the parlements and the other sovereign courts, still possessed an organizational form so essential to his government that even Louis XIV could not dispense with it. The importance of that fact can scarcely be exaggerated, and its effects were to be felt almost from the moment the old king died. While he lived, however, even this organized section of the aristocracy was incapable of bringing its group interests to bear on the making of governmental policy. In a later chapter, we shall be concerned with the aftermath of the ordinance of 1667 and the letters patent of 1673 which in combination practically deprived the *noblesse de robe* of all power to interfere in the legislative process.[13] Suffice it to say, at this point, that these measures, by limiting the courts to their strictly judicial functions and by relegating remonstrances to the feeble role of complaints to be submitted only after the new law in question had gone into effect, made sure that here too the Second Estate would be helpless on the political level.

Even in the military sphere, where the position of the *noblesse* had once seemed unassailable, the reign saw the culmination of a process begun with Charles VII's introduction of a paid standing army two-and-a-half centuries earlier. If that culmination was not one of complete exclusion of the nobility, it was partly because the younger sons of the class still provided a valuable reserve pool, especially for the cavalry. The old feudal reliance on the vassal's service, owed to his king as suzerain, had long been a legal fiction when the War of the League of Augsburg saw its virtual abandonment. In the Archives Nationales there exists a parchment which convokes, in the archaic phrases of the *ban et arrière-ban*, the nobles of Champagne and Brie for the spring campaign of 1693. In the margin the unmistakably eighteenth-century hand of a royal archivist has added: "Elle n'a pas eu lieu depuis."[14] By 1697 the institution had fallen into disuse in other provinces as well.[15] Even before this

[13] Isambert, Jourdan, and Decrusy, *Recueil des anciennes lois françaises* (Paris, 1823-1829), XVIII, 103-180, and XIX, 70-73.

[14] A.N., K. 121^{B}, no. 24.

[15] M. Marion, *Dictionnaire des institutions de la France aux XVIIe et XVIIIe siècles* (Paris, 1923), 34. Paul de Rousiers reprints a *ban et arrière-ban* summons sent to Limousin in 1696, the last which he found in preparing his delightful little family history, *Une famille de hobereaux pendant six siècles* (Paris, 1935), 212. There exists in the Bibliothèque

date, the army reforms of Louvois had generalized the system of permitting commutation payments from the nobility, who by thus swelling the war-chest were in effect hiring substitutes. The arrière-ban convocations to be seen in the *Cartons des rois* for Louis XIV's era include articles specifying the commutation rates; and it is worth noting that the royal officials prepared their lists of assessable nobles with special emphasis on heads of families and eldest sons, in other words, those most apt to pay the fees rather than enter a period of military service.[16]

This transformation of a feudal right from a recruiting mechanism into a form of tax was characteristic of the whole economic policy of the government, as will be clearly seen if one turns to what had happened to the traditions of chivalry, in the original sense of the word. The king could ennoble any subject by the issuance of letters patent, the vestige of a once personalized, oral grant of honor and privilege. The sale of such letters to rich commoners prepared to part with the requisite *finances* had been practiced increasingly by the harassed monarchs of the sixteenth century; [17] but no era previous to Louis XIV's had witnessed so thorough an exploitation of all such supplementary sources of royal income.[18] This commerce in nobility yielded the crown financial returns not only at the time of the initial sale, but also whenever recent *anoblis* were confronted with a general revocation of letters of nobility and forced to buy letters of confirmation or related types of dispensations in order to escape its effects. There were nine separate revocations under Louis XIV, now

---

Nationale (Ms. fr. nouv. acq. 21707) a manuscript "Rôle d'arrière-ban," dated 1754; but this appears to have been a short-lived fiscal expedient which has left no trace on the military history of the Seven Years' War. Cf. Louis Tuetey, *Les officiers sous l'ancien régime, nobles et roturiers* (Paris, 1908), 1 ff.

[16] A.N., K.119 contains assorted correspondence and assessment rolls dealing with the convocation of 1675. No. 28[1] is a letter from Louis XIV to the Duc d'Enghien which states that, "ayant considéré la grande dispense à laquelle la convocation du ban et arrière-ban engage ma noblesse," the king will exempt any noble prepared to pay the sum of one hundred livres.

[17] See. J.-R. Bloch, *L'anoblissement en France au temps de François Ier* (Paris, 1934).

[18] The most notable mass editions of *lettres de noblesse moyennant finances* were those of January 1660—two persons in each *généralité*; March 1696—five hundred persons (each to pay six thousand livres); May 1702—two hundred persons; and December 1711—one hundred persons. L. N. R. Chérin, *Abrégé chronologique d'édits, règlements, etc., concernant le fait de noblesse* (Paris, 1788), 133, 213, 255, 305.

covering all letters of a given class (for example, those sold to the municipal officers of the privileged towns), now annulling all those issued for money since an arbitrary date thirty or forty years in the past.[19]

It was this constant display of the government's bad faith and fiscal ingenuity which for a time near the end of the reign made it necessary to coerce prospective buyers into accepting *lettres de noblesse* and has led one writer to remark that the king made noblemen as he made Catholics: with *dragonnades*.[20] This, it should be pointed out, however, was a temporary phenomenon, limited principally to the years of the War of the Spanish Succession, when the revocations were too frequent to encourage prospective buyers of nobility and when the other fiscal demands of the government had become excessive. It is only in an edict of October, 1704, that we find the crown withdrawing one hundred of the two hundred letters placed on sale in 1702, "lesquelles n'ont point encore été levées."[21]

The various revocations were of course warmly greeted by the old noble families; but it would be a mistake to assign these royal announcements much importance as a means of reducing the total number of noblemen. Exemption from a revocation, including that of 1715, which theoretically annulled every grant made *moyennant finances* since 1689, could be bought for a price—in 1715 it was six thousand livres—and the price seems generally to have been forthcoming.[22] The same was true of the great *recherche* instituted by Colbert in 1665 to detect usurpers of noble status and thus to increase the market value of bona fide grants, while at the same time squeezing additional funds from convicted defendants.[23] An adverse judgment

[19] The earliest such edict of revocation discovered by Chérin or any subsequent researcher is 1583. Those under Louis XIV came in 1643, 1664, 1666, 1667, 1669, 1692, 1705, 1706, 1715. See Chérin, *Abrégé*, under those dates.

[20] Charles L. Louandre, *La noblesse française sous l'ancienne monarchie* (Paris, 1880), 41.

[21] Chérin, *Abrégé*, 276-277.

[22] A.N., Z[1A]. 134-144 and 524-633 (records of the Cour des Aides of Paris) contain several hundred letters of confirmation or exemption, registered at this court by recipients anxious to ensure the retention of their tax privileges as noblemen. The letters display a perfunctory uniformity which testifies to the standardized system under which they were sold by the royal secretaries.

[23] This inquiry was interrupted from 1674 until 1696, then resumed until 1729, when it was officially declared at an end, effective January 1, 1727. Chérin's *Abrégé* supplies the main legislative texts; but a much more complete collection of original documents,

by the investigating commissioners could be nullified by the purchase of letters of confirmation or rehabilitation, which gave the prosperous usurper retroactive royal sanction for his previously illegal claims of rank. La Bruyère wrote sourly of this practice:

> Réhabilitations: mot en usage dans les tribunaux, qui a fait vieillir et rendu gothique celui de lettres de noblesse, autrefois si françois et si usité. Se faire réhabiliter suppose qu'un homme, devenu riche, originairement est noble, qu'il est d'une nécessité plus que morale qu'il le soit; qu'à la vérité, son pere a pu déroger ou par la charrue, ou par la houe, ou par la malle, ou par les livrées; mais qu'il ne s'agit pour lui que rentrer dans les premiers droits de ses ancêtres.[24]

Far more important in its immediate repercussions than the sale of these various types of letters, however, was the fact that Louis XIV's reign had seen the first serious effort to harness privileged groups to their share of the tax load. It was the beginning of a struggle destined to continue, with increasing bitterness, down to the very outbreak of the Revolution. Since the middles ages, the French nobility had enjoyed immunity from ordinary taxation, an immunity based on the theory that the aristocracy's public contribution took the form not of money, but of military and other governmental services. The oldest written document on the status of nobility which Chérin found for his great collection was a copy of letters patent, issued by Philip IV in 1295 and stating that no noble, "whether chevalier, prelate, seigneur or damoiseau," would be required to pay any tax on chattels, provided he was not engaged in trade.[25]

This immunity, always irritating to those who did not share it, became impossible to maintain intact during the great wars of Louis XIV's last years. By previous standards, they were total wars; and the budget they demanded dwarfed any ever seen before in France. In 1695, a celebrated declaration established the *capitation*, or head tax, payable by every French subject in an amount corresponding to his place on the attached schedule of twenty-two classes.[26] The

---

at least for the initial stages, will be found in A.N., E. 2664, "Arrêts ou projets d'arrêts du Conseil du Roi relatifs à la recherche des usurpateurs de la noblesse." The other form of documentation still in existence is the huge file of genealogical dossiers in the Cabinet des Titres of the Bibliothèque Nationale.

[24] *Les caractères*, II, 164. [25] *Abrégé*, 9. [26] See below, 32-33.

outcry provoked by this precedent-breaking law had not yet subsided when the crown demanded the *dixième* of 1710.[27] This levied a flat ten percent on all gross incomes, with an indifference to the subject's rank which seemed to privileged persons a leveling factor of revolutionary dimensions. No threat less menacing than the Anglo-Dutch-Austrian alliance could have made the edict viable in France at that date;[28] and concerted demands for its total withdrawal waited only upon deliverance from Marlborough.

Looking backward from 1715 across the long expanse of the preceding reign, French noblemen thus saw their class excluded from civil offices, reduced to a breathless reliance on the king's pleasure, cowed by an initial show of royal power, prevented from exerting group pressure on high policy, diluted and degraded by wholesale commerce in titles, and squeezed for military commutation payments, for confirmation fees and latterly—horrendous innovation! —for taxes. Yet the class survived as a privileged stratum of the population. It survived because the sponsor of all these humiliating and crippling measures had never for a moment entertained the thought that it could or should be liquidated.

4

In the French monarchical tradition, the reliance of the crown on the broad masses of the population has very often been over-emphasized. At any rate, Louis XIV was no more inclined than were the two Napoleons later to cut loose from all groups which derived special benefits from maintaining the general *status quo*, however much they might rail at its momentary features. This was no Hobbesian sovereignty, equalizing all subjects through the equality of their subjection. Complaining, potentially dissident, in many respects parasitic, the nobility still received flattering mention in royal writs as the chief support of the throne. Perhaps the king was sincere in occasionally describing himself as the first gentleman of the realm,

[27] Isambert, *Recueil*, XX, 558-559.

[28] For evidence of the nobility's resistance to these new taxes, one has only to refer to *Correspondance des Contrôleurs généraux avec les intendants des provinces, 1683-1715* (Paris, 1874-1897), 3 vols., based on documents in the Archives Nationales and edited by A. M. Boislisle and P. de Brotonne.

though there is reason to take his phrase with some reservations. Even if, as seems to me more probable, he felt himself infinitely beyond comparison with any part of the population beneath him, there remained ample cause for his encouragement of envy and emulation as motive forces in his era's idea of the good society. The crown, safely out of range of even the most vaulting ambition, enjoyed the very solid advantages, fiscal as well as political, of dispensing the rewards for which this honorific system provided.

While he broke his courtiers to docility, therefore, the king saved many of them from bankruptcy through pensions and sinecures.[29] True, the petty noble of the provinces scarcely benefited from this exalted form of dole; but those who did so benefit, the *grands* of Versailles, sons of the greatest and once most dangerous territorial houses, were the very subjects whom a rigorous extirpator of aristocratic prestige would have had to degrade before all others. He withheld administrative offices but conferred a variety of household titles, honorific costumes, and distinctions defined by the rules of *préséance*, all the more prized because Louis himself never forgot one nor, until his last tired years, knowingly permitted a case of infringement. To the twentieth century mind these trappings may seem poor recompense for what had been lost. In a society to which the symbols of authority still represented a great advantage for its ultimate recovery, however, they were not to be taken lightly.

This same type of substitution occurred with regard to the highest courts of law; for while the reign saw them effectively denied all power to interfere in royal legislation, it also saw the regularization of their members' titles of nobility. Specific legislation in the 1640's

[29] The question of royal largesse under the *ancien régime* is an infinitely complex one, since the extent to which these gifts artificially retained numbers of incompetents in the privileged elite has only been touched upon by Marie Kolabinska, *La circulation des élites en France* (Lausanne, 1912), 111 ff. For our present purpose, the important point is that Louis XIV continued to lend financial aid to preferred nobles even at the height of his military difficulties; the records of the *Contrôle général* show that in 1708 and 1709 he granted roughly three million livres in pensions to officers of his troops and another two million listed simply as gratifications and paid to courtiers. The combined sum represented no less than 12 percent of the total privy purse, which had also to pay not only the *gages* of the great officers of the crown and the expenses of the royal household but also the gigantic sums required for the maintenance of the court and the upkeep of all the royal palaces and châteaux. A.N., G^7. 919. For the impressively long civil list of 1715 see B.N., Ms. fr. 6803.

and 1650's, the confirmations accorded in the course of the great inquest of the 1660's and after, the constant flow of *lettres d'honneur* and *lettres de vétérance*, all combined to place the noble status of the *robins* beyond any further doubt as to its technical legality.[30]

Aristocratic privileges in matters of taxation were far from eradicated. Reduced perhaps, by the capitation and the dixième; but those taxes were decreed only under the most extreme conditions of wartime necessity and even then with apologetic preambles which confirmed the old immunities as still valid in principle. The all-important exemption from the *taille*, the basic direct tax of the realm, was never called into question by the king.

As for the army, the commutation of the feudal levy in favor of noblemen whose comforts and responsibilities made the hearth more attractive than the campfire did not prevent their sons and younger brothers from crowding into select cavalry regiments or entering the accelerated preparation for line commissions which their birth conferred. Even the hard-bitten Louvois would have needed the king's unwavering support in order to break the pernicious confusion of two sets of ranks in army units, the one military, the other social. That support, at least with the requisite consistency, he never received; and it is not difficult to imagine the disciplinary atmosphere created by insolent sons of great lords when commanded by a senior officer of less exalted origin.

But whatever their shortcomings as soldiers in other respects, the nobles of France never failed under Louis XIV to display, and lavishly, the reckless, wasteful courage which their whole tradition called forth. Fighting under the eyes of their fellow noblemen and acutely aware of ancestors who had ridden to battle, if not in all cases with Godfrey of Bouillon, at least with Henry IV and Condé, these men took losses of staggering severity when judged by the standards of the time. The most cursory glance at the casualty lists of Neerwinden or Malplaquet will suffice to prove the point.[31] The fact that this *bravoure* was exactly what their monarch considered essential to the

[30] See below, 59 ff.

[31] Such lists may be found in the Marquis de Quincy's *Histoire militaire du règne de Louis le Grand* (Paris, 1726), 8 vols., and in J.-F. d'Hozier, *L'impôt du sang ou la noblesse de France sur les champs de bataille* (Paris, 1874-1881), 5 vols.

glory of his throne doubtless had its share in maintaining his belief in the class's indispensability. When in 1693 he established the military order of Saint Louis, it was to supply additional prestige and monetary rewards to those whose individual acts had best accorded with the nobility's fighting past. Louis XIV, who was perhaps in a strong enough position to have controlled the *noblesse d'épée* without having to divert its energies through constant warfare, was himself too thoroughly convinced of the value of martial prestige to consider using such restraint. The weaker regimes which followed his never were able, though they were often more inclined, to curb warhawks such as clustered around Belle-Isle in the 1740's. Hence the pressure of the fighting section of the aristocracy remained a serious problem in the foreign policy of the old monarchy down to its very end.

All these conflicting measures and policies with regard to the noblesse leave a total impression of considerable confusion; but it is, I think, the only impression justified by the evidence. The fact that the treatment of nobles during Louis XIV's reign fails to display a single, easily specified direction does not make that reign any the less momentous in the history of the French aristocracy. The effects of just this ambivalence were to emerge repeatedly during the succeeding era.

5

The situation created by the death of the king brought into sharp relief several problems previously kept in the background by the long military crisis and by Louis' own techniques of governing. As already observed, this had been far from a leveling absolutism. By 1715 it was clear that for all the unifying efforts of Colbert and for all Bossuet's soaring praise of common loyalties, the Great Reign had in most respects actually deepened the divisions separating various segments of the population. In 1698 Avocat-Général d'Aguesseau, future chancellor of France, said in his first mercurial, or harangue to an opening session of the Parlement of Paris:

> L'homme est presque toujours également malheureux, et par ce qu'il désire, et par ce qu'il possède. Jaloux de la fortune des autres dans le temps qu'il est l'objet de leur jalousie; toujours envieux et toujours envié . . .
>
> Tel est le caractère dominant des moeurs de notre siècle: une inquiétude

généralement répandue dans toutes les professions; une agitation que rien ne peut fixer, ennemie du repos, incapable du travail, portant partout le poids d'une inquiète et ambitieuse oisiveté; un soulèvement universel de tous les hommes contre leur condition; une espèce de conspiration générale dans laquelle ils semblent être tous convenus de sortir de leur caractère.[32]

This emphasis on externally designated rank, working beneath the decorous surface of a regulated society, had exacerbated consciousness of private prestige until even within the nobility, a unitary class in legal theory, economic jealousy and gradations of honor had drawn sharp lines of mutual hostility. During the whole life of the pre-revolutionary monarchy, these lines never completely vanished; but they were destined to lose their political significance in a remarkably short time and thus to give to the eighteenth century one of its most striking phenomena of change. In 1715, however, with the sole exception of a few recently ennobled administrators, all the groups enjoying noblesse had for a half-century been so successfully excluded from the political arena that there could be no immediate realization of where actual power lay. Only trial by battle would determine which of these groups had been left with the capacity for leadership in the forthcoming counter-offensive of the *privilégiés.*

The very inevitability of such a counter-offensive derived from an aspect of the pre-1715 period which deserves a word of explanation at this point. It has, I trust, been made sufficiently clear that this study does not proceed from any conception of the Great Reign as a tremendous departure from all previous traditions, either of the crown or of the nobility. Very often what at first appears to have been a peculiar aspect of the Ludovican age, on closer examination is revealed as merely the extension or intensification of some much older trend. In one respect, however, the attitude of the privileged groups had undergone a significant modification during the era of Richelieu, Mazarin, and especially Louis XIV: these groups were now convinced that political security could only be achieved by the exercise of political power. This is the message constantly reiterated by Boulainvilliers, by Fénelon, by Saint-Simon and by a series of less significant writers for the nobility. A class for centuries content to seek exemption from the law now realized that its aim must be to

[32] Henri-François d'Aguesseau, *Oeuvres* (Paris, 1754-1789), I, 44-45.

have a hand in making the law. The ability to participate in legislation, even if only in the sense of interference with it, had become the basic desideratum of the aristocracy as a whole.

But perhaps equally important was the fact that in 1715 a momentous reign and a long series of wars had ended without completely breaking any tradition and hence without imposing any new value system on the rival parties which now confronted one another. Louis XIV had wrought changes, but he had achieved nothing which made impossible the revival of old concepts. If the War of the Spanish Succession had ended in the total defeat and subsequent foreign occupation of France, as seemed quite possible in 1709, the ensuing period might have witnessed a thorough re-assessment of the bases on which political life rested. Instead, the war which came to a close in 1713-14 ended on a note of compromise, save for the remote colonial losses. The new brooms of the Regency were thus in fact exceedingly old brooms, long stored in various closets, but now once more apparently quite suitable for the needs of their respective owners. No stern necessity forbade the pleasures of nostalgia.

So the contest for leadership within the nobility, an essential part of the broader contest for power in the polity as a whole, was to take the form of old claims noisily reenunciated. The heritage of the Grand Siècle, however, had one more condition to impose. The two ladders of titled prestige and political functions remained in place. With Louis XIV and his great ministers now gone, the scale of grandeur could resume its significance as an important index of political influence; but it was never again to be the sole basis of power. Ultimately, the most potent group in the aristocracy must be one which combined relatively high—not necessarily the highest—positions on both ladders. The French peerage, for example, only one rank below the royal family in the pyramid of honor, was to make a determined bid for leadership, and to fail.[33] It failed because it had no assured place in the hierarchy of government and because another group of nobles had emerged from the era of Louis XIV with an infinitely more formidable combination of attributes.

That group was the high noblesse de robe, the personnel of the

[33] See below, 173 ff.

sovereign courts. The story of the resurgence of the French nobility is first and foremost the story of how the high robe was to demonstrate its power to obstruct the monarchy and win general recognition as the indispensable defender of privileged interests. The fact that it occupied this position by the 1770's and 1780's has long been accepted by historians; but its rise to prestige and influence during the first half of the century, a development which provides one of the dynamics of that period, is much less familiar. So my analysis of the aristocratic reaction becomes primarily an analysis of the high robe within the aristocracy, albeit with frequent pauses to examine the parts played by other segments of the nobility. Before leaving the situation as it existed in 1715, it will be necessary to obtain some general understanding of the noblesse as an order, then look more closely at the institutional structure of the sovereign courts, and finally define the special place of their members within the noble class. Only thereafter will it be possible to move on to the peculiar advantages, political, social and economic, which explain the magistracy's pivotal role, and to the actual account of how it was able to take over both tactical and intellectual leadership of the French aristocracy.

Chapter Two

The Structure of the Noblesse

1

In the middle of the eighteenth century, when the amiable Mr. Thomas Nugent published his guidebook for continental travels, he thought it prudent to insert the following comment: "The French," he warned his aristocratic young English readers, "include all their gentry under the general title of nobility or noblesse."[1] The remark is interesting, not only because it provides an example of national differences in terminology, but also because it reveals how sprawling and difficult of comprehension, even for a contemporary, the French noble class had become.

If one goes to late seventeenth and early eighteenth-century sources asking "What is a nobleman?" he will find poets, lawyers, and philosophers crowding about him with a confusing range of definitions to offer. "Nobility means nothing if it does not mean virtue," La Bruyère insists.[2] "Nobility is the mark of descent from medieval warriors and, before them, from the Frankish conquerors of Gaul," replies Boulainvilliers. "Nobility is the public recognition of great attainments" . . . "Nobility is wisdom"[3] . . . "Nobility is proximity to the sovereign power" . . . "Nobility is the fraudulent excuse of privilege" and so on endlessly, with variations determined by points of view and degrees of enthusiasm for the class.

All these theories, however, have in common one serious weakness for present purposes. Each is urging a conception of nobility, but not one helps to define a nobleman as he would have been defined

[1] *The Grand Tour* (second edition, London, 1756), IV, 13.

[2] See above, 9, n. 9.

[3] Charon in *De la sagesse*, quoted by Alphonse Chassant, *Les nobles et les vilains du temps passé* (Paris, 1857), 18.

under French law prior to 1789. The real basis—the only one, for example, on which a challenged title of noblesse could actually have been defended—must instead be sought in writers concerned with just such concrete problems of investigation and proof.

"Nobility," wrote Guyot in his great *Répertoire universel*, "is defined as a quality which the sovereign power imprints upon private persons in order to place them and their descendants above other citizens."[4]

One of Colbert's *traitants* for the Grande Recherche of 1665 and after, A. Belleguise, has left us an even clearer statement of the absolutist doctrine concerning nobility:

Nature creates neither nobles nor commoners (*roturiers*); the condition which it bestows upon men is that of freedom, and if we note any other difference among them, it is rather an effect of the sovereign will, a recompense for virtue, or the result of civil laws than a privilege of birth. The Romans, the French, the Germans and other nations would not have made different laws for the acquisition of nobility if it were a right which one possessed upon coming into the world. . . . Differentiation of status is a pure result of the prince's authority and the civil laws.[5]

Recognition, then, by the sovereign power. Here, at least, is a criterion for nobility which makes sense in terms of the historical situation at the end of Louis XIV's reign and at the same time explains how a distinctly official problem such as tax exemption could be bound up with what at first glance might appear to be simply an honorific status in society. But recognition how expressed? For a summary of the actual mechanics of proof, it is necessary to turn once more to Belleguise, the inquest official.[6] That dour but extremely

[4] *Op. cit.*, XII, 65.

[5] *Traité de la noblesse et de son origine, suivant les préjugés rendus par les commissaires députez pour la vérification des titres de noblesse* (Paris, 1700), 1-2.

[6] In keeping to Belleguise in the present discussion, I am intentionally avoiding the academic complexities of some other possible sources, who broke down the legal bases of nobility into countless, often artificially refined classifications. Gilles-André de La Roque, for example, offered twenty different types in his *Traité de la noblesse, de ses différentes espèces, etc.* (Rouen, 1678); and modern writers, such as Sémainville in his *Code de la noblesse française* (Paris, 1860), have retained that method of approach. Others have based their subdivisions on types of landholding or on titles. The value of Belleguise seems to me to lie in the fact that he posits only a few basic distinctions which the working investigators actually employed.

informative agent has left a precise summary of the principles, some drawn from earlier legal writers, others arbitrarily announced by the king, still others derived from local customs, upon which the commissioners in various districts based their decisions.

An individual called before the royal commissioners to establish his family's nobility might base his claim to confirmation on either of two general types of proof. The first was concrete, documentary evidence that the king had at some date explicitly ennobled the family and that no intervening revocation had nullified the *anoblissement*. If the king had ennobled by simple letters patent, writes Belleguise, the letters must be produced and shown to have been duly registered by the appropriate law courts. If, on the other hand, the king's will had been revealed by his having repeatedly bestowed high functions on the family, by *collation des grands offices*, whether in the armed forces, the administration, or the judiciary, then proof took the form of ancestors' letters of provision for the requisite number of offices at the specified level of dignity.[7] Finally, still under the heading of explicit ennoblement, came the comparatively rare acts of investiture *by the king* (the much more common investiture by royal judges had no such effect). If a commoner purchased a duchy, marquisate, county or other titled fief, and if the king personally received his homage and fealty, the document confirming this investiture became solid proof of the new vassal's nobility.[8]

The second general category of evidence applied to noblemen who could not produce the original grants to their respective families; for in addition to the tens of thousands of relatively new, or at least traceable, noble houses there were certain others whose claims rested on immemorial status. That is to say, in the earliest available documents their ancestors had already been treated as "placed above other citizens," to use Guyot's phrase. For purposes of judging this *noblesse de race*, which all its hauteur did not exempt from royal investigation, Belleguise sets down a series of working rules. He says that the commissioners specifically rejected the argument of prescription as being "contraire aux interests du Roy & au droit commun." No matter how long a usurpation had gone undetected, it was to be condemned;

[7] See below, 61 ff.

[8] See also La Roque, *Traité de la noblesse*, 405-406.

no matter how old an evidence of previous *roture* might be, it was sufficient to warrant a fine and forfeiture of title, unless the subject could fall back on some proof of explicit ennoblement. For noblesse de race, proofs might include special types of documents, as for example summonses to the arrière-ban, inasmuch as these were evidence of peculiarly noble military service. Such proofs had originally to date from 1560 or earlier; but since this was presumed to represent a period of time elapsed when first imposed in the 1660's rather than an unalterable date, the rule of one hundred years as a minimum age for indirect documentary evidence became general for later investigations. The mere qualification *nobilis* or *noble homme* in an old deed, baptismal record or marriage contract was rejected as inconclusive (from an historical point of view, rightly so); but in documents dating from the fifteenth century or earlier the then still undepreciated terms, *scutifer* and *miles*, were acceptable as prima facie evidence of medieval nobility.

The only other major problems to be considered in renewing or withholding royal sanction were those connected with possible loss of a family's original nobility by intervening generations. A line connected with a noble house through a bastard could not claim to enjoy nobility except by virtue of explicit *lettres de noblesse.*[9] *Déchéance*, or degradation to non-noble status, accompanied conviction for a capital crime whether or not the death penalty was inflicted, though it touched the felon's descendants only in cases of *lèse-majesté.*[10] An ancestor might also have cost the family its rank by some act of *dérogeance*, in other words, by having ceased to "live nobly." The endless shadings and special types of dérogeance need not concern us; but it is worth noting that in the eighteenth century, a nobleman still lost his noblesse and that of all progeny not yet conceived (the medieval concept of tainted blood being recognized by law in favor of earlier children) if he adopted any manual craft save the famous exception of glassmaking[11] or if he entered "for

[9] Article 26 of the Règlement des Tailles of 1600, Isambert, *Recueil*, XV, 226-238.

[10] Sémainville, *Code de la noblesse*, 707-708.

[11] The peculiar case of gentlemen glassworkers has never been completely explained, though La Roque (*Traité de la noblesse*, 351-353) claims to have found references in Pliny to the noble status of Gauls thus employed. The truth probably is that the dispensa-

sordid gain" into either retail commerce or the exploitation of another party's land.[12] Even in these instances, however, a family against which previous dérogeance had been established might still vindicate itself if it could produce subsequent *lettres de réhabilitation* in which the king had recognized some later ancestor's return to the gentle life.

Even the preceding short excursion into the law of nobility suggests how complex could become the problems of legal conflict, disputed evidence, charges of perjury and judicial bias. Many of the cases were bitterly fought all the way to the king's antechamber. Many others hung in abeyance for decades. Neither the Grande Recherche nor the founding of the *Armorial Général* in 1696, with Charles d'Hozier as *Juge d'Armes* to register all escutcheons, succeeded in fixing with perfect precision the legal boundaries of the nobility as a class. The fact remains, however, that in 1715 a half-century of emphasis on the sort of investigation Belleguise describes had left both nobles and government officials more conscious than ever before in French history that there were such boundaries and that all who lay within them had something in common, even if it was as yet little more than a sense of being distinguished from the unprivileged mass of the population outside.

---

tion grew out of the special needs and prestige system of French Renaissance society, since the fundamental texts date from the sixteenth century. Guyot, *Répertoire*, 110.

[12] The whole conception of dérogeance is a singularly complex one. Funck-Brentano, *Ancien Régime*, 138, points admiringly to the French nobility as the aristocracy of service and economic sacrifice par excellence, in contrast to the voracious English lords, whom he sees deep in commerce. A more plausible explanation for this continuing set of taboos would seem to lie, first, in the Renaissance kings' determination to keep the noblesse a purely military caste, thus harnessing the inherited ideals of chivalry to the needs of the Italian Wars, and second, in the insistence of the early modern bourgeoisie that the nobles must compensate for their fiscal privileges by refraining from competition in trade. The opening of maritime and wholesale commerce to noble participation in the seventeenth century reflected urgent national needs and the relative indifference of the small bourgeois in that direction. For legislative texts and interpretations, see La Roque, *Traité de la noblesse*, 254-257 and 339-383; Guyot, *Répertoire*, 110-112; and Chérin, *Abrégé*, *passim*. The basic law on *dérogeance* for our period was Louis XIV's edict of 1669, authorizing wholesale and maritime commerce (A.N., K. 119, no. 6[3]), renewed in 1701 (Isambert, *Recueil*, XX, 400-402).

2

If the boundaries of noble rank were determined by the sovereign's recognition, the significant content of that rank, from the point of view of the aristocracy itself, the crown and the people, lay in the special privileges which it carried. Much has been written, for example, concerning the taille exemption; and at one time it was thought by some historians that freedom from this tax might be taken as an unmistakable sign of nobility under the ancien régime. It has long since been proven that exemption from the taille was no such infallible mark, for there were numerous instances in which it was accorded to persons who did not thereby acquire the other characteristics of noblemen.[13] But this is not a crucial point. What is important is that all noblemen were in some degree exempt.

The reader will not be inclined to overlook the importance of this provision. The taille privilege not infrequently appeared to be the irreducible core of noblesse, as seen by the noble himself. The Comte de Boulainvilliers, for example, complained that despotism and egalitarianism had debased nobility "à une pure chimère, ou à l'exemption des Tailles."[14] To the crown, it represented a concrete motive for seeking to prevent usurpations of rank. And to the people, since the total amount of the taille due from a given *généralité* was communicated to the intendant by the government and then assessed pro rata upon all *taillables* of the sub-districts, the privilege represented an abuse felt annually by the individual's purse.[15] The injustice was less in those provinces (Dauphiné, Provence, Languedoc) where the taille was *réelle*, that is, assessed on land regardless of the holder's rank, rather than *personnelle*, as in the north, where a noble could remain wholly untouched.[16] But even in the *pays de taille*

[13] A.N., Z[1A]. 135, fol. 377 v[0], for instance, contains letters patent of Henry IV which in 1595 conferred on one Sieur de Lisle personal exemption from the taille without bestowing full noblesse. La Roque, *Traité de la noblesse*, 258, cites the possibility of taille-exempt commoners.

[14] *Essais sur la noblesse de France* (Amsterdam, 1732), vii.

[15] The aristocrats' claim that in practice the effect of exemptions on the non-exempt was negligible has been convincingly refuted by Marcel Marion, *Histoire financière de la France depuis 1715* (Paris, 1914), I, 5 ff.

[16] A.D., Haute-Garonne, C. 816, for example, is an order in council of 1642 emphasizing the taille liability of nobles for roturier lands in Languedoc; see also Guyot, *Répertoire*, 105.

réelle, every noble could claim exemption for an average of four *charrues* of his land. While this represented only a tiny fraction of a great lord's total holdings, it practically freed the small *hobereaux*, to the growing disgust of roturier farmers who could see little else to distinguish their fortunate neighbors from themselves.

Nobles enjoyed several additional privileges which, though not comparable in importance to freedom from the taille, nonetheless represented considerable advantages. They were exempt from the *corvée*, or forced labor. They were also exempt from militia service, as well as from the necessity of quartering royal troops.[17] These privileges, once the arrière-ban had lapsed,[18] left them wholly free from compulsory military contributions in either money or services, save in short periods of the most extreme crisis. They also enjoyed a variety of special tax privileges, differing widely from one province to another but through most of the eighteenth century including everywhere the *franc-salé* or exemption from the regulations of the *gabelle* on salt. Furthermore, within the feudal land system, every noble escaped the heavy *franc-fief* payments which the crown exacted from the roturier buyer of a fief, or portion thereof, for as many as four generations after the actual purchase.

Judicial privileges represented a valuable part of the noble's *droit*, since the right to go directly to the higher royal courts saved him the expenses of preliminary hearings in the lower. He could, for example, always be heard in first instance by a royal bailli or sénéchal, the intermediate level of the court hierarchy; but he was never judiciable in last resort at this level or even that of a *présidial*. In general, he could count on easy access to a parlement or other sovereign court for an affair involving his interests.

Finally, the nobleman, any nobleman, enjoyed honorific rights of

---

It must be conceded to Boulainvilliers that, like Vauban, he recognized the inequity of the tailles *personnelles* and in a memorandum to the Regent in 1719 urged extension of the tailles *réelles* as a basis for reforming the distribution of taxes. *Mémoires présentés au duc d'Orléans* (The Hague and Amsterdam, 1727), I, 75-119.

[17] A.N., M. 638, no. 2, Extrait des réflexions sur la Milice, lists as automatically excused "tous les Nobles . . . vivans noblemens, ainsy que leurs Enfans" and "tous les officiers des Cours," including the lower jurisdictions staffed by non-noble magistrates. See also Jacques Gebelin, *Histoire des milices provinciales (1688-1791)* (Paris, 1882), 73 ff.

[18] See above, 11-12.

préséance and *préeminence* in public gatherings. In church he was entitled to special additional honors if he happened to be the patron seigneur of the parish. Since these distinctions helped to dramatize his rank and underline his local position, they had a direct relationship to his other, more concrete, privileges and thus retained a far greater importance both for him and for the community than may be immediately apparent to the twentieth century mind.[19]

In this brief recapitulation I have been compelled to pass over not only the myriad of special rights attaching to the status of nobility in various localities but also the strictly seigneurial honors enjoyed by a manorial lord within his own holdings. In fact, the basic list of universal privileges given above would almost certainly not have satisfied any individual French nobleman as a description of his full range of attributes. The preceding summary, however, will have made clear just why the designation "noble" was prized in France. Obviously much more than honorific distinction was at stake.

3

Given this trend toward greater legal precision in defining both the boundaries of the class and its privileges, one might expect to find much simplified the problem of making a numerical estimate of the nobility. As a matter of fact, the question of the number of noble Frenchmen in 1715 is exceedingly difficult to answer. Many of the estimates of the past appear highly unreliable when examined in terms of their sources and the computing methods employed. Vauban, writing in 1707, started with some regional figures and went on to assume a more or less uniform distribution of two noble families per square league. His total of 52,000 families or 260,000 individuals is certainly too high, because of his inadequate allowance for the tremendous local variations in density of population. Coyer in 1756 blithely passed over any real methodological explanation in setting the figure at 400,000.[20] On the other hand, as late as 1789, Abbé

[19] The elaborate ceremonial honors which applied to the high nobles at court are not relevant to the present discussion since they actually set their holders apart from the rest of the nobility.

[20] Carré, *La noblesse de France*, 14-17, treats Vauban's, Coyer's and numerous other estimates.

Sieyès made an estimate of only 110,000;[21] but as Carré points out,[22] the guesses of the Revolutionary period ran low because of reliance on the 1789 voting lists, which represented only *possédants fiefs* rather than all noble persons.

Although a manuscript *nobiliaire* for some early eighteenth-century province[23] or a local study by a modern scholar[24] will occasionally provide suggestive ratios and subtotals, here again the regional variations constitute a serious danger to generalizing efforts. Even the great collection of surveys prepared by the intendants for Louis XIV's grandson, the Duc de Bourgogne, between 1698 and 1702, although in many respects a priceless source, are useless for the present purpose because most of the intendants listed only the principal titled lands and secondarily the principal local families.[25] One has merely to page through these memoranda to perceive the absence of any truly quantitative approach—this was an age which still would rather classify than count.

It is my own feeling that the original volumes of the *Armorial Général* are a better numerical source, at least for the first years of the eighteenth century, than has generally been conceded. I am quite aware of the ridicule which has been directed against the series, especially because of its editor's alleged willingness to accommodate his professional conscience to the desires of wealthy usurpers. Boileau, for example, wrote:

> N'eût-il de son vrai nom ni titre ni mémoire,
> D'Hozier lui trouvera cent aïeux dans l'histoire.[26]

[21] *Qu'est-ce que le Tiers Etat?* (Paris, 1789), 39.

[22] *Loc. cit.*

[23] Nobiliaires of differing dates and degrees of completeness exist, of course, in most departmental archives and in the manuscripts collections of some public libraries in France. There are, in addition, several volumes for our period in the Archives Nationales, MM. 689-702, covering Brittany, Limousin, Picardie, Amiens, the Rouen area, Provence and Touraine.

[24] In this connection I have found especially valuable Louis Jalenques, "La noblesse de la province d'Auvergne au XVIIIe siècle," *Bulletin historique et scientifique de l'Auvergne* (Clermont-Ferrand), 1911: 366-385; 1912: 72-80, 158-172, 232-244; L. Hulmel, "La noblesse de l'Avranchin au XVIIe siècle," *Revue de l'Avranchin* (Avranches), XVIII (1914) 353-364 and XIX (1920), 16-41; and Henri Frotier de La Messelière, *La noblesse en Bretagne avant 1789* (Rennes, 1902).

[25] A.N., H. 1588[8-17, 19-23, 25-28, 30-31, 33-35, 39, 42-45, 46]. Boulainvilliers, *État de la France* (London, 1737), 6 vols., originated as a summary of these bulky reports.

[26] *Satires*, 52.

Regardless of its flaws and possibly some frauds, however, the *Armorial* when published did represent official recognition. Later in the eighteenth century, many bona fide noblemen failed to register their arms because of the fee involved; but in Louis XIV's lifetime, security of noble status required the observance of formal requirements.[27] In d'Hozier's thirty-four great manuscript volumes at the Bibliothéque Nationale,[28] there are some 60,000 names covering the years 1697 to 1709 and arranged by provinces, though this figure should be reduced by about 2,000 to allow for duplicate entries of the same names under different provinces. The remaining 58,000 names represent heads of families, some elder sons, and certain younger brothers grown famous in the church or the army. Fortunately, a French scholar, Édouard de Naurois, has supplied the last link required to make this figure meaningful by comparing d'Hozier's figures with more detailed lists available in scattered localities.[29] His conclusion is that d'Hozier had treated as "genealogically significant" and hence deserving of mention in his *Armorial* an average of approximately 3 out of every 10 noble persons then living in France. When this ratio is applied to the 58,000 names, the result is a total of something over 190,000 individuals. The France of 1715, with a total population of almost exactly 20,000,000,[30] would thus have had one noble to approximately 100 commoners. It is worth re-emphasizing that these figures, although the most reliable I have been able to arrive at, are by no means beyond dispute (especially in view of eighteenth-century variations); but the ratio of 1 to 100 seems to me to give a fair idea of the proportion of nobles to roturiers when Louis XV came to the throne.

[27] A.N., M. 608, contains a dossier of Louis XIV's armorial regulations. It should be pointed out that Louandre, *La noblesse française*, 138-139, takes precisely the opposite view from that which I have expressed; for he insists that not until the period 1738-1768 did most nobles pay the fee and register their arms. He bases his opinion on the introduction to the ten-volume printed edition of the *Armorial*, which appeared during those years, the first volume in 1738 and the last in 1768. The vicissitudes described in that edition, however, refer partly to the publishing problem as such; and a quantitative comparison of these volumes with the 1697-1709 manuscripts will show, I think, that the more informative period is the earlier one.

[28] Mss. franc. 32194-32227.

[29] *Les classes dirigeantes* (Paris, 1910), 75.

[30] E. Levasseur, *La population française* (Paris, 1889), I, 202-206.

4

Whatever may have been the theory of corporate solidarity, 190,000 people, scattered from Flanders to Navarre and from Brittany to the Alps, comprising royal ministers, military commanders, judges, churchmen, needy rural gentlemen and scarcely more opulent soldiers of fortune, obviously did not constitute a unit in the society and politics of eighteenth century France. The royal investigators themselves subdivided the order in terms of differing origins: (1) nobility by immemorial possession; (2) nobility certified by royal letters patent; (3) nobility of the robe, based on judicial offices; and (4) *noblesse de cloche*, derived from offices in a dozen privileged town governments.[31]

Much more important to contemporaries was the differentiation of noblemen in terms of wealth. Here we are happily possessed of an excellent source, the royal declaration of January 8, 1695, many times renewed, which established the capitation or universal head tax.[32] In this document the entire French population, except for paupers, was divided into twenty-two classes, each containing subjects whose ability to pay was presumably about equal. Such categories were of necessity crude, and no doubt considerable injustice was done in certain cases. (The framers displayed a tendency to equate professional or honorific titles with personal wealth more confidently than actual conditions would seem to have warranted.) Nevertheless, the scale does represent a serious contemporary effort to estimate the relative taxability of different groups, including the various sections of the nobility.

Class 1, each member of which was assessed 2,000 livres, was reserved to the Dauphin, other princes and princesses of the blood royal, ministers and tax farmers general—an interesting combination of monster fortunes. In Class 2 (1,500 livres) we encounter a robe nobleman, the first president of the Parlement of Paris, here bracketed with princes, dukes, marshals of France, the "Great Officers of the Crown," and the intendants. Class 3 (1,000 livres) contained not

[31] Belleguise, *Traité de la noblesse*, *passim*.

[32] A.N., K. 121^{B}, no. 30^{2}. Oddly enough, Isambert gives only the date and title of this important enactment in his *Recueil*; but the text has been reproduced by Boislisle, *Correspondance des Contrôleurs généraux*, I, 565-579.

only the chevaliers of the Ordre du Saint-Esprit and the lieutenants general of provinces but also the next level of high magistrates: *présidents à mortier* of the Paris Parlement, first presidents of the other sovereign courts in Paris, first presidents of the provincial parlements. To Class 4 (500 livres) were assigned a long series of royal functionaries, including the *conseillers d'état*, the *procureurs-* and *avocats-généraux* of the Parlement of Paris and the presidents of all the other Paris sovereign courts. Classes 5 and 6 (400 and 300 livres, respectively) continued the grading of robe officials, as well as other officers too numerous to list in this context. Not until Class 7 (250 livres), that is to say, below practically all the magistrates of presidential rank in the entire kingdom, does there appear a solid grouping of non-robe nobles: all the marquises, counts, viscounts and barons not otherwise classified. Immediately thereafter were placed the councilors of the five sovereign courts in Paris (Class 8, 200 livres) and those of the provinces (Class 9, 150 livres). In Class 10 (120 livres), after most of the high robe but nevertheless representing the upper stratum of rural nobles, come those seigneurs who had the patronage of churches, the *gentilshommes seigneurs de paroisse*.

Below this level the tax drops steadily through ranks of lower officials, municipal as well as royal, until in Class 15 (40 livres) appear the castle- or fiefholding gentry. There is then another break, so far as the nobility is concerned, until the latter reappears in one of the most revealing sections of the entire text: Class 19, where gentlemen who hold neither fiefs nor châteaux are assessed 6 livres each, in common with "town artisans of the second order, owning shops and employing journeymen." The last three classes, ending with a 1 livre charge for dayworkers and private soldiers, contains no nobles; but the distance between a duke at 1,500 livres and a poor hobereau at 6 is surely great enough! I am aware of no other single piece of evidence which illustrates so strikingly the distribution of noblemen in the French income range.

5

Taking into account the diversities of wealth, profession, and rank, I can now take another step, essential to an understanding of what happened within the nobility as a whole between 1715 and

1748, that of distinguishing several groups which constituted the *politically significant* aristocracy. Under this heading should be placed the greatest nobles de race, the chief military officers, the top of the ecclesiastical hierarchy, and the high noblesse de robe, using that term in its most precise sense to designate the owners of judicial offices in the sovereign courts. From this enumeration I have purposely omitted what Philippe Sagnac has termed the "noblesse des hautes fonctions gouvernementales,"[33] that is to say, the appointive officers of the administration—ministers, councilors of state, intendants—some ennobled when commissioned, others descended from old families, but all now dependent on royal favor and identified with royal policy. The distinction between these men and the high robe noblemen has often been overlooked, and it is true that under Louis XVI it was to lose much of its significance. Under Louis XV, however, it was still of crucial importance. When a d'Aguesseau or a d'Argenson, a Turgot or a Maupeou entered the administrative hierarchy of non-venal offices, he crossed from the aristocratic to the king's camp.

Even excluding the administrators, it is perhaps anticipating history to speak of an "aristocratic camp" in 1715. Deep lines of division still separated some of its most important elements when Louis XIV died. Indeed, the fading of these lines was to be a subsequent change which can only be appreciated in terms of the nobility's initial lack of unity. But in discussing a noble class comprising almost 200,000 individuals, it is important to remember that the political cutting edge of that class was much smaller. Only if bishops, dukes, marshals, and high magistrates achieved some degree of tactical unanimity could the aristocracy again exert serious political pressure. More than that, the aristocracy was desperately in need of an institutional base. It is just here that the judiciary becomes important.

[33] *La formation de la société française*, I, 37 ff., and *passim*.

Chapter Three

The Sovereign Courts

1

The structure of French government in the eighteenth century has been variously described by a series of metaphors, all of them designed to convey the impression of a complexity bordering on utter confusion. Behind this situation lay the long process of accretion inherent in the crown's efforts to maintain control of its unavoidable delegations of authority. By the time of Louis XV, that process had produced a bewildering array of governmental organs, many of them fallen into contempt and near uselessness, but each still asserting its claim to control over some portion of the conduct, the personal property, the taxes, the disputes or the physical services of the French population. The social concomitant of such conditions was the existence of numerous groups possessing the titles and trappings of power originally vested in their offices, though the power itself had been wholly or partially transferred to new personnel.

In order to understand the full extent of the confusion, however, it is necessary to bear in mind several other historical circumstances which had left their marks on the institutions existing in 1715. One of these was the practice, characteristic of medieval government, of attaching judicial functions to almost all administrative agencies. A *grenier à sel*, for example, was at once a storage depot for salt under the official monopoly, a collection office for the gabelle, and a jurisdictional unit for the trial of accused offenders against that tax. Moreover, the effects of the long reign just ended were apparent in the tremendously over-expanded bureaucracy, swelled by the thousands of sinecures which the government had sold to increase its momentary income. Chancellor Pontchartrain is credited with a remark to Louis XIV which illustrates the spirit of this policy, even as it calls to mind another great entrepreneur of two centuries later: "Sire, every time it pleases Your Majesty to create an office, God creates a fool to buy it."[1]

To these factors there must be added the infinite number of regional variations, deriving from the manner in which the modern French monarchy had been formed. Five hundred years of piecemeal conquest, inheritance, purchase and negotiation, all necessary to bring the great fiefs of the middle ages under the effective control of the crown, had everywhere bequeathed local peculiarities. In such great and once practically independent areas as Brittany, Languedoc, Provence and Burgundy, provincial estates still enjoyed varying degrees of control over the distribution of the tax load. In Normandy and Gascony, the vestiges of protracted English rule had never wholly disappeared from legal customs and legal forms. French Flanders, the Free County, and Alsace, all incorporated under Louis XIV, retained institutions largely developed under Hapsburg rule—either Spanish or Austrian—and now simply subordinated to a top layer of French sovereignty. Little wonder that the total effect should have been one of seeming chaos.

Nevertheless, French government did function. Inefficient, to be sure, loaded down with overlapping and conflicting features, it still managed to provide greater power for the king and greater protection for the people than did any of its rivals on the continent, with the possible exception of the new Prussian monarchy. We are thus forced to conclude that somewhere in all this welter of administrative and judicial bric-à-brac there must have existed certain institutions which displayed a substantial degree of uniformity and which represented effective allocations of power. Aside from the central ministries built by Louis XIV's great lieutenants, and still powerful under lesser men, there were, it seems to me, two institutions in the early eighteenth century standing clearly above and apart from the rest. One was the network of provincial intendants. The other was the system of sovereign courts. It was the latter which contained the

[1] Louis Jalenques, *Bulletin historique et scientifique de l'Auvergne*, year 1911, 375.

politically significant portion of the noblesse de robe and which thus constitute the organizational core of the present investigation.

2

The number of such courts between 1715 and 1748 remained constant at thirty-one: fifteen parlements (including three provincial councils distinguishable only by name), nine *chambres des comptes*, four *cours des aides*, two *cours des monnaies* and the *Grand Conseil*. They were "sovereign" in that each judged by direct delegation from the king and could be overruled only by his intervention; for the intricate and often ill-defined hierarchy of appeals normally terminated in this highest judicial level, allowing always for action by "the king in council." I am concerned with the personnel of these courts primarily as a social and political force outside the courts themselves; but since the noblesse de robe drew its power in part from its professional functions, and since those functions provided not only its organizational form but also the basis for its strong corporate consciousness, it would be well to have some idea of how these courts were distinguished and how distributed.

Clearly the most important were the parlements, the high courts entrusted with competence over the greatest civil and criminal trials, with extensive administrative powers growing out of their police supervision and with the registration of new acts of royal legislation.[2] The age and jurisdictional area or *ressort* of each of the twelve parlements and three parliamentary-type councils of 1715 may be seen in the following list:

[2] The basic collection of judicial records of the Parlement of Paris is Series X in the Archives Nationales, a mountain of documentary material into which the individual researcher can delve only in search of specific points of information. It has been indexed by subject down to the early eighteenth century in Le Nain's 101 manuscript volumes, B.N., Mss. fr. nouv. acq. 8324-8424, and has been catalogued by number in the *Répertoire numérique des archives du Parlement de Paris*, published by the Ministère de l'Instruction publique et des Beaux-Arts (Paris, 1889). A.N., K. 707-713, are boxes dealing with various provincial parlements; but the main collections for this purpose are to be found in Series B, subdivision "Parlement," in each of the relevant departmental archives—Haute Garonne for the Parlement of Toulouse, Isère for that of Grenoble, Gironde for that of Bordeaux, etc.

Location	*Continuous existence since*	*Provinces*
Paris	1302 (date of separate statute, though *Olim* rolls date from 1254)	Picardy, Champagne, Brie, Île de France, Perche, Beauce, Maine, Touraine, Sologne, Berry, Nivernais, Anjou, Poitou, Aunis, Rochelois, Angoumois, La Marche, Bourbonnais, Maçonnais, Auvergne, Forez, Beaujolais, Lyonnais
Toulouse	1443 (after intermittent periods of separate existence in fourteenth century)	Languedoc
Grenoble	1451	Dauphiné and Orange
Bordeaux	1462	Guienne, Gascony, Limousin, Périgord, Saintonge
Dijon	1476	Burgundy
Rouen	1499	Normandy
Aix	1501	Provence and Barcelonnette
Arras (conseil provincial)	1530	Artois
Rennes	1553	Brittany
Pau	1620	Navarre and Béarn
Metz	1633	The Three Bishoprics (Metz, Toul, Verdun)
Colmar (conseil supérieur)	1657	Alsace
Perpignan (conseil supérieur)	1660	Roussillon
Besançon	1674 (previous existence under the Empire)	Franche-Comté
Douai	1686	French Flanders, Hainaut, Cambrésis

The chambres des comptes, like the parlements, had emerged late in the thirteenth century from a functional specialization within the medieval *curia regis*, that of Paris having been given corporate form under Philip IV, several years earlier than the original parlement. Their principal responsibility was supervision of the king's finances, as well as exploitation of the royal domain. As courts, they exercised sovereign jurisdiction over disputes arising in connection with the domain and had to verify the accounts of all agencies charged with handling the "royal deniers." As recording depots, they registered edicts bearing on these subjects and maintained the official registers of pensions, gratifications and grants of privileges, as well as the declarations of fealty and homage, *aveux*, and *dénombrements* required by feudal law of all who held property of the crown.[3] This broad competence had been seriously dimished on some sides, especially by the encroachments of the *contrôleur-général* and the intendants; but it was still considerable under Louis XV. The Paris Chambre des Comptes enjoyed a discernible but vague superiority, based on its age and the large size of its ressort, over its sister companies in Rouen, Blois, Nantes, Montpellier, Aix, Grenoble, Dôle and Dijon.

The cours des aides had a very different background; for their origin lay in the *généraux des finances* set up by Étienne Marcel's rebellious estates general of 1355 in order to supervise the collection and use of moneys voted to the crown by that assembly. They had quickly lost their original appearance of being check mechanisms, however; and before the end of the fourteenth century, Charles V had geared them into the regular machinery of royal government. Over the centuries they had declined steadily in number, as their functions had been transferred to special chambers of one parlement or chambre des comptes after another. In 1715, there remained four which were still independent bodies, at Paris, Clermont-Ferrand, Montauban, Bordeaux. Their jurisdiction covered all matters relating to such taxes as the gabelle, the taille and the various imposts on commercial transactions or goods in passage—*aides*, *octrois*, *traites*.

[3] A.N., Series P, contains the archives of the Paris Chambre des Comptes. An inventory of late ancien régime *hommages* and inventories presented as aveux and dénombrements is in the same depot, A.N., PP. 3, 4, 4bis and 7 ff. Provincial collections, as in the case of the parlements, are to be found in the various departmental archives, Series B.

Since there existed subordinate courts (*élections*, greniers à sel, *juges des traites*) to hear such cases in first instance, the cours des aides spent most of their time in considering appeals. Like the chambres des comptes, however, they also had important registration duties, covering especially letters of nobility insofar as the latter involved tax exemptions.[4]

To hear cases based on charges of counterfeiting and to decide the disputes for which the fluctuating royal coinage furnished abundant cause, there were two cours des monnaies, one at Paris, the other at Lyon, with ressorts covering roughly the northern and southern halves of the kingdom, respectively. Unlike the preceding three types of courts, the *monnoyes* enjoyed a competence sufficiently clear-cut in its special nature to make conflicts with the others extremely rare. On the other hand, they were sovereign only in civil matters, their penal sentences being subject to review by the Parlement of Paris.[5]

A more complicated case is that of the Grand Conseil; for although it was generally termed one of the sovereign companies, it unquestionably displayed some features which might seem to place it in a different category. It was, to begin with, a relatively recent offshoot of the royal council, having received its corporate form only in the last years of the fifteenth century.[6] Furthermore, it did not possess any important sphere of independent jurisdiction, since its principal function was to judge those cases which the king had "evoked" on grounds of the older courts' unsuitability, either because of conflicting rulings or because of some suspicion of bias. It also had a pot-pourri of detailed assignments, including cases involving consistorial benefices, the oaths of fealty of bishops and archbishops, the litigations of the great religious orders and finally, that peculiar levy on holders of specified privileges, which was instituted in 1723 on the basis of Louis XV's "joyeux avènement," but which, with its re-assessment year after year, tended to make that event seem progressively less joyous.[7]

[4] A.N., Z^{1A}, contains the Paris Cour des Aides' archives. Elsewhere, Series B must be consulted.

[5] A.N., Z^{1B}, contains the archives of both cours des monnaies. Cartons 728-779 of this series concern the Lyon court, which was merged with that of Paris in 1771.

[6] It was rendered sedentary at Paris by an edict of 1497.

[7] A.N., Series V^5, contains the Grand Conseil's archives.

Part of the difficulty here arises from the fact that not every case evoked by the king was assigned to the Grand Conseil. Some he judged in his Council of State, or more correctly, through a special section of it, the *Conseil des Parties*. There existed no automatic rule of thumb for distinguishing which affairs went to which tribunal. However, an examination of their membership rolls reveals a basic difference between the personnel of the Grand Conseil, on the one hand, and the Conseil des Parties, on the other. The latter was staffed by conseillers d'état, men selected from the royal administration and commissioned to serve as judicial advisers to the king in this privy council. The *conseillers au Grand Conseil*, on the other hand, owned their offices and were chiefly recruited from the lower courts, from the legal profession and from the other sovereign companies. Moreover, they not infrequently left the Grand Conseil again in order to take positions in those courts. They thus formed part of that interwoven complex of personnel in the high judicial service; and, as will emerge later, they displayed considerable solidarity with the Parlement of Paris in its political activities under the Regency, as well as in the religious crisis of the 1730's.

3

Any system such as the above, which left the fiscal jurisdiction of the parlements large but ill-defined, which failed to distinguish clearly between the types of disputes which a chambre des comptes might claim as against a cour des aides, and which reserved to the Grand Conseil a shadowy right to numerous cases normally assigned elsewhere, was bound to produce conflicts. When to these institutional complexities are added the various courts' pride in their corporate traditions and jealousy concerning their physical areas of jurisdiction, there is no occasion for surprise at the frequency with which the sources refer to hostility among the sovereign companies. Behold the Chambre des Comptes of Dijon, serving notice in the autumn of 1715 that it would not defer to the Parlement of Burgundy in the order of exit from a memorial service for Louis XIV, to be held in the Sainte-Chapelle at Dijon. Nothing less than letters patent signed by the Regent were required in order to settle the quarrel—as usual, in favor of the Parlement.[8] Similar disputes occurred between the Paris Cour des Aides and the Chambre des Comptes,[9] the Grenoble Chambre des Comptes and the Parlement of Dauphiné,[10] the Cour des Aides of Bordeaux and the Parlement of Guienne,[11] to mention only three of the countless examples.

On occasion a question of ressort boundaries, rather than one of precedence, might be the cause for hard feelings. Thus when the Utrecht settlement transferred the Briançonnais from France to the Duke of Savoy, and thereby reduced the jurisdictional area of the Parlement of Dauphiné, the latter body promptly revived old claims to the principality of Orange, which had until then been treated as an annex of Provence.[12] The Parlement at Aix responded with an angry counter-memorandum,[13] and the dispute had to be evoked by the king in 1714. Fortunately for all concerned, Victor Amadeus had on his side ceded to France the Valley of Barcelonnette, so that it was possible for a royal order in council to restore peace by awarding Orange to Dauphiné, as demanded, and compensating the Parlement of Provence with Barcelonnette.[14]

Most famous of such feuds was that between the Parlement and the Chambre des Comptes of Paris, out of which, over several centuries, had come a voluminous file of polemical memoranda from both sides.[15] As a matter of historical fact, the Chambre des Comptes' claims to seniority were well-founded; but during the eighteenth century the principal focus of the contest was jurisdictional. When judged by the cases heard in the two courts, the Parlement was an

[8] E.-F. de La Cuisine, *Le Parlement de Bourgogne* (Dijon, 1857), II, 358.

[9] B.N., Ms. fr. 7014, Mémoire pour la Cour des Aydes de Paris contre la Chambre des Comptes.

[10] A.N., K. 714, no. 36, Mémoire sommaire des titres et raisons, etc.

[11] B.N., Ms. fr. 21567, Déclaration du Roy portant règlement entre la Cour de Parlement & la Cour des Aydes de Bordeaux, 24 août 1734. Printed (Paris, 1734).

[12] A.N., K. 710, no. 59*bis*, Mémoire pour le Parlement de Dauphiné contre le Parlement de Provence au Sujet de la Juridiction de la Principauté d'Orange.

[13] Louis-Hector, Maréchal de Villars, *Mémoires et correspondances inédites* (ed. Marquis de Vogüé, Paris, 1884-1904), VI, 50–51. Villars was governor-general of Provence.

[14] Jacques de Coursac, *Choses et gens du Parlement d'Orange* (Paris, 1934), 88.

[15] B.N., Ms. fr. 18514, Pièces relatives au cérémonial de la Chambre des Comptes et à la préséance du Parlement sur la Chambre des Comptes (1430-1639), in the Théodore Godefroy papers.

infinitely more important institution.[16] In the eyes of the general public at least, the Parlement had a great superiority over a court which seemed over-staffed for its dwindling volume of feudal cases and which often displayed attitudes as anachronistic as the oaths of homage and fealty inscribed on its registers. In 1741, for example, just after the Parlement had enacted a limited measure for poor relief, justified as a police regulation to combat vagrancy, there was published an *Arrest de la Chambre des comptes portant deffense de lever aucuns deniers sur les sujets du Roi sous prétexte de l'arrest du Parlement, du 20 Décembre 1740*.[17] The popular reaction, as noted by Barbier, was prompt and outspoken. On various walls about the city appeared a characteristic specimen of Parisian doggerel:

La chambre qui n'a la police
Que sur omelette et saucisse,
Vient de casser étourdiment
Votre arrêt, gens du Parlement.

Pour faire à ces grimauds la nique,
Et pour écarter la critique
De ce sénat ignorantin,
Rendez, comme jadis, vos arrêts en latin![18]

Now the theory upon which all the sovereign courts based their proudly enunciated claims was obviously one of equality at the top level of the judicial organization. In reality, however, the thirty-one companies were far from equal. On the contrary, a quite discernible pattern of relative importance emerges if one visualizes them in a scheme of concentric circles, representing degrees of power and influence, with the Parlement of Paris at the very center. Around that greatest of the courts and comparable though never equal to it, was a sort of inner circle composed of the Grand Conseil, the Paris Chambre des Comptes and the so-called *grands parlements*: Rouen, Rennes, Bordeaux, Toulouse and Dijon. The next, somewhat less exalted ring

[16] The old dispute over precedence had by no means died out in the eighteenth century, however, as witness the ponderous Mémoire du Parlement contre la Chambre des Comptes, prepared by the former in response to renewed ceremonial claims of the latter, apparently in the mid-1740's, A.N., U. 911.

[17] B.N., Ms. fr. nouv. acq. 22246, fol. 180-183.

[18] E.-J.-F. Barbier, *Journal historique et anecdotique du règne de Louis XV* (ed. A. de la Villegille, Paris, 1847-1856), II, 285-286.

would include the Paris Cour des Aides and Cour des Monnaies, the parlements at Aix, Grenoble and Besançon, as well as the chambres des comptes at Dôle, Montpellier and Nantes. Finally, there was a less significant fringe of individual companies in smaller provincial towns and weaker companies in large centers, as for example the Parlement of Navarre, the Cour des Monnaies at Lyon, or the Cour des Aides at Bordeaux.

Nor is this a wholly artificial pattern, imposed for convenience at the distance of two centuries. Gradations of prestige among the sovereign courts were reflected in the lives of their members, including the formation of family alliances. A member of the Cour des Aides at Montauban was thought to have made a good marriage for his son, all other things being equal, if the bride's father was installed in the Grand Conseil. And the latter magistrate, if he had a son of his own, might simultaneously be negotiating with a proud parent on the bench of the Parlement of Paris. This is only an arbitrary and much simplified example of combinations which could in fact become infinitely complex, but which nonetheless reflected a recognizable hierarchy of institutional prestige.

4

Something of the atmosphere in which the old sovereign companies carried on their functions still lingers in the maze of chambers, corridors and courtyards of the Paris Palais de Justice. Most of the detailed remnants of that earlier period have vanished; but a visitor looking across to the Île de la Cité from the Seine's right bank finds the long wall which faces him broken by the vertical lines of two pointed towers set close together. Between these are the windows of the Grand' Chambre (and later of the Revolutionary Tribunal). Once inside the confines of the Palais itself, he can identify the official residence of the First President of the Parlement, separated from the courtyard of the Sainte-Chapelle by the square mass of the Chambre des Comptes. Also in the Palais before the Revolution were facilities for the Cour des Aides, the Cour des Monnaies and no fewer than eight subordinate tribunals.[19] At the very center of this complex

[19] Henri Stein, *Le Palais de Justice et la Sainte-Chapelle* (new edition, Paris, 1927); and F. Rittiez, *Histoire du Palais de Justice de Paris* (Paris, 1860).

may still be traced the foundations of the original royal dwelling, a reminder that until the time of Philip the Fair the courts, when indeed they were resident in Paris at all, had occupied parts of the king's own palace, and that not until later in the fourteenth century had Charles V moved the royal household completely to the Louvre.

What the modern visitor cannot find reproduced, however, is the shouting, clattering, brawling population of hucksters and small shopkeepers, prostitutes and public scribes who once made the area within the outer walls a town in itself—the "world of the Palais." Only occasionally had this crowd to pause in its affairs when there was a resplendent procession of magistrates to be stared at as it wound through the Cour de Mai en route to a ceremonial mass in Notre Dame, or a condemned prisoner to be jeered at as he began the grim journey to where the wheel awaited him, across the river in the Place de Grève.

The only Paris sovereign court not lodged in the Palais was the Grand Conseil, which had its own quarters in the Hôtel d'Aligre on the Rue Saint-Honoré, just a few steps from the Louvre itself. It was this latter circumstance which in earlier times had aggravated the feeling that the Grand Conseil was not wholly a part of the order of sovereign courts, that it drew its strength too directly from the royal presence; but in the eighteenth century, when the Household remained in the outlying châteaux, save for Louis XV's childhood in the Tuileries, the royal presence was as far from the Hôtel d'Aligre as it was from the Palais de Justice.

In the provinces, court facilities were naturally less extensive. At any rate, those of Dijon failed to impress Baron von Pöllnitz, writing in 1732 from the secure heights of that slightly garrulous condescension with which he described all his travels:

> The palace where the Parlement meets is very old and one of the most miserable in the kingdom. I do not know whether it was here that the old dukes of Burgundy used to reside, but if so, they were not magnificently housed.[20]

[20] *Mémoires* (Amsterdam, 1735), III, 145. The Palais de Justice at Dijon, constructed over a period covering almost the entire sixteenth century, should not be confused with the Palais des Ducs, used by the Provincial Estates of Burgundy in the eighteenth century. Bib. Dijon, Ms. 781; also Pierre Perrenet, *Le Palais de Justice de Dijon* (Rennes, 1936).

Most of the major centers possessed royal buildings large enough for all the local courts; but, except for the fine Palais at Grenoble and Rouen, they were more impressive for age than for charm or comfort. In Toulouse, the parlement sat in the Château Narbonnais, latterly a crown possession but in medieval times the dwelling place of the successive counts Raymond.[21] Even these dark but still awesome piles were not everywhere available. Where there was no suitable building belonging to the king, some former ecclesiastical establishment generally had to serve, as in the case of the Refuge de Marchiennes at Douai or the Maison des Capucines at Pau.

5

General patterns of interior organization varied from one type of sovereign court to another, though the similarities within each category were more important than the differences. The Grand Conseil and the two cours des monnaies were "semestrial," split into two roughly equal parts with one panel responsible for business arising in the winter semester and the other taking over the court's functions during the summer term.[22] In the chambres des comptes the commonest scheme was that of division into two or more *bureaux*, of which the first normally considered only the weightier and more involved disputes. The same system obtained in the large Paris Cour des Aides, where the first of the three chambers heard the most important cases and was staffed by the senior councilors.

The internal structure of the parlements was much more involved and, from a political point of view, more significant. Only the councils of Artois and Roussillon (at Arras and Perpignan, respectively) were small enough to require no subdivision. Elsewhere each parlement had its *grand' chambre*, heir to the original *Chambre des Plaids* of Paris and focus of the company's judicial and political operations. In the grand' chambre, made up of the first president, the présidents à mortier, and the senior councilors, were heard the oral pleadings of

[21] Henri Bruno Bastard-d'Estang, *Les Parlements de France* (Paris, 1858), I, 184 ff., supplies a variety of details on physical facilities.

[22] The Parlement of Metz was also semestrial, as was that of Brittany until rendered *ordinaire* by an edict of 1724. B.N., Ms. fr. 21567, fol. 150, Edit du Roy portant Réunion des deux Semestres du Parlement de Bretagne.

the avocats and the reports on matters referred to it by the lower chambers. Here too, with the junior councilors frequently but not invariably in attendance, were debated the new edicts communicated by the crown for registration. The Grand' Chambre of the Parlement of Paris derived additional prestige from the fact that on its high benches might sit the fifty-odd *ducs et pairs de France* in their capacity as "councilors-born." But even in the provinces, where this peculiar distinction was lacking, the grand' chambres everywhere considered the cases most likely to attract public as well as royal attention.

Over a period of several centuries, the increasing volume of incoming business had resulted in the creation of several other types of chambers: (1) *chambres des requêtes* to consider cases brought before a given parlement by holders of the royal letters of *committimus* which conferred access to the sovereign courts in first instance; (2) *chambres des enquêtes* to study prepared briefs and supply examining magistrates in affairs requiring questionnaires to local officers or interrogation of witnesses; (3) the *tournelle*, usually composed of officers regularly assigned to requêtes or enquêtes but commissioned in rotation to consider criminal appeals;[23] (4) *chambres des vacations* to carry on the routine business of the company during the September and October recess.[24]

The most extreme case of internal complexity was that of the Parlement of Paris, which contained, in addition to its Grand' Chambre, two chambres des requêtes and five chambres des enquêtes

[23] In the Parlement of Languedoc, to cite the inevitable exception, appointments to the Tournelle were "ordinary" rather than rotating.

[24] The ability of no more than a dozen presidents and councilors to substitute for one hundred or more during two full months requires a word of explanation. Even during the regular sessions, the actual judicial business of the various chambers seems to have been conducted by relatively small working teams of councilors, while many of the younger, wealthier, or simply less interested members appeared only for major trials and great ceremonies. In the notes of Bertin du Rocheret, president of the élection of Épernay, there is a useful list of members whom this judge considered significant in each of the chambres des enquêtes at Paris: for two of the chambers, which in theory had about twenty members each, he notes only six names apiece; for two others, seven apiece; and for the last, eight. B.N., Ms. fr. nouv. acq. 1313, fol. 55. Given the customary slowness of parlementary justice and the possibility of postponing troublesome affairs until after the full court had reconvened, the members of the "vacations" could manage to collect their extra fees without suffering unduly from their sacrifice of a holiday.

(reduced to three in 1756), not to mention its Tournelle and chambre des vacations, both of which drew on the personnel of the other eight divisions. The Parlement of Languedoc had one chambre des requêtes and three chambres des enquêtes. Other companies for the most part varied only in the number, not in the type, of constituent chambers. The Parlement of Dauphiné alone retained a superficially different organization, its chambers simply being numbered first through fourth; but in actual division of functions they corresponded closely to their parallels elsewhere.[25]

Within each sovereign court the individual officer occupied a position carefully defined in terms of its functional title and his seniority at that rank. The names varied somewhat among the different categories of courts, but the same general levels of titular hierarchy were present in each of them. At the very top stood the first president. Just below him, and entitled to act in his absence (in order of seniority), were the other presidents of the court, sometimes as many as twelve, as in the Paris Chambre des Comptes, though more commonly numbering only five or six in the provincial companies. The parlements displayed one peculiarity in this regard: their présidents à mortier were a special group attached in each court to the grand' chambre and sharply distinguished from the presidents of the subordinate subdivisions. Then came the *gens du roi*—the procureur-général and the two to four avocats-généraux—frequently referred to simply as the *parquet* because at ceremonial sessions they addressed the court from the small center space of floor. This was the team of legal officers who represented the king's interests, supervised criminal prosecutions and police functions in the ressort, and were responsible for the registration of all instructions from the crown.[26]

[25] It should be pointed out that special chambers for fiscal affairs were attached to the parlements of Metz, Burgundy, Brittany and Dauphiné, which had absorbed the functions of previous cours des aides; the Parlement of Navarre had an extra chamber for cases elsewhere handled by the chambres des comptes.

[26] The chief gens du roy were sharply distinguished by their official status from the numerous private procureurs and avocats at a given court and by their noble rank from their subordinate *substituts*. Among themselves, however, the separation of status and function was much less clear. In theory, the procureur-général had *la plume* and the avocats-généraux, *la parole*; but in the eighteenth century all took turns both at oral pleading and at preparing written briefs for the crown. (Cf. the notes of Président de Harlay, B.N., Ms. fr. 16819, fol. 121.) In ceremonial distinctions the senior avocat-

The deliberative mass of a court was composed of the councilors, always led by their dean, who was entitled to extra income and special honors, including that of presiding over the court in the absence of all the presidents. In a parlement the councilors of the grand' chambre (both lay and ecclesiastical) and the presidents of the subordinate chambers, who took rank with them, stood far above the junior councilors of requêtes and enquêtes, who could advance to the grand' chambre only in order of seniority. In the chambres des comptes there were titles of specialization: *maîtres des comptes*, *correcteurs des comptes*, *auditeurs des comptes*. These various distinctions, however, should not obscure the fact that in the classification *conseiller* we have a general term covering at least 80 percent of the high robe officers.

There is no need here to go into great detail concerning the other sovereign court members who were classed as nobles of the high robe: the *greffiers-en-chef* (from one to five per company), who supervised the clerical staff, dispatched correspondence, and saw to the distribution, in some cases the printing, of judgments and resolutions; the *premier huissier*, master of ceremonies in the original sense of the term; and the officers of the chancellery attached to each court—*garde des sceaux*, *contrôleur*, *notaires-secrétaires*—who like the gens du roi were special agents of the crown, in this instance charged with affixing the royal seal to outgoing instructions and rulings.[27]

Finally, if only to emphasize the institutional contact between robe and non-robe noblemen which sovereign court organization permitted, mention must be made of the various honorary officers who were entitled to sit in the various companies: peers of France in the Parlement of Paris, the local governor and lieutenants general in each provincial parlement, the archbishop of Toulouse and the abbot of Saint-Sernin in Languedoc, the bishop of Dijon (from 1731) and

---

général enjoyed a traditional precedence; but the procureur-général, who alone was empowered to sign documents originating with the parquet, was the actual chief of the group. The best special study on this subject is that by Gustave Saulnier de Pinelais, *Les gens du roi au Parlement de Bretagne* (Rennes-Paris, 1902).

[27] In the Joursanvault papers concerning Franche-Comté, B.N., Ms. fr. nouv. acq. 8795, there is a list of chancellery officers at the Chambre des Comptes of Dôle in the 1730's which shows one garde des sceaux, four contrôleurs and twelve secrétaires, the latter two sets of officers divided into four teams, each serving three months per year.

the abbot of Cîteaux in Burgundy, the bishops of Rennes and Nantes in Brittany, and so on. By a custom inherited from the medieval Norman *Échiquier*, the lord of Pont-Saint-Pierre was entitled to sit as honorary councilor in the Parlement at Rouen, letters patent of 1692 having confirmed the holder of this fief in the title of "eldest of the house of Roncherolles" and hence "first baron of Normandy."[28] Finally, there were the two *chevaliers d'honneur* installed in each sovereign court, save the Parlement of Paris, by an edict of July 1702, "in order to tighten the bonds which ought always to exist between the noblesse de robe and the noblesse d'épée."[29] True, Louis XIV's interest had lain primarily in the fiscal returns from this sale of new offices, and in many instances not *nobles de race* but scions of wealthy robe families had purchased places as chevaliers d'honneur; but it was of some importance for the future that certain great feudal houses—Beaufremont and Oyselay at Besançon, for example—now had representatives in the strongholds of the robins.[30]

The above discussion represents the bare minimum of institutional detail necessary for an understanding of the various factors involved in individual judicial careers of the early eighteenth century. Against the background of different categories of sovereign courts—parlements, chambres des comptes, cours des aides, cours des monnaies, Grand Conseil—and titular ranks—first president, president, procureur- or avocat-général, councilor, greffier-en-chef, huissier-en-chef, chancellery officer—we begin to perceive a comprehensible pattern of advancement in otherwise confusing changes of title and transfers from one court to another. The element of geographical movement is particularly striking, for it bespeaks a greater degree of communication and interchange of personnel among the various provincial courts than has generally been assumed to have existed.[31] Thus we find Geoffroi-Macé Camus de Pontcarré leaving his councilorship at

[28] B.N., Ms. fr. 21567, fol. 185. See also Louis de Merval, *Catalogue et armorial des présidents, conseillers, gens du roi et greffiers du Parlement de Rouen* (Evreux, 1867), xx.

[29] Bastard d'Estang, *Les parlements*, I, 153.

[30] B.N., Ms. fr. nouv. acq. 9770, fol. 118, Lancelot papers; A.N., U. 992, fol. 73, papers of President Denis.

[31] It is interesting, in this connection, to read the late seventeenth-century notes of First President de Harlay (B.N., Ms. fr. 16819, fol. 149-150) on ceremonial distinctions accorded visiting robe officials in various parlements. The total impression is one of considerable circulation.

the Parlement of Paris in 1730 in order to become first president of the Parlement of Rouen. The previous year Matthieu Montholon, one-time councilor in the Grand Council, more recently first president of the Parlement of Navarre, had set off from Pau to take up the same office in the distant Parlement of Metz. When Aimard-Jean Nicolai succeeded his grandfather as first president of the Paris Chambre des Comptes in 1734, he vacated a lower position in a more powerful court, to wit, a councilorship in the Parlement of Paris; and First President Claude de Monnier at Dôle had in 1731 received the same relative promotion—in his case, from the Parlement of Franche-Comté. The Paris Cour des Monnaies had been presided over since 1727 by a former councilor of the Grand Conseil, Étienne-Alexandre Chopin de Gouzangré.[32]

Not all the high offices, to be sure, were occupied by newcomers from other courts, this being a circumstance encountered most frequently, though not solely, in the first presidencies, which the king could fill with officers of his own choice. Taken as a whole, presidencies and the high places of the parquet went more often than not to officers already members of the court in question. But the examples given in the preceding paragraph, all selected, incidentally, from just the middle ten years of my prescribed period, will perhaps suffice to show what went to make up the *noble de robe's* conception of advancement.[33]

6

Any attempt to reconcile the relatively extensive circulation of officers with the sharp disputes which frequently broke out among the various sovereign courts, must, I think, begin with the fact that the high noblesse de robe was in 1715 far from being a thoroughly unified caste. Rather it was a network of local companies, held together

[32] These examples, as well as countless others, may be found in that obsequious but extremely valuable little compilation by "Louis Chasot de Nantigny," *Tablettes de Thémis*. This work, a veritable *Who's Who?* of high judicial personnel, is even more valuable in manuscript (B.N., Ms. fr. 32985-32986) than in the printed form (Paris, 1755), 3 parts in 2 vols; for the anonymous author's notes, in addition to including numerous lists omitted from the 1755 edition, show clearly that he gathered his material in the 1740's, that is to say, during the period treated in the present study.

[33] For information concerning the movement of numerous officers from one court to others, see especially Emmanuel Michel, *Biographie du Parlement de Metz* (Paris, 1853).

by the fitful intercourse of correspondence and personnel transfers, differentiated within itself by the forces of organizational jealousy and local pride. These latter forces are not to be dismissed lightly, for they were basic to the behavior of the sovereign courts, as, indeed, to that of all widely distributed institutions under the *ancien régime*. Nevertheless, the high robe did represent a corps with certain common values and a steadily increasing awareness of professional, as well as social solidarity. It is in this sense that the total numerical strength of sovereign court officers becomes a factor of importance.

Just how many such officers there were at any given moment between 1715 and 1748 can only be estimated with a substantial allowance for error. The data for this purpose consist of lists of officers received into the various companies over periods ranging from one to four centuries, scattered attendance rolls for specific assemblies, and an occasional note made by some magistrate interested in determining how many colleagues he had. Jottings of this latter type are obviously not a complete source; and the attendance figures are similarly imperfect, because they never indicate the names of absentees. Even the reception lists present a problem, in that only the most carefully prepared give the essential information as to when each officer died or resigned his place.[34]

[34] The most important single source of numerical data for the sovereign courts as a whole during our period is "Chasot de Nantigny's" manuscript of *Les Tablettes de Thémis* in the Département des Manuscrits of the Bibliothèque Nationale (already cited). Also worth noting among the unpublished sources are B.N., Ms. fr. 21567, Édits et listes concernant les cours supérieures, notes of President de Harlay; A.N., MM. 821, Généalogie des Magistrats du Conseil et du Parlement; B.N., Ms. fr. 24113, Liste de membres du parlement de Rouen; B.N., Ms. fr. 26478, Liste d'officiers du Parlement de Metz (1633-1754); B.N., Ms. fr. nouv. acq. 5273, Organisation du Parlement de Navarre, à Pau; B.N., Ms. fr. 32142-32143, Catalogues des présidents, conseillers et officiers de la Chambre des Comptes (1296-1757); A.N., KK. 888, Noms de tous les officiers de la Chambre des Comptes qui ont possedé une mesme Charge; B.N., Ms. fr. 32318, Mémoires pour servir à l'histoire du Parlement de Rouen, de la Cour des Aides, de la Chambre des Comptes et du Bureau des finances de Rouen, principalement des officiers de ces juridictions; B.N., Ms. fr. 32991, Listes des premiers présidents, présidents, conseillers et autres officiers de la Cour des aides; B.N., Ms. fr. 7723, Tableau chronologique de tous les officiers de la Cour des Aydes de Paris, depuis son etablissement; B.N., Ms. fr. 22623, États de la Cour des monnaies en 1712; B.N., Ms. fr. 14015, Genuit des conseillers du Grand Conseil, depuis l'an 1483 jusques à present (1756); B.N., Mss. fr. 32987-32990, Guiblet's Histoire des présidents, procureurs et avocats généraux, conseillers, et autres officiers du Parlement de Paris et du Grand Conseil.

To supplement these original documents, which leave many sovereign courts unac-

In the parlements, noblesse de robe was enjoyed by officers numbering as many as 185 in Paris and as few as 16 in Perpignan, with Toulouse, Rennes and Rouen having more than 100 apiece and with Bordeaux, Dijon and Metz only slightly smaller. The total for all fifteen in the early eighteenth century came to approximately 1,250,[35] exclusive of the non-professional nobles and the non-noble subordinate officers. The chambres des comptes, ranging from the 215 officers at Paris and Montpellier's 138 down to the 19 at Blois, provided about another 800. The cours des aides, less numerous as well as smaller on the average, were staffed by just under 150 officers; that of Paris had 69 in 1715, while Montauban, Clermont-Ferrand and Bordeaux had 33, 29 and 17, respectively. The cours des monnaies were established with the same number of positions in each: 41 or a total of between 70 and 80, allowing for periodic vacancies. In 1715 the number of robe officers in the Grand Conseil was still fixed at 63,[36] though here again vacancies often made the actual figure lower. Combining these statistics, one can say that the total number of nobles de robe in the sovereign courts remained somewhere over 2,000

---

counted for, one must turn to various monographs on individual companies. Aside from these, there are several other printed works which contribute to our numerical information; *Listes des membres du Parlement* (Paris, various dates), B.N., Lf^{25}.31; *Liste générale de Nosseigneurs du Parlement de Bretagne depuis son Erection en 1554, jusqu'en 1725* (Rennes, 1725), B.N. Lf^{25}.93; Mlle. Denys, *Armorial de la Chambre des Comptes* (Paris, 1780, second edition), 2 vols., B.N., Lf^{27}.6A (Réserve); and H. Géraud, "Parlements, Conseils, Chambres des comptes et Cours des aides," *Annuaire historique* (Paris), III (1839), 141-185.

35 Somewhat lower estimates for this all-important category are given by Carré, *La Fin des parlements*, 2—1,100—and by Édouard Barthélemy, *La Noblesse en France avant et depuis 1789* (Paris, 1858), 64-65—only 1,037. However, it should be pointed out that both these writers were using estimates of magistrates actually in office in the late 1780's, Carré having relied on the figures given by Necker, and Barthélemy, on those of Chérin. Even though these later totals include the Parlement of Lorraine, at Nancy, created in 1775, they reflect the number of vacancies which were never filled after the crisis of the Maupeou suppression of parlements, 1771-1774. When to this factor is added the influence of increasing exclusivism, which tended more and more to leave offices unfilled because of the inability of any outsider to secure the approval of the established officers, the larger number for the earlier years of the century becomes comprehensible.

36 Between 1690 and 1738, the Grand Conseil had a regular first president and eight presidents. But in the latter year, the crown suppressed these offices and returned to the pre-1690 system of detailing a conseiller d'état and eight maîtres des requêtes to fulfill the same functions, on short-term commissions which simply detached them temporarily from the king's council. Thereafter, only the conseillers au Grand Conseil and the gens du roi were, properly speaking, members of the noblesse de robe.

and never exceeded 2,300 during the first half of the eighteenth century.

If these two thousand or more individuals are to be taken as the true *haute robe*, how should they be distinguished from the rest of the French magistracy? The answer lies in the special rank and powers of the sovereign, as opposed to the lower, courts. The phrase, "noblesse de robe," is one of those convenient bits of historical vocabulary which are always easier to employ than to define with precision; and the same is true of the even broader designation of "robe," for the whole of pre-1789 judicial personnel, from great noblemen on parlementary benches down to humble greffiers in remote *prévôtés*.

Under the circumstances, one is forced to recognize the universal tendency of social or professional groupings to be separated by indistinct and wavering border areas rather than by concise boundaries. Below the sovereign court positions, there existed, as will be seen in the later discussion of the technical bases of nobility, a number of other judicial offices which conferred noblesse on their occupants, either immediately or after two or three generations in the same family. This was true of the presidencies and treasurer-generalships in the twenty-six *bureaux des finances*[37] and of the offices in the Châtelet (technically only the prévôté of Paris, actually one of the most important courts in the realm). It was also true, though less automatically, of a fluctuating number of presidencies, lieutenancies and councilorships in almost 100 présidiaux, 300 subordinate bailliages,[38] and the literally countless lower courts which provided their more prosperous members with excuses to purchase nobility. Taken as a whole, these subordinate nobles de robe unquestionably represented a number many times as large as that of the sovereign courts' personnel. The fact remains that it was the thirty-one great companies described in the preceding pages which alone displayed that combination of political power and social prestige which is of central significance for my study.

[37] Chérin, *Abrégé*, *passim* (for each of the above-mentioned categories, see his index for relevant legislation).

[38] Cf. Armand Brette, *Recueil de documents relatifs à la convocation des États généraux de 1789* (Paris, 1894-1915), II, 547-555, for a "Tableau des bailliages" which brings the total number of units at that level to 455.

There is also need to distinguish the high robe from the numerous and tightly organized corps of private avocats, the men who had secured admission to the bar and whose monopoly on pleading rights made them as essential to judicial functions as were the court officers themselves. In the pages of Barbier and Marais, both practicing avocats at the Parlement of Paris, one may follow the fraternity of the bar in its various conflicts, now against the courts on a matter of procedure, now in support of them against a measure of the government. Some of the most famous avocats, Bourjon and Lorry and Babille, for example, have remained figures of note in French legal history. Nevertheless, these men and their much less vocal colleagues, the procureurs, remained, except for sons of nobles de robe who might be serving short apprenticeships before ascending to the bench, fundamentally bourgeois, private practitioners. One has only to contrast the sentiments of Barbier with those of his contemporary, President Hénault,[39] to perceive the differences of outlook. The attitude of sovereign court judges toward the avocats seems generally to have been at best one of condescension and at worst one of contempt.

7

What it meant to be a member of a sovereign court, as distinguished from any other group in French society, was nowhere so clearly revealed as in the meticulous ceremonial rules which governed the public life of a high noble de robe. His official costume was strictly regulated. At home, he might be indistinguishable from any other prosperous gentleman, except for his flat clerical neckpiece or *rabat*. On the street, he could generally be identified by the broad-brimmed felt hat which most members of his order preferred to the fashionable tricorn; and he might also affect a long outer cloak, though under the Regency and following, these cumbersome garments became much less common than they had been during Louis XIV's time.[40]

[39] Charles-J.-F. Hénault, *Mémoires* (ed. F. Rousseau, Paris, 1911).

[40] Saint-Simon, *Mémoires*, IV, 405-406. Louis XIV, in an edict of 1684, which was to be read in every sovereign court twice a year, had admonished the high magistrates to "s'attirer du respect par la sagesse de leur conduite aussy bien que par la dignité du caractère dont nous les honorons" and went on to specify the manteau for all public appearances, including especially church services. B.N., Ms. fr. 16581.

When sitting in court to consider routine business of the day, he would wear simply the black gown and broad hat which constituted the "petit habit." But when his court re-convened at the solemn *rentrée* after the autumn recess,[41] when it assembled to attend a Te Deum or to receive a distinguished visitor, then his own position and that of his company were dramatized for all to behold.

On the 19th of June 1717, for example, Peter the Great made a visit to the Parlement of Paris and was presented with an impressive spectacle of traditionalistic pride and self-conscious grandeur.[42] The czar and his retinue, escorted by a welcoming delegation from the court, entered the still empty Grand' Chambre and were led to prepared places in the two high pleading cubicles or *lanternes* at opposite corners of the room. Then, while the red-robed peers filed into their high benches, using the special entrance which permitted them, at the cost of some rather precarious climbing tactics, to escape the regular rules of precedence, the robe personnel began its entry in full regalia. Leading the procession came the first president and the présidents à mortier, each in his crimson robe, ermine *épitoge* and the distinctive bonnet from which the title was derived (a soft, bowl-shaped headgear of black velvet trimmed in gold, with the bulbous tip of the crown protruding at the top, to complete the appearance of an apothecary's mortar and pestle). Next to enter were the scores of councilors, carefully arranged in order of seniority, with the *doyen* and the presidents of the lower chambers in purple robes and ermine capes, the lay councilors in fur-edged capes and bonnets of crimson with velvet-lined robes of the same color, and their ecclesiastical colleagues in scarlet-violet. The gens du roi followed, practically indistinguishable from the lay councilors who had preceded them or the greffiers-en-chef, who now entered at their heels. Last of these sumptuous figures was the first huissier, in a simpler red robe but easily distinguished by his cap of cloth of gold. While

[41] The exact date of the rentrée varied somewhat in different courts, but most of the great parlements, including Paris, Toulouse, Bordeaux, Dijon and Rennes, reconvened on November 12, the day after Saint Martin's.

[42] The *procès-verbal* from the minutes of the *Conseil Secret*, highest form of parlementary audience short of the royal *lit de justice* itself, may be seen in the Archives Nationales, X^{1A}, 8434. Selections have also been printed in *Le Mois littéraire et pittoresque* (Paris), June 1902, 581.

the presidents assumed their places in the high benches opposite the peers and while the councilors took assigned seats in the lower tiers, the long column of lower functionaries and the black-gowned avocats completed the procession.

This type of ceremony, be it remembered, was repeated several times a year in each of the courts. A visitor to Clermont-Ferrand on the morning of Pentecost or to Pau when a Te Deum was to be sung for the birth of a Dauphin would have witnessed a remarkably similar display, without the peers, of course, but with the addition of the king's generals and the chevaliers d'honneur in their black habits, white-plumed hats and dress swords.[43] If the occasion were a rentrée after St.-Martin's or after Easter, the court members would be further reminded of the duties and privileges of their calling by *mercuriales*, delivered by the procureur-général and perhaps by a president, one of the avocats-généraux or the dean of councilors. The mercuriales given by d'Aguesseau while avocat- and later procureur-général in the Parlement of Paris, "La dignité du magistrat" (1700), for example, or "Les moeurs du magistrat" (1702), "L'homme publique" (1706), "La vraie et fausse justice" (1708), give a good insight into the professional pride which they were intended both to express and to increase.[44]

My insistence on treating the personnel of the sovereign courts as a distinct part, by far the most important part, of the noblesse de robe will perhaps not appear unduly arbitrary if one now recalls the chief characteristics of those courts, viewed simply as judicial companies: first, their distribution and the criteria by which they were designated sovereign; second, the fierce particularistic pride which sometimes set them at odds with one another; third, the circulation of officers which signalized their increasing unification, even in the face of such disputes; fourth, the parallel subdivisions and systems of ranks within

[43] See, for example, *Usages de la Cour des Aides de Clermont-Ferrand* (Clermont, 1853, reprinted from a document in the Archives Départementales of Puy-de-Dôme), B.N., Lf[28].2; also B.N., Mss. fr. 18513-18533, Recueil sur le Cérémonial, Godefroy papers.

[44] *Oeuvres*, I, 75-86, 97-108, 118-124, 140-148. There exists a little-known mercurial by Montesquieu, delivered before the Parlement de Bordeaux in 1725 but printed at Geneva only in 1777, B.N., Lf[25].102; also, for an example for a different class of court, we may refer to one by Avocat-Général Lefranc of the Montauban Cour des Aides, delivered at the *rentrée* of 1727 and printed the next year, B.N. Lf[28].4. A.N., K. 704 contains other mercurials.

them; and finally, the pomp which dramatized their special combination of powers and prestige. The members of these companies formed an exalted stratum of public officials, in important respects quite distinct from any other portion of French society in 1715. No single aspect of their position, however, is more significant from the present point of view than the special place they occupied within the nobility at the death of Louis XIV.

Chapter Four

The Magistrate as Nobleman

1

THE MOST important single fact about the high robe's nobility in 1715 was that in legal terms there was no longer any doubt about it. Admission to the full social status of gentlemen might still be dependent on individual wealth and marriages rather than on high office alone, although even here the old sentiment that "les conseillers sont nobles et leurs petits-fils gentilshommes"[1] was rapidly becoming meaningless, because so many eighteenth-century councilors were also grandsons of councilors. In any event, recognition of the sovereign court magistrate's nobility rested on an impressive combination of legal bases: fifteenth- and sixteenth-century precedents, pronouncements of the great jurisconsults, and, more recently, the combination of express legislation and judicial confirmation. The course of late seventeenth-century developments in this regard had already led a commentator at the end of Louis XIV's reign to write: "since that time, there is, it seems to me, no longer any excuse for confusing the magistracy with the Third Estate."[2] At the time these words were written, a full century had passed since the Estates General of 1614, when last the high robe had figured among the commoners; the very passage of time had brought its own, in this case exalting, influence to bear in support of a group which had never for a moment relaxed its own pressure for higher honors.

Although direct written evidence of magistral nobility in the medieval period is naturally scarce, there is reason to believe that beginning in the thirteenth century at the latest, certain non-noble legists who had worked their way to the highest ranks in the king's

[1] Bastard d'Estang, *Les Parlements*, I, 260.

[2] B.N., Ms. fr. 10789, Du rang de la robe, 399.

service received royal grants of personal and in some cases hereditary noblesse. The king's informal action in conferring such dignity on an individual robin might have reflected either gratitude, the desire to provide subordinate officials with an example of loyalty's rewards, the administrative necessity of making the judges less vulnerable to the scorn of titled subjects, or a combination of all these motives. In the sixteenth century, with the progressive elaboration of legal distinctions in such works as André Tiraqueau's *Tractatus de Nobilitate*[3] and the growing need for precise criteria in tax exemption cases, formal *lettres de noblesse* in favor of high magistrates became increasingly common. Among the papers of the Paris Cour des Aides for 1558, for example, we find letters from Henry II solemnly ennobling "nostre cher et bien amé maistre Nicole Berthe, advocat en nostre Cour de Parlement et demourant en nostre ville de Paris," as a reward for the "bons et agreables services qu'il a par cy devant faitz et fait chacun jour en son estat."[4]

Involved in this and similar cases, however, was a degree of royal caprice, or individual payments for individual favors, which could not indefinitely be reconciled with the organizational needs of a developing government. Beginning with the reign of Henry IV, there was elaborated a complex but nonetheless relatively coherent system for determining questions of noble rank among high robe officers. The key to this system lay in gradations of dignity, that is to say, in the differing periods of time and/or number of successive generations which a robe family must have served at a given official level before it could claim full, hereditary nobility. This conception emerges clearly, albeit in negative form, from the great *Règlement des Tailles* of 1600:

> It is forbidden that any person assume the title of esquire (*écuyer*) and introduce himself into the corps of nobility, if he has not issued from a father and grandfather who have served the public in certain honorable charges from among those which, according to the laws and customs (*moeurs*) of the kingdom, are capable of initiating nobility.[5]

[3] (Paris, 1549). Jacques Brejon, *André Tiraqueau* (Paris, 1937), 47 ff.

[4] A.N., Z1A. 528. This particular case was one of "perfect," i.e., immediate and transmissible, noblesse; for Berthe is elevated "ensemble sa posterité et lignée masles et femelles, nez et a naistre, decendans de lui en bon et loyal mariage."

[5] Isambert, *Recueil*, XV, 234.

This, however, was obviously too vague to provide the sort of sharply defined standards needed in cases of dispute. Furthermore the reference to existing "laws and customs of the kingdom" indicated a more or less submerged body of jurisprudence which, along with Henry IV's edict itself, called for the regularizing efforts of contemporary theorists.

Of the latter, I shall here cite only the two most important, partly because they were to become the decisive authorities for later reference, partly because their views reflect not only scholarly care but also a broad acquaintance with how the courts were actually ruling and on what grounds. The first, Jean Bacquet, in his *Droit d'anoblissement*,[6] begins with a distinction between "nobles de race" and "nobles par benefice du Prince," then goes on to classify the latter according to several sub-categories, beginning with those ennobled by letters patent and arriving thereafter at "Estats, Dignitez & Offices." He lists the maîtres des requêtes, the officers of the parlements, chambres des comptes, cours des aides, and the trésoriers généraux de France as functionaries ennobled by their offices. But only at the third generation in such functions can a family be said to have acquired hereditary nobility, or so Bacquet interprets recent decisions by the Paris Cour des Aides in tax cases.[7] This was the principle to which the legists had assigned one of their cherished phrases from Roman law: "Patre et avo consulibus."[8]

Much more complete than Bacquet was Charles Loyseau, whose *Cinq livres du droit des offices* (Paris, 1610) and *Traité des ordres et simples dignitez* (Paris, 1613) constitute an incomparable fund of information on public functions and nobility as conceived by the early seventeenth century. One of his most important contributions was that of supplying an exact set of terms for distinguishing those functions which he believed to confer immediate, hereditary noblesse from those which carried only personal noblesse for their incumbents

[6] *Oeuvres* (Lyon, 1744), II, 343-364. The original edition appeared in 1608.

[7] *Ibid.*, II, 348. "Quand les ayeul & père successivement ont esté pourveus des estats & offices susdits, & sont decedez pourveus desdits estats & iceux exerçans, les enfans peuvent jouyr de tous les drois, autoritez, privileges, franchises & immunitez dont jouyssent les nobles de race."

[8] A.N., M. 785, no. 1[2], an anonymous memorandum, De la noblesse de robbe, in the Mirabeau papers, contains a full historical discussion of this famous expression.

during the first two generations. The following officers he recognized as invested with "perfect" nobility the moment they took office: the Great Officers of the Crown (Chancellor, *Connétable*, *Grand Maître*, *Grand Chambellan*, *Grand Amiral*, *Grand Écuyer*, etc.); those of the Household (*Grand Aumônier*, *Grand Maître des Cérémonies*, *Grand Fauconnier*, *Grand Louvetier*, etc.);[9] members of the Conseil Privé, and hence by extension all presidents of sovereign courts, to whom Loyseau assigns the rank of privy councilors.[10] Also exalted by their offices but entitled to only personal nobility are, among others, the secrétaires du Roy and the councilors of sovereign courts. In the *Cinq livres*, from which the above is extracted,[11] the doctrine of *patre et avo* is not adduced; but Loyseau employs it in his *Traité des ordres*, where he cites councilors of sovereign courts among those officers whose family nobility can become transmissible in the third generation of successive occupancy.[12] The concept is here more precisely defined than in Bacquet; for not only does Loyseau clearly distinguish the offices requiring three generations from those of the higher class, he also cites a rule of either twenty years service or death while in office as the requirement for each generation.

It is not always easy to determine the concrete importance of the legists' theories, inasmuch as later legislation reveals considerable confusion even in official quarters about the very niceties of doctrine which had been set down with such confidence by the jurisconsults. But it would be a grave mistake to assign their writings only academic significance. Down to the end of the old monarchy, one finds them, especially Tiraqueau, Bacquet and Loyseau (as well as the later codifier, La Roque), quoted at length in judicial opinions, beside precedent-making decisions of the courts themselves. In questions of social rank, as in all else, French jurisprudence remained throughout

[9] By the early eighteenth century, of course, these crown and household dignities had long since lost their importance as ennobling instruments. The office of Connétable had been suppressed by Richelieu in 1627. The rest were now always filled by members of great families (in the case of the Chancellor, great robe families) and in some cases princes of the blood royal. Thus, three successive Ducs de Bourbon-Condé, greatest of the *Princes du sang*, were Grands Maîtres from 1685 to 1770; and the Grand Amiral from 1683 to 1737 was the Comte de Toulouse, Louis XV's legitimated great uncle. For a discussion of these offices, see Barthélemy, *Noblesse en France*, 198 ff.

[10] The same list appears in La Roque, *Traité de la Noblesse*, 401 ff. The first edition of this work appeared in 1678.

[11] *Op. cit.*, 109-110. [12] *Op. cit.*, 69.

the ancien régime an amalgam of Roman fomulas, case law, local custom, and legislative texts as reported and expanded by authoritative interpreters.

The weight of theoretical commentaries had thus been placed behind the high robe's nobility very early in the seventeenth century. Succeeding decades saw it further buttressed by a combination of legislative and judicial recognition. In 1639, for example, a special taille law for Dauphiné endorsed the *patre et avo consulibus* rule as a test for transmissible nobility among officers of the Grenoble Parlement, Chambre des Comptes, Cour des Aides (then separate) and Bureau des Finances.[13] It was during the first years of Louis XIV's troubled minority, however, when the Queen Regent and Mazarin were desperately bargaining for political support, that the sovereign courts received their detailed charters of nobility. Hence the 1640's and 1650's were a period of crucial importance for the background of this question.

The basic grant was embodied in an edict of July 1644, which conferred perfect nobility on all presidents, councilors, gens du roi and greffiers-en-chef of the Parlement of Paris.[14] This was quickly followed by similar concessions to Grand Conseil officers in December of the same year[15] and to the Paris Chambre des Comptes in January 1645.[16] The extension of these privileges to other sovereign courts arose out of the Fronde crisis, or rather out of the efforts of Anne of Austria and her minister to liquidate it. A declaration of June 1649, for example, announced in the young king's name that, in view of the loyalty displayed by the Parlement of Burgundy:

> Nous avons dict & declaré, disons & declarons, que noz Presidents, Counseillers, Advocats & Procureur General, le Greffier en Chef, les huict Notaires & Secretaires de nostre-dicte Cour presentement pourveus desdicts Offices, & qui le seront cy-après soyent Nobles & les tenons pour telz, voulons & nous plaist qu'ils iouyssent & leur Vefues [sic] demeurans en viduité, leur posterité & lignée tant masles que femelles, nez & a naistre, des mesmes droits, privileges, franchises, immunités, rang, sçéance, prééminence que les autres Nobles de Race, Barons, Gentils-hommes de nostre Royaume. . . .[17]

[13] Chérin, *Abrégé*, 103. [14] *Ibid.*, 109. [15] A.N., K. 694, no. 2. [16] Chérin, *Abrégé*, 110.

[17] Bib. Dijon, Ms. 1059 (128), in historical notes preceding Abbé Boullemier's Succession des offices du Parlement, fol. 54.

Similar documents for the Chambre des Comptes of Dijon, in 1650,[18] and for the Parlement of Normandy later the same year,[19] show a definite governmental policy of bartering blanket recognitions of nobility for support or at least passivity in the civil war. In some parlements such grants came only later; Metz in 1658;[20] Franche-Comté in 1692, completed in 1694;[21] Flanders not until 1713.[22] Similarly, the chambres des comptes received their individual concessions over a period of several decades, Nantes in 1669, for example,[23] and Montpellier in 1690.[24] The various cours des aides kept pace;[25] but the two cours des monnaies, alone among the sovereign courts, had to wait until after Louis XIV's death before they finally received such grants of noblesse in 1719.[26]

All this detailed legislation is apt to leave a confused impression on the modern reader's mind, as indeed it often did on a seventeenth-century Frenchman's, especially after the inevitable revocations and subsequent confirmations under Louis XIV had done their baffling work. It will be noted, for example, that most of the royal declarations cited above had initially conferred perfect nobility on all specified courts in the first generation, momentarily passing over Bacquet's and Loyseau's treasured formula of *patre et avo consulibus.* A general edict of 1669 restored the third generation rule for councilors and below;[27] but this in turn was rescinded by another edict in 1690,[28] only to be re-established in August 1715,[29] so that the old requirement was technically in force, though actually seldom mentioned, during the period under examination. This sort of confusion, however, while characteristic of legislation under the *ancien régime*, should not obscure the central fact that by 1715, whatever uncertainties about technical points might arise in borderline cases, there remained no

[18] Bib. Dijon, Ms. 781(464), Père Gautier's Notice de la Chambre de comptes de Dijon, 298.

[19] For the text see Merval, *Catalogue et armorial . . . du Parlement de Rouen*, xxii–xxv.

[20] Chérin, *Abrégé*, 131-132; Emmanuel Michel, *Histoire du Parlement de Metz* (Paris, 1845), 290-291.

[21] Chérin, *Abrégé*, 200-201, 209; B.N., Ms. fr. 21567, fol. 129. Besançon had been incorporated into France after the mid-century legislation; but its parlementaires had been noble under the Hapsburg Empire and needed only to be confirmed by Louis XIV.

[22] Chérin, *Abrégé*, 305; G.M. Pillot, *Parlement de Flandres* (Douai, 1849), II, 309-320.

[23] Chérin, *Abrégé*, 184. [24] *Ibid.*, 195. [25] *Ibid.*, 96, 104, 195, 197 and *passim.*

[26] *Ibid.*, 335. [27] *Ibid.*, 183. [28] *Ibid.*, 195. [29] Guyot, *Répertoire*, 75.

question that practically all officers of sovereign courts were, in the eyes of the law, noblemen beyond a shadow of doubt.

Official proof of this appears in the results of Louis XIV's Grande Recherche concerning fraudulent claims of rank. In Toulouse, for example, I have examined eleven cartons of *Jugements d'usurpation de noblesse* imposed by the intendant, Lamoignon de Basville, between 1697 and 1716, without finding a single case of a high robe officer thus condemned.[30] In the parallel series of *Jugements de maintenue*, on the other hand, there are mentioned innumerable officers of the Parlement of Languedoc, the Chambre des Comptes at Montpellier and the Cour des Aides at Montauban—all confirmed in their nobility.[31]

It is perhaps worth re-emphasizing at this point what I have already had cause to indicate: that the two thousand or more sovereign court officers in service when Louis XIV died were by no means the only functionaries who had benefitted from the theoretical writings, legislation, and investigators' decisions just described. They and their predecessors had conquered the legal status of noblemen during the seventeenth century in company with the maîtres des requêtes, the presidents of bureaux des finances and their subordinate *trésoriers de France*, and the superior officers of the Châtelet at Paris.[32] Technically, they shared their rank with the hundreds of secrétaires du roy, holders of *charges sans fonction*, whose noblesse had been established as early as 1484 in a sweeping pronouncement by Charles VIII.[33] Finally, there was the special category of nobles de cloche or municipal officials ennobled as *maires*, *échevins* or *capitouls* of the *bonnes villes*, which in the eighteenth century still included Poitiers, Angoulême, St-Maixent, Tours, Toulouse, Lyon, Angers and Nantes.[34]

[30] A. D. Haute-Garonne, C. 503–513. Many such judgments for the Généralité of Toulouse were printed by Baschi d'Aubais in his *Pièces fugitives* (Paris, 1759), II.

[31] A. D. Haute-Garonne, C. 499-502.

[32] Chérin, *Abrégé*, 104, 209, 348 and *passim*. There were between 700 and 800 noble officers in the bureaux des finances alone, Carré, *La noblesse de France*, 9.

[33] A.-L. de Laigue, *Les familles françaises considérées sous le rapport de leurs prérogatives honorifiques* (Paris, 1815), 45-46.

[34] Guyot, *Répertoire*, 82-83. The lists of privileged towns given by Laigue, *Les familles françaises*, 20; by Nimal, *Nobles et noblesse* (Paris, 1892), 43-44; and by Barthélemy, *La noblesse en France*, 65-66, are considerably longer. These authors, however, have included all the towns which ever received automatic nobility for their highest officers

Enough has been said of the sovereign courts' special rôle, however, so that it scarcely seems necessary further to justify looking more closely at their members' peculiar position in the French aristocracy. For now that they are solidly placed within the boundaries of noblesse as defined by law, there arises the problem of defining distinctive rather than common characteristics. In other words, where did the high robe of 1715 fit into the whole nobility and in what respects was it set apart?

2

As a nobleman, the *parlementaire* (using this term in its eighteenth-century sense to denote any sovereign court officer) enjoyed all the standard privileges discussed in Chapter Two.[35] In addition, however, he had special rights which he did not share with non-robe noblemen. As a royal councilor he benefitted from the privilege of committimus, which empowered him to carry personal litigations either directly to a parlement or, if he was a member of the Paris Parlement, all the way to the king's own privy council—in other words, ironically enough, above the jurisdiction of his own court.[36] Once he had served twenty years in office, he could obtain royal *lettres d'honoriat* which even after his resignation would assure him free access to the palais de justice, admission to his old court's deliberations, and retention of his professional titles and honors.

Some fiscal exemptions were so narrowly confined to the parlementaire as to appear forms of political blackmail paid by the government. He was exempt from a wide range of feudal dues collected by the crown, including the *lods et ventes* which the non-robe noble ordinarily still paid for royal permission to sell any portion of a fief.[37] And the royal declaration of September 1723, which announced the famous tax on offices, land grants, and commercial privileges "à

and have largely ignored the numerous suppressions, such as those affecting La Rochelle, Niort and Saint-Jean d'Angely, in the seventeenth century.

[35] See above, 27-29.

[36] B.N., Ms. fr. nouv. acq. 1643, fol. 228, gives the text of the royal declaration of 1724 confirming this general right of *committimus au grand sceau* in favor of officers of the Paris Parlement. Also in A.N., K. 137, no. 14^3.

[37] Bib. Dijon, Ms. 1059 (128), fol. 57, the grant of nobility to the Parlement of Burgundy in 1649, uses the phrase "tous droicts seigneuriaux et feodaux" in enumerating the exemptions bestowed therein.

cause de l'Avénement du Roi à la Couronne," specifically excused all officers of the parlements, chambres des comptes, Grand Conseil, cours des aides, and cours des monnaies.[38] From a purely fiscal point of view, it is not difficult to see why high robe office might appear attractive even to a member of the wealthier aristocracy. The parlementaires had achieved a position of special privilege within the ranks of the privilégiés themselves.

3

The question of the extent to which a high robe magistrate thought, looked, and acted like the typical nobleman quite naturally suggests a second question: whether or not there *was* any special manner in which a typical nobleman had to think, look, and act. Enough has been said of the internal diversity of the sprawling noble class to suggest caution in positing any "typical" characteristics, except for legal recognition as noble and a general set of prerogatives. The list of attributes which were essential parts of the concept "living nobly" is undoubtedly much shorter than some writers have assumed. It was not necessary that a family have a *devise*, such as the Beaumanoirs' "J'aime qui m'aime" or the Pontecroix' more cryptic "Naturellement," in order to qualify as gentle. Some, of course, had proudly retained medieval or at least medieval-sounding war cries, such as the Montmorency's "Dieu aide au premier baron chrétien!" or the Levis' singularly unoriginal "Dieu aide au second baron chrétien!"[39] But a president or councilor could and generally did eschew these more bizarre vestiges of chivalry. Similarly, although he duly registered his escutcheon in the *Armorial général*, he was on solid enough ground not to feel called upon to fabricate, as did more than one enthusiastic noble de race, a fantastic genealogy to prove his descent from a Roman emperor, a Greek or Biblical hero, or a Germanic king.[40]

No precise code of dress was at work to unify the nobility in its

[38] Chérin, *Abrégé*, 341-343.

[39] Laigue, *Les familles françaises*, 214-217; Louandre, *Noblesse*, 135-136.

[40] For some amusing examples of such genealogies, see Nimal, *Nobles et noblesse*, 31-37. Also valuable is the Vicomte de Marsay's *De l'âge des privilèges au temps des vanités* (Paris, 1946).

external aspects. The history of French sumptuary legislation is long and complex, but the very frequency of legislative enactments forbidding roturiers to use certain types of adornment (there were nine laws concerning furs, silks, laces and jewelry between 1601 and 1667) is the best possible proof of how completely they had been ignored.[41] Nevertheless, a high robe officer stood out from the general populace by the rich materials of his dress, while the rabat at his throat, the frequent though by no means inevitable absence of a sword, and the customarily square cut of his periwig also set him apart from a *noble d'épée*, even after Louis XIV's insistence on the public wearing of robes had become a dead letter.

By 1715, as I shall have cause to note again when examining the evolution of robe families, a substantial percentage of sovereign court officers had obtained prestigious titles by the simple expedient of paying the crown to erect their greatest land holdings into baronies, counties or marquisates. Certain of the highest designations still remained closed to the robe, as to most other nobles. In 1717, for example, there were 12 princes, 53 ducs et pairs, 10 ducs *non pairs*, 11 marshals of France, and 5 cardinals, all of whom could claim titular superiority to the highest placed magistrate.[42] But as a group the personnel of the sovereign courts stood well up in the hierarchy of designations, with their professional titles as an added element of distinction. To a proud chevalier in a truly old family these titles might not constitute perfect gentility; but even before 1715 they were already in the cask and aging. All that was needed was the passage of time.

In their choice of names as in their titles, the magistrates had by 1715 drawn closer to the rest of the noblesse; for the "de" had appeared mysteriously in scores of families. Nevertheless, the characteristic seventeenth-century preference of the robe for Biblical or Roman first names had not yet and in fact never did completely yield to the invasion of François', Philippes and Hyacinthes. In its titles and names, as in most other respects, the high magistracy bore the marks of honor equal to that of all save the highest noblesse de

[41] Chérin, *La noblesse considérée sous ses différents rapports* (Paris, 1788), 49-57; Louandre, *La noblesse française*, 97 ff.

[42] A.N., K. 619, no. 6, Estat des rangs.

race; but shadings of difference had by no means wholly disappeared.

The change in the high robe's way of life, destined to bring it progressively closer to that of other aristocrats in the eighteenth century, was already adumbrated in the era of Louis XIV's passing. Already the more facile presidents, councilors, and gens du roi had begun to make their mark in salon society and to display the skill in conversation, gaming, and lovemaking which that society demanded. Even on the rougher side of noble mores certain of the younger magistrates had begun to take their place. Their participation in the dangerous pastime of dueling had already drawn an expression of Louis XIV's wrath, directed specifically against *gens de robe.*[43] Hunting, the noble's sport par excellence, was becoming more and more accessible to magistrates as they extended their landholdings ever farther into the broad, wooded fiefs of rural France. Yet care must be taken not to read into the individual practices of certain robe nobles the one-sided victory of the seventeenth-century fighting noble's way of life. That way of life was already moribund as an absolute standard for aristocratic living, and for the upper nobility at least, another was taking shape, one in which the high robe was to contribute almost as much as it absorbed.

Did the high robe think as other nobles thought? Again a question which perhaps suggests too much solidarity among the rest of the noblesse. In 1715, however, there were certain marked differences between the magistral mind, as it is revealed in letters, memoirs and judicial minutes, and that of such articulate nobles de race as Saint-Simon, Dangeau, and Boulainvilliers. Both groups had a keen sense of privilege and the desire to protect it. Both were resentful of ground lost under Louis XIV and eager to make the most of the opportunity offered by his death. But in the case of the robe the bourgeois roots were too deep not to call forth a strong *rentier's*, businessman's reaction to the fiscal crisis confronting the new government, while the nobles d'épée with only a few exceptions favored sacrificing investors by declaring the crown bankrupt. The seventeenth-century strain of Jansenism was still strong in the magistracy—probably stronger than it was by the 1730's when it became a major political issue for the sovereign courts. Hence the

[43] A.N., K. 121^{B}. 37^{4}.

religious and moral tenets of the robe could not fail to be considerably different, more austere, self-conscious, personalized, than those of a Jesuit-trained noble de race. Of differences in mental outlook enough evidence will emerge for the years just after 1715 to make the subsequent drawing together a truly striking development.

Taken as a whole, the names, titles, dress, habits and daily pursuits of the sovereign court officers in 1715 combined to form a pattern quite different from that of a non-robe noble living nobly. Some magistrates still worked hard, albeit at a profession which carried no reflection on their nobility. Even a marquis or count with several seigneuries and a good pack of hounds for his vacations in the country was not apt to be confused with retired colonels or the ruffled heirs of territorial houses as long as he was also called "Monsieur le Conseiller," was named Marc-Achille or Jean-Baptiste, wore a rabat and flat dark hat in town, and during several months of the year went early each morning to his duties at the palais. Only when these characteristics become less clear-cut, in the course of the eighteenth century, can one speak of increasing social assimilation.

4

Familiar to every student of French history, of course, is the traditional hostility between the robe and the sword, between men who were acutely aware of their high judicial dignities and other men who felt themselves superior to all whose status rested on anything but valor, actual or ancestral. Assigning the parlementaires their particular place in the nobility thus involves at least a brief consideration of what various types of nobles themselves thought that place was or should be. For an initial impression of the "robe-épée line," which will occupy a large place in the remainder of this investigation, it is necessary only to glance at a few of the writers who signaled its existence under Louis XIV. La Bruyère, with his characteristic dislike of excess, frankly deplored the jealousy between the two groups: "I know not whence comes the reciprocal scorn of the robe and the sword."[44] And Primi Visconti, that nimble-witted

[44] *Les caractères*, I, 352. "La noblesse expose sa vie pour le salut de l'État et pour la gloire du souverain; le magistrat décharge le prince d'une partie du soin de juger les

adventurer who had stepped, as it seemed, from the Italian Renaissance into the Grand Siècle, remarked in 1679, with the exaggeration so essential to his flamboyant intelligence: "No citizen who devotes himself to law [in France] enjoys any consideration . . . only he who follows the career of arms appears noble."[45] The smug pages of Chevigny's catechism for courtiers provide still another evidence of the separation, this time as noted in 1706:

Q. "What is nobility?
A. "It is a quality which a prince has accorded to one of his subjects as recompense for some outstanding act.
Q. "How many kinds of nobility are there?
A. "Two, that of the sword and that of the robe.
Q. "Which is the more esteemed?
A. "That of the sword . . . because it is acquired only after frequent risk of life."[46]

The same distinction, the same tendency to equate "noblesse" with "noblesse d'épée," save in matters of legal definition, runs through official documents of the period. De Bezons' inquest for Languedoc, for example, divided the body of recognized noblemen into a "classe illustre," a "classe d'ancienne race," a "classe de robe," and a small "classe de la cloche" (for those ennobled by service as municipal capitouls of Toulouse).[47] Intendant Le Bret, reporting in 1715 on individuals in Provence who might be considered for various royal commissions, first lists several gens de robe, then goes on to say: "As for *gentlemen*, I perceive only one who might be proposed."[48] Another intendant, Boucher of Bordeaux, was probably typical when he mentioned "parlementaires" and "nobles" separately throughout his correspondence with Paris, 1715-1721—though significantly enough, he was already concerned over their common opposition to royal measures.[49]

---

peuples: voilà de part et d'autre des fonctions bien sublimes et d'une merveilleuse utilité." However, La Bruyère himself was on occasion scornful of robe nobles. Cf. Maurice Lange, *La Bruyère, critique*, 248-251.

[45] *Mémoires* (Paris, 1909), 252-253.

[46] *La Science des Personnes de la Cour*, 38-39.

[47] Guyot, *Répertoire*, 95.

[48] Villars, *Mémoires*, VI, 67.

[49] A.D. Gironde, C. 3145-3147.

Needless to say, the high magistracy had claims of its own. The haughty tone of François Bertaut's polemic, *Les Prérogatives de la Robe*, published at Paris in 1701, would not appear to concede any qualitative superiority to the noblesse d'épée. According to Bertaut, the highest function of the crown was that of administering justice, since the magistrates had inherited the most exalted activity of the medieval monarchs: "Even the costume of *Messieurs du Parlement* is that of the [earlier] kings, princes, dukes-and-peers and chevaliers."[50] In Rome and now in France, he asserts in conclusion, the robe stood and stands higher than the sword, since sooner or later in any dispute "arms must give way to justice."[51] A more conciliatory tone pervades a memorandum prepared by the Parlement of Paris early in the Regency to refute the claims of the peerage, but the same insistence on magistral dignity is basic to the arguments presented: "There is only one sort of nobility. It may be acquired differently, by military services or by those of judicature; but the rights and prerogatives are the same, for the robe has its honors no less than does the sword."[52]

Notwithstanding these strong and apparently confident statements, however, the Regency opened with the noblesse d'épée, and especially the dukes-and-peers, still arguing loudly that the robe's social inferiority was beyond question. Here, for example, are the first lines of a pro-peerage memorandum of 1716, interesting for its ironical use of the Parlement's words from the treatise quoted above: "There is only one sort of nobility, which cannot be acquired by judicial services. One may respect merit when one encounters it in magistrates, but as to birth . . . they will never be regarded as other than honorable bourgeois who enjoy the privileges of noblemen."[53]

Saint-Simon, whose loathing of the robins constituted one of the few dependable lines in that mercurial intellect, is a source to be used with caution in this regard as in many others. Time after time in his *Mémoires* he brought to bear on the Parlement of Paris as a whole and its leading members in particular the full range of his wit, scorn, invective and transparent mendacity. The writing, of course, is brilliant, though one suspects that few other noblemen

[50] *Op. cit.*, 66. [51] *Ibid.*, 378. [52] A.N., MM. 818^1, 365.
[53] A.N., K. 622, no. 7, Lettre de M^r —— à un de ses amis.

spent so much thought and effort on debasing the robe.[54] Nevertheless, it is interesting to read his statement that "for as long as non-ecclesiastics and non-nobles have constituted a third order in the state . . . no magistrate has ever been a deputy [to an Estates General] for anything except that third order."[55] The charge was historically accurate, given the fact that the last Estates General had been held over 100 years earlier; and it is important as an expression of the most extreme type of anti-robe sentiment when Louis XV's reign began.

5

In only one French province were the pre-1715 relations between robe and non-robe nobles notably more cordial than those outlined above. This was in Brittany, where the subsequent movement toward amalgamation was to be less striking than elsewhere because the process had been largely completed before the eighteenth century began.

It would not be true to say that noble birth had always been an absolute requirement for admission to the Parlement at Rennes or the Chambre des Comptes at Nantes. Numerous Breton families of Louis XV's era certainly owed their original noblesse to high offices in the magistracy; but many more were old aristocratic houses which had simply added high offices to their other attributes. As early as the sixteenth century it had already been relatively difficult for a roturier to enter the sovereign courts of Brittany.[56] The *non-originaires* who had been placed in those companies by a mistrustful

[54] It should be pointed out that Saint-Simon did not refuse the magistrates some honors, but he placed them well down in his order of ranks. In his memorandum of 1712 on "Un projet de restablissement des trois estats du royaume de France" (*Écrits inédits* [Paris, 1882] IV, 217-242), for example, he organized a system for determining precedence in ceremonial processions: first, the princes of the blood, then the peers (and their eldest sons), then the *Grands Officiers de la Couronne*, the bishops and the marquises in succession; only after all these would come the first president of the Paris Parlement, marching with the counts, and still farther back, the other sovereign court officers, equated by title with the viscounts, barons and baronets. Like most of Saint-Simon's other hierarchical visions, this processional code remained nothing more than a characteristically detailed flight of its author's imagination.

[55] *Mémoires*, XXV, 334.

[56] Pol de Potier de Courcy, *Nobiliaire et armorial de Bretagne* (Rennes, 1862), I, 2.

monarchy after the union with France in 1532 had quickly sunk their roots and joined their interests to those of the local aristocracy.

By Louis XIV's reign the Parlement and the Chambre des Comptes had in fact become all but inaccessible to common-born aspirants. An *arrêt* of the former court, given at Rennes in 1678, announced that "sous le bon plaisir de Sa Majesté, il ne sera reçu aucuns presidents, conseillers, ni gens du roy en icelle qui ne soient d'extraction noble ou de condition advantageuse."[57] Saulnier has found only three cases of bourgeois recruits to the Parlement after 1671, when the *grande réformation* of the Breton nobility was completed.[58]

This is not to say that there was no separate robe class in Brittany. On the contrary, there existed a proud confraternity of high magistrates who were exceedingly sensitive on the subject of their official prerogatives.[59] Perhaps they were all the more formidable because some, such as Monsieur de Lambilly, former page to the king, joined "à le fermeté du magistrat l'audace d'un mousquetaire."[60] In any event, the Breton robe had to overcome no slurs on its gentility. It dominated the Second Estate in the provincial assemblies. It phrased the demands of the noblesse to the crown and lashed at the intendant for every transgression against vested privilege. Its officers sat at banquets and café tables with other noblemen, gambled and hunted with them, discussed politics and agriculture with them, shared their theater boxes, and not infrequently won entry to their wives' boudoirs.

The special case of Brittany is important not only as an exception to the general situation in 1715, but also as an adumbration of what to a greater or lesser extent was to be the trend all over France in the decades which followed. This closing of aristocratic ranks in the face of royal and popular pressures was exceptional only in the sense

[57] *Registres secrets*, quoted by Saulnier de la Pinelais, *Gens du roy*, 46. The ambiguous final phrase offered a loophole for rich bourgeois perhaps; but very few appear to have benefited from it.

[58] *Le Parlement de Bretagne* (Rennes, 1909), I, lxi.

[59] In a "Lettre au Régent du 24 avril 1718, à propos de l'exil de Lambilly et de Rochefort," the Parlement complains that these councilors had been arrested by "un homme d'épée, au préjudice des prérogatives de la robe qui exempte les magistrats de la juridiction militaire, prérogatives qui intéressent la magistrature entière." A.D. Ille-et-Vilaine, B. 71, quoted by Le Moy, *Le Parlement de Bretagne*, 15.

[60] Frotier de la Messelière, *La noblesse en Bretagne*, 51.

of time, not in that of direction. The integration of the robe into high society at Rennes and Nantes had come early, but it was not to be unique.

6

The nobility of a sovereign court magistrate at the accession of Louis XV was admittedly a complex quantity. It was technically secure in legal terms, though still subject throughout most of France to hostile and often contemptuous references by nobles whose own rank derived from military service or immemorial possession. The high robin enjoyed the standard fiscal and honorific privileges of a noble, plus others which were peculiar to his judicial office. He claimed unqualified nobility and had begun to adopt many of the characteristic amusements, manners and attitudes of the old aristocracy; but he was distinguishable by his dress, his duties and his basic outlook, which still bore the marks of a special heritage—urban, commercial, Jansenist. He was no longer purely a royal functionary; he had moved far from his bourgeois origins; but he was not yet fully an aristocrat. Down to 1789 itself, something of this mixture of attributes was to remain characteristic of the high noblesse de robe. The eighteenth century, however, was to see the proportions altered, the emphasis shifted increasingly away from the old elements of austerity, industry and thrift toward those of elegance, social hauteur and a feudalized conception of privilege.[61]

Robe-épée hostility, actualized in the form of physical conflict, had been serious enough to occasion the 1704 edict,[62] directed specifically against judicial officers who had been provoking duels with military personnel, to the detriment of the king's service in time of war. In provincial towns it was not unusual for feuds between royal judges and members of the old local nobility to continue for decades, with the aid of every weapon from litigation to armed attacks by hired cut-throats. But such violence was already becoming rare, as the savagery of seventeenth-century aristocratic mores yielded to a

[61] Egret, *Parlement de Dauphiné*, I, 20 ff., agrees that the eighteenth century saw the critical shift in magistral attitudes.

[62] See above, 69.

combination of royal police power and the emphasis on refinement instead of bravado. The edict on dueling of 1704 seems to have required little subsequent enforcement in the major towns which possessed sovereign courts. Like the frenetic strictures of Saint-Simon, it is interesting primarily as a basis for gauging subsequent changes.

BOOK TWO

THE SOURCES OF HIGH ROBE POWER

Chapter Five

The Right to Remonstrate

1

It is easy to forget, in tracing the political performance and the social evolution of the high noblesse de robe, that the parlements and their sister sovereign companies never ceased to be primarily courts of law. All the political pronouncements of the Parlement of Paris between 1715 and 1753 have been reproduced in a single volume;[1] whereas summaries of the same court's "jugements civils," to mention only one of the more important technical subdivisions, take up 434 large manuscript volumes for the same period.[2] A collection such as Brillon's voluminous *Dictionnaire des arrests des Parlemens de France* (three volumes, published at Paris in 1711, greatly augmented—to six volumes—in 1727) provides a good idea of the accretion of case law. In addition, the high courts, particularly the parlements, exercised a wide range of administrative responsibilities based on their loosely defined police powers: forbidding inhabitants of Marseille to leave the stricken city during the plague of 1720,[3] regulating the legal status of actors and actresses in the Toulouse Opera,[4] restricting Paris bakers to no more than two varieties of bread for the duration of the 1740 wheat crisis.[5]

The modern historian, however, must look elsewhere for a full explanation of the high robe's imposing place in the chronicle of the

[1] *Remontrances du Parlement de Paris au XVIIIe siècle* (ed. Jules Flammermont, Paris, 1888), vol. I.

[2] A.N., X[1A]. 823-1256.

[3] Villars, *Mémoires*, VI, 89.

[4] A.D. Haute-Garonne, B. 1348.

[5] Charles, Duc de Luynes, *Mémoires* (ed. L. Dussieux and E. Soulié, Paris, 1860-1863), III, 255.

late ancien régime. That place depended heavily on the magistracy's judicial and administrative functions, of course; but it depended even more on the ability to interfere with certain actions of the crown and to arouse general support for such interference. The first would have been impossible without the robe's institutionalized role in the legislative process. The second would have been impossible without the robe's great weapon of propaganda: the right to remonstrate.

2

Although the sovereign courts often expressed themselves publicly on matters not formally submitted to them for consideration, a new act of government came within their official purview only when it was communicated to them for registration. Registration was in itself nothing more complicated than the procedure by which a court entered new ordinances, edicts, declarations, orders in council and letters-patent on its records and ordered their communication to the subordinate jurisdictions of its ressort. It was, in other words, the mechanism by which the will of the sovereign with respect to any concrete issue was incorporated into the "published" body of law. When the king, either alone or in council, ordered some decision to be framed in the form of a written enactment, it was drawn up by the royal chancellery clerks for his signature and that of a secretary of state—in minor matters, this secretarial counter-signature was often the only genuine one. The document was then sealed by the chancellor or by the garde des sceaux and copies dispatched to the procureurs-généraux of all appropriate sovereign courts, with orders to have it registered. Once an individual court had voted the registration, the greffier-en-chef certified this fact by a formal endorsement, entered the substance of the law in the court's registers, and had copies or relevant extracts sent on to the lower tribunals. In theory, discretion was thus reserved to the crown. The courts had only to receive, record, transmit and enforce.

For almost as long as any of them had been in existence, however, the sovereign companies had prided themselves on the right to delay registration of a questionable law while they presented their objections to the king and awaited his response. Flammermont has summarized in convenient form the procedure for drafting remonstrances,[6] and the boxes of such documents in the Archives Nationales contain numerous firsthand accounts of the preceding debates themselves.[7] In a parlement (the other courts had simpler arrangements) much routine registration was done by the grand' chambre acting alone; but when an act which threatened to require remonstrances was presented by the procureur-général, the first president could summon the entire personnel of the court to meet in an *assemblée des chambres.* Even if the premier did not think such was called for, it might be demanded by a joint deputation from the enquêtes and requêtes, usually well informed as to pending business in the grand' chambre. After the law had been read to the assembled magistrates, any one of several courses might be adopted: its immediate registration might be voted; it might be entrusted to a *rapporteur* or to a special commission for study pending a second assembly; or, if the immediate reaction was strongly hostile, a commission to draft remonstrances might be formed on the spot. These decisions were all reached by oral vote, each president and councilor opining in order of seniority, with the youngest and often most rebellious thus accorded the strategic advantage of speaking last.

Draft remonstrances, after a careful editing by the first president, had still to pass a final reading before the chambers. Once approved, they were delivered to the king by a delegation of presidents, who normally carried a written memorandum but who during the early eighteenth century rendered the message verbally whenever Louis XV could be induced to listen.[8] Having been apprised of a court's objections, the government might dispatch letters which modified the contested points. It was much more likely to send *lettres de jussion*, ordering registration in the original form. In the provincial

[6] *Remontrances*, I, lxxv-xcv.

[7] A.N., K. 696 and 698 for the period 1715-1748. B.N., Mss. fr. nouv. acq. 22241-2, Mélanges sur l'histoire des Parlements, contains most of the same items, as does B.N., Ms. fr. 7547. B.N., Mss. fr. nouv. acq. 8432-8439 is President Lamoignon's collection of remonstrances 1720-1764.

[8] Duc de Luynes, *Mémoires*, IX, 415, notes in 1749 that the most recent set of remonstrances had been submitted in writing and adds: "Il paroit que l'on veut supprimer l'usage de les faire verbalement."

companies such orders, sometimes repeated several times, never failed between 1715 and 1748 to achieve the desired result. In the case of the Parlement of Paris, however, the crown not infrequently encountered complete refusal to yield until the king appeared in person at a *lit de justice*. Once the monarch had taken his place on the high, canopy-covered cushion from which the ceremony took its name, the court's delegation of sovereignty was suspended—*adveniente principe, cessat magistratus*. After the chancellor had read the detailed registration order, the king repeated the standard phrase: "Je vous ordonne de ma propre bouche d'exécuter tout ce qui vient de vous être dit."[9] Even this ceremony did not always conclude the matter; for the parlement might continue to protest in subsequent memoranda, and the crown might resort to extraordinary measures of coercion. In recognized institutional terms, however, the lit de justice was the final word in court.

The above summary deals with a subject so familiar to students of pre-revolutionary French history that it would scarcely deserve discussion here, were it not for the fact that this well-established pattern was to be revived in 1715 after a long and significant interruption. As has been pointed out in an earlier connection,[10] Louis XIV had reduced the whole process of registration to little more than a formality. His letters-patent of 1673 had in effect stripped the right to remonstrate of its meaning; for after laying down a time schedule under which all the stages of registration had to be completed within seven days, the enactment went on to forbid any officer, on pain of expulsion, either to raise or to entertain objections.[11] Over the entire period of forty-two years the courts had never missed an opportunity to protest against the hated restrictions, but in vain; for the regulations concerning remonstrances seem to have been more sternly enforced than many other arbitrary enactments of the same era.[12] Not until Louis XIV died did the magistrates at last see the opportunity to recover their old powers. Recover them

[9] A.N., K. 698, no. 10. [10] See above, 11.

[11] Isambert, *Recueil*, XVIII, 105-106.

[12] A.N., K. 695, no. 21, Portraits des Mrs. du Parlement de Paris (by Pellisson?), provides impressive evidence of the bitter energy and frustrated ambition which characterized many of the leading robe figures during Louis XIV's reign. Printed in Depping, *Correspondance administrative*, II, 33 ff.

they did, with a sweeping new sanction from the crown which enthroned remonstrances once more as a key factor in French politics.

As might be expected, the center of the change was the Paris Parlement; and the lever was a matter of strictly judicial function. With the accession in 1715 of a five-year-old child, there was abundant historical support for the claim to the regency put forward by Philip, Duc d'Orléans, as nephew of Louis XIV and first prince of the blood. But the duke's ambitions faced a formidable obstacle in the explicit wishes of the late king, whose testament elaborated a plan for a relatively broad regency council; and that document had been entrusted to the Parlement of Paris for safekeeping. It was this body alone which could annul the testament and at the same time accord the would-be Regent the degree of public recognition which he needed in order to overcome the ambitions of the other Bourbon princes, including the King of Spain. Despite the warnings of his friend, Saint-Simon, Orléans chose to accept the danger of future difficulties in return for the support which was momentarily indispensable.[13] His discussions with First President de Mesmes and his colleagues unquestionably had settled the bargain even before the old king died.[14]

On September 2, 1715, barely twenty-four hours after Louis XIV's death, the Parlement fulfilled its part of the agreement by voting to set aside the testamentary provisions for a limited regency, on the grounds that the late ruler had intended to leave room for discretion and that in any event the Duc d'Orléans was entitled by his birth to exercise sovereign authority during the minority of Louis XV.[15] On the 15th of the same month, the Regent paid the price for this decision by issuing the Declaration of Vincennes in the new king's name:

> Voulons . . . que lorsque nous addresserons à notre Cour . . . des ordonnances, . . . notre dite Cour, *avant que d'y procéder* [italics mine], puisse nous représenter ce qu'elle jugera à propos pour le bien public. . . .[16]

[13] Saint-Simon, *Mémoires*, XXVII, 172-173.

[14] Saint-Simon, *Mémoires*, XXVII, 172; XXIX, 27; Philippe de Courcillon, Marquis de Dangeau, *Journal* (ed. Soulié, Dussieux, et al., Paris, 1854-1860), XVI, 162-165.

[15] A.N., K. 696, no. 2, Procez verbal de ce qui s'est passé au Parlement le lundy 2e septembre 1715. Cf. Leclercq, *Histoire de la Régence*, I, 97 ff.

[16] Isambert, *Recueil*, XXI, 40-41.

This authorization to remonstrate, once conceded to the Paris Parlement, was quickly extended to the other sovereign companies as well.[17] After almost a half-century of silence, the high courts had recovered their voice.

3

The political narrative of the first decades after Louis XIV's passing furnishes numerous examples of how the magistracy used its newly re-acquired powers. In 1717 it obtained the suppression of the dixième, that unclass-conscious tax so hated by the nobility. The following year it inaugurated its struggle with John Law by defying the Regent and his Scotch protégé over an issue of monetary depreciation, only to be humbled and forced to register the disputed edict at the lit de justice of August 26, 1718, immortalized in some of Saint-Simon's most brilliant pages.[18] In 1720, this time with Law's *Système* in full disintegration, the sovereign courts of Paris again opposed him on two enactments. Beginning July 21 the Parlement was exiled to Pontoise, twenty miles northwest of the capital; and while relaxing for almost five months in that over-burdened community, it became even more seriously embroiled with the government by seeking to block a royal declaration drafted by the future Cardinal Dubois and designed to revive the anti-Jansenist policy. Only after Law's ruin was complete and after the Parlement had yielded on the religious issue (under threat of a further "translation," this time to Blois) was it permitted to re-enter Paris, in December 1720.[19]

Five years later, on June 8, 1725, another lit de justice was needed to force registration of the edict establishing a *cinquantième* or 2

[17] Bib. Grenoble, Ms. 1601 (6337), for example, contains a letter from the Regent to the Parlement of Dauphiné, dated September 28, 1715, and expressing the crown's "cordial desire" to have the court's advice and cooperation.

[18] *Mémoires*, XXXV, 21-22; 31-33, 35-158, 168-237. The Parlement's own procès-verbal, as well as numerous background documents are in A.N., K. 696. Other contemporary accounts of the 1718 crisis are supplied by Dangeau, *Journal*, XVII, 370-372; Barbier, *Journal*, I, 9-14; Jean Buvat, *Journal de la Régence* (ed. E. Campardon, Paris, 1865), I, 518-528.

[19] In addition to the sources mentioned above, two others are important for the Pontoise episode: Hénault, *Mémoires*, Appendix II, and 53 ff.; "Duc de Richelieu," *Mémoires* (ed., actually written by Soulavie, London-Paris, 1790-1793), III, 44ff.

percent tax on all net incomes;[20] but in this instance the real victory went to the robe, for its display had touched off such intense, albeit confused popular resentment that the government was immediately compelled to cripple the originally quite equitable measure by numerous modifications.[21] The period from March, 1730, to September, 1732, was one long crisis, this time over the religious question again, with Louis XV and Cardinal Fleury confronted by the courts, Gallican as always and as always led by the Parlement of Paris. Before it came to an end, the episode had involved two lits de justice, the arrest of several particularly outspoken councilors (including the famous orator, Abbé Pucelle), and finally the temporary exile to a dozen different towns of all the members of the chambers of enquêtes and requêtes—a total of 139 officers. A settlement was finally reached, with the more cautious Grand' Chambre agreeing to accept Fleury's declaration of 1730 against Jansenism in return for the suspension of disciplinary restrictions. One of the most unregenerate of the younger councilors, immediately after his return from exile, signified his scorn at this surrender of his elders, including First President Portail, by affixing the following notice to the gate of the Palais de Justice: "Palais à vendre—On avertit le public que le portail n'en vaut rien, que la grande chambre est sans lumière, et que le parquet en est pourri."[22] Actually, however, the victory belonged to the Gallican-Jansenist and parlementary forces, for the government henceforth contented itself with purely formal support of Unigenitus.[23]

For the remaining sixteen years of my prescribed period, sovereign court politics played a less dramatic part in national affairs, but the high robe was far from inactive. In 1733 and 1741, when the old dixième was revived for brief periods as a war measure, it extorted modifications which practically destroyed that measure's original threat to the nobility's immunities. It also emasculated the great project of Chancellor d'Aguesseau to codify provincial and seigneurial legal customs in the 1730's. In general, however, this period

[20] A.N., K. 698.

[21] Marcel Marion, *Histoire financière de la France*, I, 130-137.

[22] J.-F. Phélyppeaux, Comte de Maurepas, *Mémoires* (ed. Soulavie, Paris, 1792), III, 131.

[23] For full descriptions of the 1730-1732 affair, see Félix Rocquain, *L'esprit révolutionnaire avant la Révolution* (Paris, 1878), 56 ff.; and Bernard de Lacombe, *La résistance janséniste et parlementaire au temps de Louis XV* (Paris, 1948), 79-85.

was one of relative calm. As the Marquis d'Argenson remarked in 1739, "It may be observed that the government now conducts itself toward the Parlement with a very different prudence than heretofore . . . [Fleury] lets the fire die."[24] Not until 1748, when tax questions again became embittered and when anti-Jesuit forces began their assault on ultramontane policies, was the long crescendo of magistral opposition to be resumed.[25]

Out of a mass of narrative details it is possible to sift the basic issues over which the sovereign courts consistently came into conflict with the crown. It is also worth pausing for a moment to single out one subject which did *not* enter into these disputes: namely, foreign affairs. Neither the intricacies of Dubois' and later Fleury's dealings with Austria, Spain and Britain nor the intervening blunders of the Duc de Bourbon called forth a single remonstrance. When in 1718 the Spanish ambassador, Cellamare, was pushing his king's project to overthrow the Regent through a palace revolution, the Parlement of Paris might have been expected to show some interest, especially in view of its humiliation of that year. But even Saint-Simon does not accuse the magistrates of complicity;[26] and before Cellamare's arrest, various parlements had already formally condemned several pamphlets circulated by Spanish agents.[27] Only the Parlement of Brittany, deeply involved since 1717 in the local rebellion, can be said to have considered foreign affairs and then only because of Philip V's offer of Spanish aid to the Breton insurgents.[28] But note that even here the issue was essentially one not of foreign sympathies but of particularistic feelings arising out of problems of taxation in that most particularistic peninsula. And if in 1744 the Parlement of Flanders greeted the arrival of the king at Douai as part of an effort to "secure the peace of all Europe,"[29] this was more because of the old worry about the northern border of its ressort than because of any highly developed theory of foreign relations.

[24] *Journal et Mémoires* (ed. E. J. B. Rathéry, Paris, 1859-1867), II. 177.
[25] A.D. Haute-Garonne, B. 1559, fols. 335-339; Bib. Bordeaux, Ms. 383, fols. 24-101.
[26] *Mèmoires*, XXXIV, 103 ff.; XXXVI, 14 ff.
[27] A.D. Gironde, C. 3625; A.D. Haute-Garonne, B. 1362.
[28] Le Moy, *Le parlement de Bretagne*, 137-143.
[29] Duc de Luynes, *Mémoires*, VI, 239.

Underlying the events of 1715 to 1748 was a set of three major concerns which could invariably be counted upon to inflame the latent oppositionism of the sovereign companies. One was fiscal and included any measure which tended to increase the total tax load, threatened to shift any considerable portion of it to the shoulders of landed groups, or endangered the position of the investing class. Hence the resistance to the dixième in 1717, 1733, 1741 and the cinquantième in 1725, as well as to John Law's devaluation of 1718 and his reduction of the legal interest rate from 5 to 2 percent in 1720.

The second basis for robe protests was local patriotism. It will be necessary to examine parlementary particularism more closely in later connections; for it was undergoing important modifications in the eighteenth century. Any direct assault on the special customs and privileges of a given province, however, was still an infallible signal for resistance from the sovereign courts of that province, as d'Aguesseau discovered to his chagrin in the 1730's.

The third consistent issue was the high robe's defense of Gallican liberties against Dubois' and Fleury's ultramontane policies, against papal claims as set forth in the bull Unigenitus, and against the activities of anti-Jansenist bishops. Properly to assess parlementary Gallicanism, and the Jansenist sympathies with which it was associated in the public mind, is one of the most difficult problems in any analysis of this period. To explain it, one must take into account the strongly Jansenist flavor of the standard robe education, which under Louis XIV had depended much less on Jesuit schools than on tutors drawn from that stratum of the lower clergy which had never lost its devotion to the principles of Arnault and Quesnel. Such a preceptor was Hamon of Port-Royal, who had trained numerous future magistrates.[30] It is also important to bear in mind that the great robe families, though now noble, had still been close to the high commercial class in the seventeenth century when that class had absorbed as a fundamental part of its ethic the austere doctrines of Jansenism. The Deacon Paris, saint of the Jansenists, about whose tomb in Saint-Médard the *convulsionnaires* swarmed nightly in search of miraculous

[30] Charles A. Sainte-Beuve, *Port-Royal* (4th ed., Paris, 1878), IV, 289 ff.

cures, was the son of one councilor in the Parlement of Paris and the brother of a second.[31]

Purely religious considerations, however, fail to explain all sides of the parlementary attitude toward church matters under Louis XV, when the high robe was partaking, perhaps more strongly than any other single group in French society, of the Enlightenment and its skeptical influences. Barbier, himself a convinced Jansenist as he defined the word, was sure that in the 1730's no more than sixty of the members of the Paris Parlement were greatly interested in the theological aspects of the quarrel.[32] Two other motives of a far more mundane nature must be borne in mind in seeking to understand the high robe's attitude. One was corporate opposition to the jurisdictional claims of bishops with regard to Jansenist sympathizers among the lower clergy. The second was resentment against papal interference in French affairs, the interference for which Unigenitus had become the symbol and in denunciation of which the Jansenist-Gallican slogans assumed their charismatic force.[33] However bitterly the high courts might resist the crown on specific issues, they still conceived of themselves as sharing in the royal prestige; and when confronted with what they considered foreign meddling, they were prepared to defend that prestige, if necessary, against the momentary preferences of the king himself. Even under Louis XIV, the one occasion on which the parlements had unanimously chosen to risk royal displeasure was in 1714, when they registered the bull Unigenitus only with a strong reservation concerning the article reasserting the pope's right to use excommunication as a political weapon against monarchs.[34] A third of a century later, in 1747, the Parlement of Paris publicly reiterated its determination to combat any effort by Rome to disregard that initial warning.[35]

To obtain something of the flavor of this proud attitude concerning

[31] Barbier, *Journal*, I, 287. For other details of robe Jansenism, see d'Argenson, *Journal*, II, 298-401 (*passim.*) and III, 39 and 48; also Rocquain, *L'esprit révolutionnaire*, *passim*.

[32] *Journal*, I, 431.

[33] The essentially Gallican, as opposed to merely Jansenist, tradition of the high robe is the subject of Jules Flammermont's *Les jésuites et les parlements au XVIIIe siècle* (Paris, 1885).

[34] Flammermont, *Remontrances*, iii. There is little reason to doubt that this reservation had royal approval.

[35] Luynes, *Mémoires*, VIII, 129.

the papacy, it is worth listening a moment to the procureur-général at Metz haranguing his Parlement in 1717:

> We are here concerned with placing limits on a foreign power which never lacks pretexts for self-aggrandizement . . . all the more specious because they seem to be founded on an authority which emanates from the Divinity and because they are accompanied by the respect which one owes to religion. . . . This is not the first time that the Court of Rome has sought to commit offenses against the authority of rulers and the liberty of the peoples. . . . History furnishes us countless examples of these enterprises, which have always failed . . . because of the firmness of the sovereign courts.[36]

4

Not only the recurrent issues but also the standard tactics of the high robe's political operations and the theories adduced in support of those tactics deserve some mention at this point. I have emphasized the right to remonstrate as a method of bringing public pressure to bear on the government. Underlying the remonstrances was refusal to register new enactments, in other words a definite if negative legislative function; in extreme crises, such as that of 1732, the complete judicial strike stood ready to hand, a crippling weapon against the royal administration. The government could not on any specific occasion be indefinitely thwarted by these expedients, whether employed singly or in combination; but there is no question that they made the magistracy the most troublesome segment of the population, from the ministerial point of view.

This was particularly true in the eighteenth century because despite their vestigial animosities among themselves the sovereign courts were tending more and more to synchronize their activities, instead of reacting independently. This growing sense of professional solidarity was reflected in the increasing tendency of provincial companies to echo views already expressed by other courts. Here, for example, is a newspaper item from 1719: "The Sovereign Council of Roussillon at Perpignan has issued a resolution against the four writings condemned by the Parlements of Paris and Bordeaux; it is understood that the Parlement of Pau in Béarn is disposed to follow

[36] Michel, *Histoire du Parlement de Metz*, 318-329.

suit."[37] The file of letters from Avocat-Général Gilbert de Voisins of Paris to other courts, 1724-1738, testifies to the steady strengthening of a communications network;[38] and the message of sympathy from the Parlement of Brittany which First President de Mesmes read to the Grand' Chambre in Paris a few days after the 1718 lit de justice was a portent of the *union des classes* policy of the 1750's and after.[39]

The importance of cumulative protests from various companies began to be apparent in 1718 when John Law's reminting edict drew remonstrances within only two weeks from the Paris Parlement, Chambre des Comptes, Cour des Aides, and Cour des Monnaies.[40] An instance which revealed wider geographical participation was that of the Scotch finance minister's reduction of the interest rate in 1720, condemned in quick succession by the parlements of Paris, Normandy, and Languedoc.[41] And in 1725 the cinquantième project was met by remonstrances from the parlements of Languedoc and Brittany as strongly worded as those of courts in the capital.[42]

For the theoretical underpinning of the high robe's tactics, the remonstrances themselves are the best source. The great brochure assembled by the Parlement of Paris in support of its political aspirations early in the Regency contains a collection of extracts from remonstrances and court records running as far back as the fourteenth century and selected in such a manner as to prove that the company had always received the kings' most deferential attention.[43] Within the period 1715 to 1748, quite aside from these ponderous appeals to history, the Parlement of Paris re-enunciated all the principal claims of the magistracy.

In the major remonstrances of July 26, 1718, for example, the Parlement asserted that the kings of France had always considered it not only the privilege but the duty of the high courts to (a) guard

[37] B.N., Ms. fr. nouv. acq. 9641, fol. 6.

[38] A.N., U. 912-913.

[39] A.N., K. 137, No. 14^{A}.

[40] A.N., K. 714, no. 57, and K. 715, unnumbered; B.N., Ms. fr. 7547 and Ms. fr. nouv. acq. 9640, fol. 164-176.

[41] A.N., K. 713, no. 4 *bis*; B.N., Ms. fr. 7547, fol. 112-123; A. Floquet, *Histoire du Parlement de Normandie* (Rouen, 1842), VI, 204.

[42] A.N., K. 138, no. 13^{4}, and K. 712, no. 70.

[43] A.N., K. 694, no. 22.

against measures opposed to the crown's real interests, (b) protect the well-being of the state as a whole, and (c) defend the much-cited but never fully explained fundamental laws of the kingdom.[44] When the Duc de La Force was seeking to escape the same tribunal's jurisdiction for his fraudulent dealings in commodities during the hectic days of the Système, the Parlement reminded the king of a further aspect of its dignity: its position as court of peers, having the right to try the mightiest of his subjects:

> Ce n'est qu'au Parlement, Sire, que les princes de votre sang, les pairs de votre royaume doivent rendre compte de leur conduite; ce n'est que sous vos yeux, dans la Cour, que nos registres appellent par excellence la Cour du Roi, que ces affaires doivent être traitées.[45]

And long before its most eloquent representative enshrined the principle of separation of powers in his eulogy of the British constitution, the high robe was making use of that principle to defend its prerogatives. Thus in 1732:

> Non, Sire, dans un gouvernement aussi sage que le vôtre, les attributs du Souverain et les fonctions des magistrats qu'il a établis ne peuvent être confondus: c'est au Souverain à donner des lois, c'est aux magistrats à les faire exécuter avec toute l'autorité dont il les a rendus dépositaires à cet effet.[46]

If this distinction between giving and executing laws seems at first glance to belie some of the Parlement's other claims, the confusion will disappear when one recalls that "execution" required, in the sovereign courts' view, their own formal registration, that is, approval, of new legislation.

But of all the robe's arguments, that of having to protect the king from his own lapses, as well as the mistakes of individual ministers, was the most difficult to answer. Even so confirmed a ministerial mind as La Vrillière's was forced to admit during the Regency that, though the king must remain master, "at bottom the magistracy is right; a ministry is vacillating . . . there is need for a guardian body [to watch over] laws and principles."[47] The aging d'Aguesseau in

[44] Flammermont, *Remontrances*, I, 88.

[45] Flammermont, *Remontrances*, I, 145. Remonstrances of March 1, 1721.

[46] *Ibid.*, I, 283. [47] Maurepas, *Mémoires*, III, 144.

some *Fragmens sur l'origine et l'usage des remontrances* which he wrote in the late 1740's, conceded after three decades of intermittent conflict with the sovereign courts that there was much to be said for a remark once penned by the first president of the Parlement of Aix: "Souffrez, Sire, qu'avec peine, et envie, nous défendions votre autorité."[48] Even on the verge of outright treason, through acceptance of Spanish aid, the Parlement of Rennes could still, in September, 1718, remind the monarch of the court's past services, including its "respectueuses Remontrances sur les dons excessifs extorquez de la bonté de quelques uns de nos Rois."[49] And attacks on Fleury, such as a famous pamphlet of the 1730's, in the form of advice from Louis XIV to Louis XV, excoriated the minister for having kept the Parlement of Paris from its proper place at the king's side.[50]

By extension, this right to defend the king's and the public's interests (in theory never at variance) could become the basis for claims of surprisingly broad scope, as revealed, for example, by the Paris Parlement's conception of its religious functions. Thus, in 1737, when the new First President Le Peletier somewhat reluctantly yielded to his company's demands and drafted a resolution condemning a Molinist pronouncement by the Archbishop of Cambrai, the preliminary reading of the document was drowned out by tumultuous shouting from the moment when the court heard the words: "... although your Parlement does not claim to be a judge of doctrine."[51] A few months later the company formally announced that it would "continue to reject the Council of Florence as non-ecumenical."[52] Some contemporaries not unnaturally wondered whether the Palais de Justice housed a law court or a consistory.

There were other expressions of the high robe's theoretical position which, though unofficial, were nonetheless important in that they stated the extremes implicit in the more careful language of the remonstrances. By far the most significant example of such literature was a pamphlet which appeared during the crisis of 1732 under the

[48] *Oeuvres*, XIII, 557.

[49] A.N., K. 137, no. 14A.

[50] B.N., Ms. fr. nouv. acq. 6505 (printed).

[51] Luynes, *Mémoires*, I, 167-168.

[52] *Ibid.*, II, 94.

title of *Judicium Francorum*.[53] Closely patterned after the *Véritables Maximes* of 1652,[54] the *Judicium Francorum* went considerably further than even that echo of the Fronde in its total claims on behalf of the Parlement of Paris. So extravagant were the assertions of the anonymous author that the Parlement had no choice but to suppress the tract and order it burned by the common hangman; but there can be no doubt that many of the magistrates had read its pages with the warmest feelings of personal approbation.

The institutional ancestor of the Parlement of Paris, writes the author of the *Judicium*, was the *Champ de Mars*, the *Märzfeld* of the Frankish monarchy, which had assembled each spring to hear the king's proposals and to pass on them in the name of all freemen. This institution, portrayed as a genuine senate, is described as having continued in existence even under the first Capetians—no source for this assertion is given, and one would be exceedingly difficult to find. In any event, "du tems de Philippe-Auguste ces sortes d'assemblées, par le Jugement desquelles tout étoit résolu, changerent de nom, & non pas d'autorité: on commença de les appeller Parlement."

Here then was a sovereign court, as old as the monarchy itself and much older than the present dynasty. Its authority was still as broad as that of the Märzfelder:

> Les Etrangers ne croyent pas la paix concluë avec nous, qu'après que le traité y a été vérifié; le Roi y envoye aussi le motifs qu'il a de faire la guerre. C'est une loi fondamentale, que rien ne peut être imposé sur les Sujets du Roi, & qu'on ne peut faire aucun officier en France, donner aucun titre nouveau, que par le consentement du Parlement, qui represente le consentement général du Peuple. Telle est la forme essentielle du Gouvernement François.

This claim to representation is absolutely basic to the entire doctrine set forth in the pamphlet:

> Nous voyons, que le Parlement a toujours été un abrégé des trois États. Nous y voyons encore aujourd'-hui l'Eglise representée par un

[53] B.N., Ms. fr. 7547 (printed, 1732). The full title is Mémoire touchant l'origine et l'autorité du Parlement de France, appellé Judicium Francorum.

[54] See Martin Göhring, *Weg und Sieg der modernen Staatsidee in Frankreich* (Tübingen, 1946), 131; and B.N., Ms. fr. nouv. acq. 7981.

nombre de Conseillers Clercs. Nous y voyons la Noblesse dans les personnes de Princes du Sang & des Ducs & Pairs de France qui sont les premiers de la Couronne; enfin le Corps entier, qui est un Corps mixte, y represente tous les Ordres du Royaume.

The advantage here taken of the century-old coma of the Estates General is of the first importance to an understanding of the courts' political attitude. It also reflects some of the ambitions which the spectacle of the British Parliament could not fail to excite in a French body so similar in name, so different in fact.

Throughout the document the familiar historical precedents keep appearing, in this case designed to prove the exalted jurisdiction which the Parlement has always exercised: Count Robert of Artois condemned under Philip VI, Jean d'Alençon under Charles VII, the Duc de Nemours under Louis XI, down to the trial of the Great Condé in 1654. The reader is reminded that Charles V, "surnommé le sage" (presumably for this reason), always honored his Parlement and that even the jealous Louis XI promised the magistrates that he would never force them to render a judgment contrary to the demands of conscience.

The remainder of the *Judicium Francorum* includes a violent attack on Fleury, a minister "who sets altar against altar" and on the royal council for its wrongs to the regular sovereign courts. (It is worth noting, incidentally, that the Grand Conseil is accepted as one of the latter.) Also in evidence is the old claim to primacy of the Parlement of Paris, which the author insists should be called "Parlement de France" and never confused with the supposedly derivative provincial parlements, much less with the other judicial companies of the kingdom. But this portion, irritating though it may have been to the rest of the high robe, is not, it seems to me, an essential part of the argument as a whole. What is essential is one of the later paragraphs which, after reviewing the judicial limitations on the caprice of monarchs, emphasizes a familiar distinction:

L'on ne peut pas dire pour cela que notre Gouvernement ne soit pas Monarchique. Les Monarchies ne sont pas toujours despotiques: il n'y a que celle du Turc qui le soit, toutes les autres que nous voyons aujourd'hui sont temperées par une espèce d'Aristocratie, qui les maintient & qui les conserve.

In the whole robe tradition, from Harlay to Montesquieu, the doctrine of aristocratic limitations on absolutism is nowhere more clearly stated.

5

In restoring the right to remonstrate after Louis XIV's death, the crown had obviously not abandoned all claims to superiority over its courts. It had retained a set of theories and a variety of physical expedients which deserve consideration beside the robe's own attitudes and performance.

The assumptions upon which the royal government proceeded were concisely set forth, for example, in the response which Voyer d'Argenson delivered in 1718 to the initial remonstrances against Law's reminting edict:

> Le Roy a fait examiner les Remontrances de son Parlement. Il les a receu avec bonté, et a esté bien aisé d'y voir sa soumission. [Hardly their substance!]
>
> Il recevra avec plaisir les avis que l'on luy donnera pour le bien de ses sujets, pourveu qu'ils ne tendent point a partager ou limiter son Autorité.
>
> Les Edits n'ont point besoin d'Enregistrement pour avoir force de Loy qui n'emane que de l'autorité qui est dans la personne du Legislateur, l'Enregistrement n'étant que pour promulger par les Cours les Edits aux Juridictions qui leur sont subordonnées.[55]

The succeeding admonition to the courts to limit themselves to their judicial duties and to abstain from interference with measures deemed necessary by the crown follows naturally from the principles thus posited.

The unidentified writer who signed himself simply "d'Ange" displayed less clarity but went into greater detail in his *Traité des Parlemens*, written in 1725. It would be difficult to imagine a sentiment more galling to the magistracy than that which he expressed in saying:

> Les Parlemens sont officiers des Rois dependans d'Eux et des loix qu'il leur plaist d'etablir en leur Etat en signe de quoy ils rendent aux Rois des

[55] B.N., Ms. fr. 7547, fol. 57.

soumissions fort particulieres comme de parler le genoüil en terre au Roy tenant son Lit de justice et autres occasions.[56]

The author then proceeds to unfurl a series of historical examples the length and repetitiousness of which go far toward explaining why his tract was never published.

On the basis of such conceptions, the government could obviously justify any measure of coercion, up to and including exile or imprisonment for lèse-majesté. Not once under Louis XV did the crown fail to obtain a contested registration even from the stubborn Parlement of Paris, sometimes through the relatively mild expedient of the lit de justice, sometimes through individual arrests, sometimes through large-scale exiles or outright translation, with the threat of final suppression in the background. Nor were all the weapons in the royal arsenal those of threat and punishment. The fact that at Paris the Grand' Chambre was notoriously more docile than the junior chambers of the Parlement explains the favor with which the royal government viewed this body's efforts at various times including 1725 and 1731 to exclude the younger councilors from its political discussions.[57] Strategically placed pensions, such as that which abruptly silenced President de Blamont in 1717,[58] could often do much to lower temperatures in the Palais;[59] and a variation of the same technique was exemplified in 1743 when the government obtained the prompt registration of fourteen tax measures by sug-

[56] B.N., Ms. fr. 10893, fol. 102 v°.

[57] Saint-Simon, XXIII, 118-121; D'Argenson, *Journal*, VIII, 26.

[58] Marais, *Journal*, I, 233.

[59] B.N., Ms. fr. nouv. acq. 1644, *Comptes des gages*, fol. 367-368, for example, supplies the following interesting figures concerning pensions to members of the Parlement of Bordeaux (all for life):

30 July 1715	to President de La Caze	1500 livres
17 June 1716	to President de Gourget	375 livres
10 October 1716	to Councilor de Tresne	1500 livres
4 May 1725	to Councilor de Marano	375 livres
24 January 1737	to President Le Berthon	6000 livres

Similarly for other courts:

Douai, 1732	to Procureur-General Vernimmen	1500 livres
Montauban (Cour des Aides) 1721	to President Lefranc	600 livres

Grand Conseil—20 pensions between 1715 and 1748.

gesting that they were essential to the payment of official salaries.[60]

The use of the first president and the gens du roi in each court was, of course, a royal device of the first importance. Directly indebted to royal appointment for their positions and well-placed to earn additional favors, these officers were peculiarly susceptible to the arguments of the Palais-Royal or Versailles. At the Parlement of Paris, successive first presidents had to combat the suspicion that they were more attached to the king's ministers than to his law courts.[61] It is not surprising, therefore, to find a secretary of state, Chauvelin, in 1734 writing confidentially to First President Boisot at Besançon regarding the parlement's opposition to the new dixième,[62] or to read d'Aguesseau's views of an outburst in the Parlement of Douai in 1737: "Il faut se borner, par rapport à nous, à ce que Monsieur le Premier Président me marque à la fin de sa lettre, c'est-à-dire à ne faire rien, quant à présent, que de se reposer entièrement sur son courage et sur sa sagesse . . . Il sera bien dédommagé dans la suite, s'il peut sortir honorablement . . . d'un combat si opiniâtre."[63]

Considering the range of penalties and rewards at the government's disposal to inflict or confer, and considering its record of at least formal victory in every instance of resistance between 1715 and 1748, it may appear surprising that no sustained application of pressure brought the sovereign courts once and for all to their knees. Part of the explanation lies in the temporizing characters of the Regent (whose undeniable intelligence could never for long overcome his voluptuous indolence), of d'Aguesseau, of Fleury, and, when he became an active force, of Louis XV himself. The absence of any issue which could be taken as a threat to the survival of the monarchy

[60] Barbier, *Journal*, II, 378-379.

[61] In the 1718 crisis, when First President de Mesmes stood by his colleagues in opposing the Regent, Barbier noted cautiously that "bien des gens doutaient encore de la sincérité de ce changement," *Journal*, I, 8, and it was only after the Pontoise interlude that the First President won the general confidence of the parlementaires. His successor, Potier de Novion, held office for only a few months during which no test of his attitude occurred; but Portail (1723-1735), Le Peletier (1735-1743), and Maupeou *père* (1743-1757) all were attacked as tools of the government at one time or another.

[62] F. Prost, *Les Remontrances du Parlement de Franche-Comté au XVIIIe siècle* (Lyon, 1936), 17-18.

[63] *Lettres inédites*, 491-493.

during the early eighteenth century also played its part in postponing a showdown. But in order fully to comprehend the impediments to royal action and to appreciate why the crown's victory of 1730-1732 was more difficult than that of 1725, itself in turn more difficult than that of 1718, it is necessary to bear in mind one other factor. This was the problem of public support.

6

The record of popular feelings toward the high courts under Louis XV is interesting in part because it is one of the points on which the modern observer can document an unmistakable change in the high robe's position. When the Regency opened, there was little evidence that many Frenchmen felt any particular esteem for the magistracy. Barbier notes that on August 26, 1718, when the Parlement filed out of the Porte Saint-Anne and across the Pont Neuf on its way to the celebrated lit de justice at the Tuileries, its members hoped for some demonstration in their favor. Instead, more abuse than applause issued from the crowd which lined the Rue Saint-Honoré to watch the sumptuous procession. John Law's popularity was approaching its zenith. "The public itself, at the beginning, was intoxicated with the imaginary profits which it foresaw [from the Système]; and, save for a handful of wise and prudent men, people generally looked upon the Parlement as an assembly of dotards [radoteurs]."[64] In the next two years, despite a report in May 1720, that the parlementaires would lead a mass march on the Tuileries to protest against the now hard-pressed financier,[65] the robe does not appear to have enjoyed any high degree of popularity. An examination of the *Nouveau Mercure* for that period shows the journalists much less interested in the magistrates than was to be the case ten years later.[66] Even the translation to Pontoise in July 1720, did not produce an immediate outburst of sympathy; and President Hénault comments indignantly that: "the people, whom our absence deprived of the sole resource which remained, nonetheless regarded our removal with indifference."[67]

[64] *Journal*, I, 384-385. [65] *Ibid.*, I, 26-27. [66] B.N., 8⁰ Lc². 37.
[67] *Mémoires*, 293.

Before it was over, however, the Pontoise exile had combined with events in Paris to make the latter months of 1720 the most important period in the early eighteenth century, from the point of view of parlementary standing with the public at large and especially that crucial segment, the people of Paris. It was known, of course, that the robe had fought John Law; and with the brokers' stalls in the Rue Quincampoix now the scene of furious riots by desperate investors in the Système, the Parlement suddenly assumed the appearance of an oracle at last heard clearly though too late. The antiquarian, Du Puy, composed an encomium which shows clearly whose prestige had profited most from the Scotchman's ruin. It was the Parlement of Paris which had acted with an

> amazing disinterestedness, a tested zeal for the interest of the prince and the people, an invincible firmness for the public welfare, a tireless attachment to the laws of the state, a limitless devotion to justice and true virtue. . . . When all classes and all conditions of the kingdom, seduced by a series of the blackest ruses and frauds imaginable, ran blindly after a deceitful lure which was to cause the ruin of all the fortunes of honest men and perhaps of the state, the Parlement alone in the midst of France held fast to the ancient laws and justice. It dared to warn the people of the snares which had been laid for them. . . . The people stopped their ears to the voice of the Parlement; they abandoned the polar star to follow the will-o'-the-wisp which has led them to the precipice.[68]

However slight the value of this purple passage as an historical judgment of either the Système or the Parlement's role in it, Du Puy's enthusiasm remains a striking example of how a negative position may under certain circumstances assume the appearance of inspired grandeur. Of equal importance was the revival of the Jansenist issue during the Pontoise period. Opposition to Dubois' declaration of 1720 dramatized the courts' position as guardians of Gallican rights; and public excitement over those rights still ran high. The support of much of the lower clergy was in itself a considerable asset for the magistrates. There is no disagreement among the chroniclers that in spite of the Parlement's having yielded to the

[68] B.N., Ms. fr. nouv. acq. 1503, 7-8.

crown's immediate demands, it nevertheless returned to Paris in a strong position.[69]

The 1720's saw the robe espousing popular causes both in the cinquantième fight of 1725 and religious disputes such as that touched off by the Council of Embrun's suspension of the anti-Jesuit Bishop Soanen in 1727. That powerful stream of religious passions, which in England was revealed by the Wesleyan revival, broke through the surface of established forms more briefly but in a more hysterical form in the ecstasies of the French convulsionnaires at Saint-Médard. Any group which consistently opposed both Unigenitus and new taxes was sure to acquire mass support. As Secretary of State Maurepas pointed out, "the people, who love to have the ministers suffer contradiction, always bestow their approval on the contradictors."[70]

The extent to which just this had happened became apparent as soon as the new crisis broke in 1730 over Fleury's renewed attempt to crush Jansenist-Gallicanism. Almost immediately a flood of popular verses began to appear, apostrophizing the high robe in terms of frenzied adulation:

> Quand Rome aux attentats s'anime,
> Portant ses coups contre nos rois,
> Vous réclamez les justes loix,
> Et le devoir fait votre crime.
>
> Fuyez cette terre ennemie;
> Mais hélas! que demandons-nous?
> Le seul frein de la tyrannie
> Ne s'en va-t-il pas avec vous?[71]

The *Nouvelles ecclésiastiques*, illegal weekly organ of the Jansenists, had long followed cases in the high courts when some curé appealed against his Molinist bishop or when a layman brought suit for refusal of sacraments. Now, however, the paper embarked on something approaching the mass canonization of the parlementaires, whose names and doings were thereafter to fill its pages. Just as the provincial parlements were taking an ever greater part in the quarrel, so pro-

[69] Barbier, *Journal*, I, 66; Marais, *Journal*, II, 27-28; Hénault, *Mémoires*, 345-7; Saint-Simon, *Mémoires*, XXXVIII, 59-60.

[70] *Mémoires*, III, 145. [71] *Ibid.*, III, 140.

vincial public opinion displayed an increased tendency to follow the reactions of Paris. Although there were some regional variations—the southeast had been relatively little affected by Jansenism, and the parlements of Grenoble and Besançon accordingly showed scant excitement over the declaration controversy—the names of Abbé Pucelle, Councilor Titon and some less remembered Jansenist magistrates became household words from one end of the kingdom to the other.

This brings to the forefront an important development which might easily be lost sight of: namely, the great advance in publicity techniques in the early eighteenth century. The *Nouvelles ecclésiastiques*, circulated in manuscript copies from 1719 until 1726,[72] but thereafter widely distributed in printed form,[73] is a case in point. The steady improvement of roads and mail services meant faster transmission of news, rumors, and arguments. The parlements themselves were by 1732 publishing almost all their major remonstrances and resolutions in printed form. The crown repeatedly but in vain rebuked the courts for these breaches of their members' oaths of secrecy, for a magistrate in a sovereign company remained in theory one of the king's confidential councilors.[74] Among the papers of First President Portail at the Bibliothèque Nationale, there is a pamphlet which furnishes an interesting example of how "inside" news from the Parlement of Paris was broadcast to the public. It is a printed reproduction of the instructions which the court's delegates took with them to Versailles for their own guidance in presenting remonstrances against the disciplinary order in council of August, 1732. Its dissemination is supposed to be a completely unofficial scoop: "Ce projet ou mémoire, qui avoit été dressé pour servir aux dernières Remontrances . . . nous étant tombé entre les mains, nous avons cru qu'il n'y avoit nul inconvénient à le rendre public." And after presenting the parlementary claims, the anonymous editor concludes: "Il nous a paru que dans cet Ecrit tout étoit grand, noble, ferme, digne d'un Corps aussi auguste que celui pour lequel il est fait . . . Le Parlement y parle comme il lui convient de parler."[75]

[72] B.N., Ms. fr. nouv. acq. 4002.

[73] B.N., 4^{0} Lc^{3}, 1-2.

[74] Flammermont, *Remontrances*, I, 446.

[75] B.N., Ms. fr. nouv. acq. 593, fol. 77 ff.

Hand in hand with the greater interest shown by the public at large and the increased technical possibilities for arousing mass excitement on behalf of such a cause as Gallicanism, there went the growing tendency on the part of the articulate, urban portion of the aristocrary and the cultured upper business class to indulge in political discussion. What could be more characteristic of an age in which the writings of Locke vied with those of Newton for popularity among educated Frenchmen, when one's "enlightenment" was signified by one's appreciation of Voltaire's praise of England or the deft satire of the *Lettres persanes*? And here was the Parlement, a well-established corps with the ability to express its views, a veritable standard-bearer for those captivated by the idea of government tempered by discussion! Pöllnitz toured the salons of Paris in May, 1732, and expressed his amazement at the changes wrought by only a few years:

> Voilà en gros la situation des affaires, & les raisons qu'allègue le Parlement pour le maintien de ses Droits, qu'il farcit d'une infinité de grands mots, comme de *motifs de conscience*, de *Libertés de l'Eglise gallicane*, & de mille expressions semblables, dont les crocheteurs mêmes vous étourdissent les oreilles, en passant dans les rues. Les Dames mêmes ont oublié pour un tems tout jargon de parure, pour ne parler que ce langage-là; & telle ne s'entretenoit que de Pompons & de Cornettes, qui aujourd'hui parle en *Avocat*.[76]

Even allowing for the undeniable faddishness of this attitude, as well as for the fickle nature of more broadly based enthusiasm, the two elements combined to work a very considerable change in the position of the high robe.

When the crisis of 1748-1749 took shape, it was with the government fully aware that to mishandle the sovereign courts' opposition might well result in general insurrection. The Marquis d'Argenson, although admittedly given to pessimism in these matters, was on this occasion no more than realistic in the views he entered in his journal. When in May, 1749, he learned that the Parlement of Bordeaux had actually forbidden all citizens to pay and all collectors to demand the new *vingtième*, he was quick to agree that this was

[76] *Mémoires*, IV, 19.

formal revolt; and he conceded that strong measures would be justified. "Mais qu'on y prenne garde," he added grimly, "cela pourrait être suivi d'une révolte populaire, car ici le parlement ne parle pas pour ses droits et pour ses hautaines prérogatives, mais pour le peuple qui gémit de la misère et des impôts."[77] There, in a few words, is the crown's great dilemma of the later eighteenth century.

It would be well to recognize the need for caution in one respect: public sentiment toward the high courts was not an uninterrupted paean of adulation. The role of tribune has never been a secure one, even when completely sincere; and in the case of the high robe there were personal interests which the populace showed no inclination wholly to forget. In 1717, for example, the avocat, Marais, reports that the Parlement had registered an edict suppressing the franc-salé, the concession of exemption from the gabelle for certain privileged groups, because it would have been too dangerous to block the measure—the people were well aware that the high robe was one of those privileged groups.[78] Parlementary pomposity seems to have provided an inexhaustible source of humorous verses and parodies throughout the period.[79] An unusually elaborate example was that by Coutellier under the Regency: *Extrait du livre VII de Rabelais; de la chronique de dom Philippe d'Aurélie et des prouesses des bonnets ronds en icelui temps.*[80]

Nor was the public attitude always one of mere raillery. More than once, with regard to individual parlements, it flared into contemptuous anger. The ubiquitous Baron von Pöllnitz has left another scrap of information from his tour of France in the eventful year 1732. In Provence he found the Parlement of Aix excluded from the general favor with which its sister companies were viewed by the Jansenists. After one of the most famous trials of the century, it had just dismissed the case of the Jesuit Père Girard, accused of having seduced a penitent, Marie-Catherine La Cadière; and Pöllnitz

[77] *Journal*, V, 409-410.

[78] *Journal*, I, 232. The franc-salé was quietly restored in 1720.

[79] A number of satirical quips and poems on this subject are to be found in *Lettres du Commissaire Simon-Henri Dubuisson au Marquis de Caumont, 1735-1741* (ed. A. Rouxel, Paris, 1882), *passim.*

[80] Buvat, *Journal*, I, 327-330.

reproduces the following quatrain, addressed to the court, as a fair sample of local sentiment:

> Pour avoir immolé le Fils du Tout-Puissant,
> Pilate moins que vous nous parut détestable;
> Il ne reçut point d'or pour punir l'innocent,
> Mais vous en recevez pour sauver le coupable.[81]

In the Joursanvault papers on Franche-Comté there is a similarly scornful attack on the Parlement of Besançon for having registered the dixième of 1741.[82]

Criticisms such as these, however, were exceptional. In general the courts knew that they could rely on the possibility of genuine revolt to buttress their protests. The effect of that knowledge was to make the threat of popular wrath a more and more common weapon of the high robe in its dealings with the government. It is just here that this digression on popular opinion finds its connection with the courts' own political record. An example of the effect which public support had on parlementary tactics is an early eighteenth-century *Mémoire pour prouver qu'il seroit advantageux de consulter le Parlement.*[83] The claim set forth therein is in itself sufficiently striking, for it amounts to nothing less than a demand for consultation concerning fiscal edicts *before* the framing of the edicts themselves—a long step from the simple right to remonstrate over registration. But even more arrogant is the concluding paragraph:

> Si la Compagnie n'est consultée qu'avec l'édit scellé a la main, elle ne croira pas avoir eu plus de part dans cette affaire que dans les autres édits qui emanent de la Volonté du Roy, et le Public en portera le mesme jugement.

The sovereign courts obviously possessed a weapon as dangerous in its way as was the government's power to imprison or to exile; and they were prepared to use it.

[81] *Mémoires*, III, 159.
[82] B.N., Ms. fr. nouv. acq. 8795, fol. 447.
[83] B.N., Ms. fr. 7547, fol. 27-40.

Chapter Six

The Ownership of Office

1

THE CHANGE WHICH TOOK PLACE in the status of the high noblesse de robe after 1715 depended on a combination of family position, wealth, and the new political opportunities discussed in the preceding chapter, all inextricably bound into a tight braid of reciprocal reinforcement. The effort to unravel so complex a phenomenon or at least to identify its several strands poses a serious problem of causal relationships. How explain the political influence without first taking into account the rôle of the sovereign courts' professional solidarity and power, which were in turn dependent on official rank, birth, and personal fortunes? But how understand the protection of this dynastic continuity and wealth, with all the attendant privileges, except by beginning with the political influence? The order in which these separate elements are teased loose and examined involves, no doubt, an unavoidable element of arbitrary choice. But this treatment need not, for that reason, be wholly disparate, if it proceeds from one aspect of the *ancien régime* which was equally crucial for the robe family, robe fortunes, and the robe's political performance. I refer to the fact that almost every sovereign court officer owned his office as a piece of negotiable property.

Few features of the old monarchy are apt to strike the modern reader as so foreign to nineteenth and twentieth century conceptions as does the trade in public functions. In Campan's novel, *Le mot et la chose*,[1] for example, the hero negotiates for a "charge" which his father has offered to buy for him from a widowed friend of the family. (In this case, the young aspirant makes the mistake of discussing

[1] (S. l., 1752), 36 ff.

the project with an acquaintance, who finds the price so attractive that he quietly buys the office for himself.) A real-life situation, identical save for the outcome with that in Campan's story, is revealed by a sale contract of 1736 in the Gironde archives, involving Montesquieu, who is fulsomely described as "chevalier, baron de la Brède et de Montesquieu, ancien président à mortier au Parlement de Bordeaux, un des quarente de l'Académie française." The philosopher is here seen buying an office of councilor in the Parlement of Guienne for his son, Jean-Baptiste Secondat, and promising to pay to Dame Charlotte Rose de Sacriste de Tombeboeuf, widow of the former holder, the sum of 27,000 livres during the next three years.[2]

The system of *vénalité des charges* or *des offices* under which such transactions took place has, of course, received exhaustive study as a general feature of French history from the late middle ages until 1789. Martin Göhring's *Ämterkäuflichkeit im Ancien Régime* surveys the problem over its whole chronological range and through all the tens of thousands of offices involved. Roland Mousnier has concentrated primarily on the crucial early seventeenth century stage, but his brilliant study offers invaluable insights into the phenomenon's later ramifications. Even more recent is K. W. Swart's *Sale of Offices in the Seventeenth Century*,[3] a scholarly synthesis which covers no fewer than nine countries, including China and the Ottoman Empire. In the present context, I am directly concerned with venality only as it affected the high robe and specifically as it helps to explain the latter's position in the early eighteenth century. The few pages which can here be devoted to the subject, however, are pivotal to the investigation as a whole. My own thinking owes so much to a short article written sixty years ago by Henri Carré that it seems appropriate to quote at the outset Carré's own conclusion:

> Venality had at last constituted an aristocracy of wealth and offices, and this aristocracy tended in the eighteenth century each day to merge more fully with the nobility narrowly defined, and to fortify the prerogatives of the latter.[4]

[2] A.D. Gironde (Notariales), notary: Roberdeau, October 22, 1736.

[3] (The Hague, 1949).

[4] "La noblesse de robe au temps de Louis XV," *Bulletin de la Faculté des Lettres de Poitiers* (Paris-Poitiers, 1890), 345.

2

It is essential for an understanding of French venality that one bear in mind a basic set of distinctions employed by pre-1789 commentators. Loyseau is extremely useful in this regard, for in his *Cinq livres du droit des offices* of 1610 he takes care to define the "vray office formé" as a "dignité avec fonction ordinaire en l'Estat."[5] The phrase, "in the state," excludes any possibility of confusing an office with a benefice. The all-important word, "ordinary," that is, conferred in full property, distinguishes an office from a royal commission, which the king can revoke at pleasure or upon the termination of a specified task.

The sale of offices, thus defined, was in the French case a tradition going as far back as the direct Capetians. By the fourteenth century the charges of bailli and sénéchal were regularly purchased by their holders, and already the royal treasury benefited from payments for higher appointments, or more accurately, *finances* in return for the issuance of *provisions*. From then until the reign of Henry IV, especially during the sixteenth century, there was a steady increase in the number of offices sold, the amounts demanded by the crown, and the degree of standardization. But this expanding volume of initial sales by the monarchy is only the simplest aspect of the pre-1789 conception of office, with its special characteristics: heredity and transferability at the will of the incumbent.

In this case, as in that of the robe's legal nobility, the late fifteenth and the sixteenth centuries had supplied a mass of special actions by the crown, and the seventeenth had followed with legislative formalization of principles deriving from those actions. The earlier monarchs had drawn profits from the transfer of offices by authorizing the sale of resignations. The would-be officeholder or *résignataire* purchased from the incumbent or *résignant* a surrender of office in his favor and then paid the king a fee for confirming this transaction through the issuance of new letters of provision. Mousnier points out the similarity between this payment to the crown and the various dues payable whenever landed fiefs changed hands.[6] The *resignatio in*

[5] *Op. cit.*, 14. [6] *Vénalité*, 28.

favorem itself, however, seems to have been most clearly inspired by the transfer of papal benefices through the same mechanism.

A distinction must be made between that portion of the *office formé*, as Loyseau calls it, which the holder could sell from that portion which, in theory at least, only the sovereign could confer. Technically speaking, all the résignant could alienate was his claim to the original finance paid for the office. That sum was supposedly recoverable if the crown chose to take back the office. In the "sale" of an office, it was the buyer or résignataire instead of the king who reimbursed the former holder and thus acquired the latter's claim to the finance. On these terms, the king could always recover control over any charge by refunding the finance to the résignant, if the transaction had not yet been completed, or to the résignataire, if it had. In actual fact, however, given the crown's reluctance to disburse funds for such purposes and the whole bureaucracy's pressure to make these resignations actual sales of functions, there was little danger of a break in the normal routine. The buyer who had secured a *resignatio in favorem* and had paid his *marc d'or* to the king seldom failed to secure his royal letters of provision in due course.

Under Francis I, however, there had appeared a compulsory clause in the standard resignations which was for a time to be of some importance. This was the famous forty-day reservation, specifying that if the résignant should die within that period after the transaction—if, in other words, the sale represented a deathbed act or anything close to it—the office would revert to the crown without indemnity to either party. Immediately, of course, wealthy résignataires began to buy exemptions from this clause, but it remained throughout the sixteenth century the most serious threat to commercial security in the purchase of an office. Even more important, it was an obvious barrier to transmission of offices by testamentary bequests within families.

For under the late Valois kings there had also become common certain variants of the *resignatio in favorem* which placed heredity even above salability. Special letters of *survivance* offered a councilor or a maître des comptes the opportunity to have his lineal heir recognized as his successor in office within his own lifetime. By the 1580's, at latest, the crown was also selling outright grants of heredity in numerous offices. It is this progression (sale of provisions, approval of resignations *in favorem*, sale of letters of survivance and finally of indefinite heredity) which makes the sixteenth century so important in the rise of the high robe dynasties to be examined in the next chapter. But it was the early seventeenth century which brought the full institutionalization of these concessions.

Henry IV had found already established a *Trésorier des Parties Casuelles*, who received all payments due the crown for the various types of letters patent described above and who supervised the sale of newly created and newly reverted offices. The name which every student of French history associates with this system, however, is that of Charles Paulet, Henry's own *Secrétaire de la Chambre;* for it was he who devised and inaugurated the plan under which the Parties Casuelles was to operate after the "Paulette" edict of December 1604. This enactment reflected on the one hand the crown's desire to convert the venality and heredity of public charges into a dependable source of income. On the other hand, it answered to the wishes of officeholders eager to obtain protection from the forty-day clause.

After 1604 each officer paid to the crown an annual tax of one-sixtieth of the capital value of his charge (the finance for which it had been sold by the crown, unless the Conseil d'État had subsequently placed a higher valuation on it). In return, the officer was assured the freedom to sell or bequeath his office at any time, including the day of his death. He no longer had to protect his family's hold on the office by paying a large finance for the concession of survivance; as long as he paid his *droit annuel* or *soixantième*, he could obtain such letters cheaply, as a matter of right. Instead of having to make a large expenditure for special letters patent, he now could pay a small sum, which varied little or not at all from one year to the next; and the capital which would previously have gone en bloc to the king could now be put into remunerative investments. As for the crown's profit, Paulet himself advanced 900,000 livres, a tremendous sum in 1604, against the first year's proceeds to the Parties Casuelles, and even this proved to be too low; for in 1615 the crown stopped farming the Paulette income and resumed direct control of collections. The main elements of this income were the droit annuel, of course, and the marc d'or, still paid by a new officer when applying for his provisions, plus the "loan" offered to the king by each functionary every nine years, when the original edict had to be renewed.[7] In addition, the Parties Casuelles not infrequently demanded supplementary finances of functionaries whose offices were alleged to have been originally under-priced.

The age of Louis XIV brought a tremendous expansion in the income from the sale and bequeathal of offices, combined with an extortionate use of every related fiscal device at the crown's disposal. The last thirty years of the reign in particular, saw that mushrooming of new charges which have already been noted in other connections.[8] The same period witnessed the geographical extension of the system into newly incorporated areas, such as Flanders.[9] The well-conceived efforts of Colbert in the 1660's to raise the standards for office, regulate the speculation in charges by setting official price tables, and reduce the weight of royal indebtedness by redeeming superfluous provisions were quickly lost in the soaring financial demands of the Sun King's quest for glory and in the great minister's own absorption

[7] The edict of 1604 had ostensibly been an extraordinary measure applicable for only nine years. In theory, it lapsed at the end of that time and had to be renewed, again for nine years, in return for a loan from all office-holders. The amount of this *prêt*, which was in fact a gift, fluctuated widely from its institution onward. Originally 5 percent of each office's value, it rose briefly to 25 percent under Richelieu, but by the eighteenth century had leveled off at something over 6 percent—denier 15 or denier 16. Göhring, *Ämterkäuflichkeit*, 96 ff. A.D. Gironde, C. 853; B.N., Ms. fr. nouv. acq. 9770, fol. 282-283. (The latter two references are for sources referring specifically to the 1730's and 1740's.)

[8] In the appendices to Monmerqué's edition of Madame de Sévigné's letters, XI, xxv-xxvi, there is an interesting example of how completely the purchase of an office might dominate a wealthy individual's plans for both social advancement and capital investment. On April 24, 1691, the intendant of Brittany, de Pomereu, transmitted to the Contrôleur-Général, Pontchartrain, the following letter from Charles de Sévigné:

"Si Sa Majesté a agréable de créer une charge de lieutenant du Roi dans le comté nantois, avec un logement dans la ville de Nantes, il y a des personnes dont le nom a l'honneur d'être connu du Roi, et qui ont servi longtemps dans les troupes de sa maison, qui en donneront cent mille francs.

"Parce qu'ils espèrent que Sa Majesté voudra bien y accorder les mêmes honneurs et prérogatives qu'aux autres charges de lieutenant du Roi de ladite province, tant dans l'assemblée des états qu'au parlement et en fixer les appointements sur le pied du denier quatorze [i.e., about 7,143 livres per year]."

In November 1693, Sévigné was duly received as lieutenant du roi and conseiller d'honneur in the Parlement of Brittany.

[9] Pillot, *Parlement de Flandres*, I, 212-230.

in other problems. Hence the edict of 1665 on legal values of sovereign court offices remained a dead letter, while the king himself made a mockery of Colbert's rules governing minimum ages for their holders and forbidding members of the same family to possess charges in the same company at the same time. In a declaration of 1676, Louis established a regular tariff of fees for royal dispensations from these statutes, depending on the number of years' minority to be overlooked or the degree of family relationship (*parenté*).[10]

The other respect in which the Great Reign influenced the conditions of office, namely, the crown's ruthless manipulation of finances, revocations of letters of provision and ceaseless demands for loans, applies particularly to the host of functionaries in lower jurisdictions: présidiaux, bailliages, greniers à sel, etc. The high robe suffered too, especially from arbitrary exactions under the guise of *augmentations des gages* (supplementary finances supposed to bear additional interest in the form of increased gages of office). But it is worth noting that when Göhring discusses what he calls Louis XIV's *Erpressungspolitik*, he is dealing primarily with the lower robe.[11] Impotent as were the late seventeenth-century sovereign courts, in comparison with their power after 1715, they were still too highly placed to suffer the worst of the Sun King's extortions. They were untouched, for example, by the great revocation of 1715, which in the last month of Louis XIV's life annulled all the privileges attached to offices purchased since 1689 for finances of under 10,000 livres, in other words, well under the value of any high robe charge.

It is, I think, fair to say that so far as *vénalité des offices* was concerned, the Great Reign was less trying for the sovereign courts than for the rest of the sprawling French officialdom. In 1715, the legal rules under which a member of the high noblesse de robe possessed his charge were substantially those of 1604, except for certain points in which, as will be seen in a moment, changes had actually been made to his advantage. The importance of the late seventeenth-century developments should not, however, be underestimated. For one thing, numerous abuses implicit in the very

[10] Bib. Toulouse, Ms. 581, Chambre des Comptes de Paris, fol. 117-118.

[11] *Ämterkäuflichkeit*, 171-239.

concept of venality had become increasingly apparent. Furthermore, the reign of Louis XIV had been for the high robe a period of class entrenchment, the markings for which had been laid down in earlier decades and the results of which were to become fully apparent in the period of Louis XV.

3

The position of the eighteenth-century sovereign courts with respect to the ownership of office displayed at least three special characteristics which must be sketched in against the general historical background. One was the practically complete escape of *high* magistrates from Paulette payments, because of what now amounted to a blanket grant of survivance for all sovereign court officers without payment of the droit annuel.[12] Thus in an official "Mémoire pour servir à l'instruction aux commis à la Recette du Prest & Droit annuel pour l'année 1732,"[13] one finds the royal collectors being ordered to open their regional bureaus by October 1, 1731, to post public announcements to that effect, and to keep office hours from seven in the morning to six in the evening for the receipt of payments by all officers of "Bailliages, Sénéchaussées, Justices Royales [e.g., prévôtés and *châtellenies*] . . . Elections et Greniers à Sel." But Article 6 of these instructions excuses:

> les Presidens & Conseillers des Cours superieures, les Presidens, Maitres, Correcteurs & Auditeurs des Chambres des Comptes, les Avocats & Procureurs generaux & Greffiers en chef d'icelles Cours & Chambres, [et] les Officiers dépendens des Pays d'Artois, Flandre & Alsace, en estant dispensez par ladite Declaration du 22 Juillet 1731.

When this peculiarly favored status of the high magistracy in relation to the heredity of charges is compared with its impregnable position vis-à-vis the legal requirements for nobility, a rather striking picture begins to emerge. In both cases, in the high robe's grip on its offices and on noblesse, the early seventeenth century had seen the formulation of precise regulations and the later seventeenth

[12] Cf., for example, the 1740 declaration of the annuel for another nine years, A.D. Gironde, C. 853, which refers to earlier exemptions for the sovereign courts.

[13] B.N., Ms. fr. nouv. acq. 9770, fol. 282-283.

century had seen a new privileged caste fortifying itself by compliance with those regulations. Now in the eighteenth century the rules had ceased to be strictly applicable to at least the top level of judicial officers. The Paulette, like *patro et avo consulibus*, lay behind them in their upward surge to power and prestige.

A second feature of the period was the tremendously increased use of dispensations from minority or parenté, or both. The government no longer posed even the token objections contained in some of Louis XIV's early edicts. In the years between 1700 and 1789, of the 324 councilors received into the Parlement of Brittany, 164 or just over 50 percent had received exemption from the 25-year age requirement (itself a reduction from the age of 27 set in 1665); and of these, 24 were only 20 years old, while 14 others were actually under 20.[14] In the Parlement of Dauphiné there were 252 officers who served in ennobling charges at some time between 1715 and 1748; of these, no fewer than 192 had been received with either age exemptions or *dispenses de parenté*.[15]

This in turn leads to the third characteristic of venality as applied to the high robe in Louis XV's first decades as king: the passivity of the crown when confronted with the spreading abuse of legislation still technically in force. One reason for royal timidity with respect to personnel standards doubtless lay in the political power of the great magistral families. Another was the danger that the Parties Casuelles would lose income if available heirs to offices were not permitted to pay the marc d'or at once, since new buyers had become less plentiful than in the earlier periods of relatively active circulation. Here again, fuller analysis must await our examination of the cash value of charges, as an aspect of robe fortunes, and the increased exclusivism of the courts, as an aspect of robe families.

One other factor in the government's attitude, however, deserves mention at this point, namely, the lack of clarity by monarch and ministers alike with regard to what venality and its abuses had permitted the sovereign courts to become. Louis XIV's feeble gestures aimed at limiting these abuses had been eclipsed by his tremendous extension of the system itself and by his lack of compre-

[14] Saulnier, *Parlement de Bretagne*, xxix.

[15] A.D. Isère, B. 2271-2275, records of receptions. Cf. *Catalogue*, Série B, II, 15 ff.

hension of Colbert's insights. An occasional personal touch shows the Sun King in direct contact with heredity of charges, as in a bit of parchment bearing the scrawled inscription:

J'ay trouvé bon que le controleur general remet presentement a son fils la fonction de la charge de president en ma court de parlement. Fait a Versailles le 21me avril 1689.

Louis[16]

The same complacency, infinitely magnified in application, is to be found in the preamble to an edict of 1693 which sanctioned venality in Flanders:

Since venality of charges was first introduced into Our kingdom and since heredity or payment of the droit annuel first assured security of title to acquirers and safeguarded property in families, it has been noted that fathers have given special care to the education of their children and have had them instructed in jurisprudence and in the other sciences necessary to render them capable of succeeding to their [fathers'] dignities and of exercising their profession for the glory and advantage of their country.[17]

The monarchy of Louis XV seems to have been less given to such saccharine pronouncements. An edict of 1724, again concerning Flanders, openly laments the effects of venality and pleads fiscal necessity as the crown's only reason for confirming it.[18] The general feeling of the royal administration after 1715 was unquestionably hostile to the system, as it clearly revealed by its efforts to reduce the number of lower offices during the Regency and later.[19] But here again intervened the special position of the sovereign courts. Only once during the first half of the eighteenth century—in 1738, when it reconverted the presidencies of the Grand Conseil from offices formés into short-term commissions—did the crown strike even a feeble blow at the high robe's hold on its charges.

There is to my knowledge only one modern writer who, though himself critical of venality, has argued that the system offered advantages to the crown commensurate with its dangers. This is Pierre de Vaissière, who asserts that on the one hand the sale of offices in full property enriched the government, while on the other

[16] A.N., K. 121, no. 48.
[17] Pillot, *Parlement de Flandres*, I, 230.
[18] *Ibid.*, I, 232-233.
[19] Göhring, *Ämterkäuflichkeit*, 240 ff.

hand, given the poverty of most of the noblesse de race, it effectively debarred the old aristocracy from acquiring public functions and thus served royal policy.[20] It is important, however, to point out that de Vaissière is here speaking of the sixteenth and seventeenth centuries. He would not, I am sure, seek to extend this formulation to the eighteenth.

For the "advantages" he describes remained such only so long as the group to be feared, from the crown's point of view, remained that which was in fact excluded from offices by the system of venality. By the reign of Louis XV, the situation had completely changed. The very techniques which had broken the original feudality of land and military prowess had ended by creating a new and in modern terms even more formidable feudality, that of public, above all judicial, functions. Once again, as with the Carolingian counts, the great medieval vassals and the governors general of past centuries, the monarchy was confronted with the need to wrench power from a too solidly entrenched group and confer it on a more dependent class of officials. Nothing less than the political emasculation of offices subject to venality and heredity was clearly called for. The failure of the crown this time to meet the challenge was to be a major factor in the progression from weakness and injustice to revolution.

4

Even before the regime of venality lay fully exposed in all its political and social implications, its effect on the institutional value of the sovereign courts themselves was becoming painfully apparent. There can be little question that, taken as a whole, the high judicial personnel of even the early eighteenth century was inferior in professional ability, dignity and industry to that of the seventeenth. This judgment should not obscure the fact that the courts under Louis XV still contained numerous officers who on occasion displayed both intelligence and integrity of a high order; nor does it leave out of account the existence of corrupt and indolent magistrates in earlier periods. But what does emerge from any study of the period

[20] *Gentilshommes campagnards de l'ancienne France* (Paris, 1925), 253.

after 1715 is the general decline in professional quality at the very time when the high robe was approaching its zenith of political influence and social prestige. The ownership of offices was in this respect matching its work of consolidation with another of degeneration.

As noted above, there were numerous "boy magistrates."[21] Some of these officers who had been received at tender ages later developed into able jurists. The celebrated President de Brosses of Dijon, for example, had become a councilor in the Parlement of Burgundy at 20.[22] A case might be made for ensuring a steady recruitment of younger men to leaven courts which could otherwise have become the preserves of senility. But the impression one gets is that of a scattering of worthwhile beginners among a host of untrained and frequently uninterested heirs of well-established robe houses.

In any case, the argument for keeping down the average age of magistrates could be sustained only if it could be proven that young additions represented the best of their generation, regardless of wealth or family background. Actually, of course, nothing could have been further from the conceptions of the *ancien régime* in general and the sovereign courts in particular. The process of admission, it is true, theoretically offered an opportunity for qualitative choice, though other factors also loomed large in the procedure. After a candidate for a high robe office had received the *resignatio in favorem* of an elder relative or had purchased it from someone outside the family, he generally repaired at once to the court in question and applied for the approval of a screening committee of its senior members. (At the Parlement of Metz, for example, this preliminary *commission d'enquête* consisted of the dean of présidents à mortier, the dean of councilors, the senior ecclesiastical councilor, and the elected syndic of the court.)[23] This group examined the individual's family background, personal fortune and past conduct, and in most cases only after receiving its informal assurance of his acceptability would he pay his marc d'or to the crown. The letters patent

[21] See above, 113. See also Floquet, *Parlement de Normandie*, VII, 321 ff.; and Carré, "La noblesse de robe au temps de Louis XV," 347.

[22] Henri Mamet, *Le Président de Brosses* (Lille, 1874), 20.

[23] Michel, *Parlement de Metz*, 269 ff.

which came back from Versailles "provided" him with the office, but only on condition that he be "jugé suffisant et capable."

So the next step was to submit the royal provisions to the court and petition the latter to examine and receive him. At a plenary session, the procureur-général presented a report, this time official, on the candidate's birth and character. Assuming that this was favorable, the aspirant was invited to *piquer la loi*, to select at random a passage from the Roman law for analysis. He was normally allowed several days in which to prepare his commentary, which he delivered to another assemblée des chambres, convened for that purpose. At this meeting the candidate was supposed also to submit to questioning on technical points of jurisprudence, after which he retired to permit the company to deliberate. Provided that the vote was favorable, he was called back, heard the first president pronounce the *arrêt* of reception, took the official oath and swore on the bible to live and die a faithful Catholic.

This procedure obviously contained elements which, depending upon how the courts placed the emphasis, permitted selection in terms either of legal competence or social acceptability. The evidence points to the latter as the decisive criterion in actual practice. In the papers of President de Harlay, for example, there are some interesting notes on receptions of new officers which repeatedly stress not only the dispensations from age and parenté rules, but also the laxness of the professional examinations in the last years of Louis XIV.[24] The same source records the scorn with which the Parlement of Paris reacted to a short-lived Chambre des Comptes plan to examine more carefully the young sons of robe houses who presented themselves for admission to the latter court.[25] My own impression, based on reading in the reception records of several sovereign courts,[26] is that by the early eighteenth century, the genealogical investigation was crucial and that the subsequent technical examination was perfunctory to the point of becoming farcical. The Roman legal texts selected seem to have been very simple and to have recurred with a frequency which excites suspicion. The "plenary

[24] B.N., Ms. fr. 16581, fol. 26 ff. [25] B.N., Ms. fr. 16581, fol. 49 ff.

[26] A.D. Haute-Garonne, B. 1344-1564; A.D. Gironde, B. I.B. 40-49; A.D. Côte d'Or, B. 12071 (noniès); A.D. Isère, B. 2271-2275.

sessions" were generally attended by only a fraction of the court's membership; and even that small group, to judge by Harlay's remarks, was often more bored than inquisitorial.

Having emphasized the worst effects of venality and heredity on personnel, I must point out two factors which served to dilute the evils of the system enough at least to account for its survival. One was the royal policy which had kept a handful of key positions out of the reach of venality. The first presidents, the procureurs-généraux and the avocats-généraux of the sovereign courts held their places not as *offices formés* but as royal commissions, for which they paid finances recoverable at the time of retirement but which they could not alienate or bequeath at will. This rule did not prevent certain families from maintaining a grip on even these posts. Ten consecutive Nicolays served as first presidents of the Paris Chambre des Comptes from 1506 to 1789; and the Joly de Fleury family established what looks like a dynastic succession of gens du roi at the Parlement of Paris itself.[27] But the fact remains that the crown never lost control of this level of authority so completely that it could not prevent the reception of absolute incompetents.

The other extenuating characteristic of eighteenth century robe personnel lay in the well-founded custom of having magistrates' sons serve a period in subordinate positions before ascending to the bench. This technique of practical training, especially in the form of service at the bar, seems to have remained much more general and to have continued much later than some students of venality have recognized.[28] At Grenoble, every one of the 78 councilors received into the Parlement of Dauphiné between 1715 and 1748

[27] In this connection, see A. Molinier's "Avertissement" to his *Inventaire sommaire de la collection Joly de Fleury* (Paris, 1881). See also "Chasot de Nantigny," *Tablettes de Thémis*, Part II, 32-33. The same work records a total of 50 *premiers* received between 1715 and 1748; of these, 22 succeeded close relatives, usually fathers. This phenomenon was much more common, however, in the less important courts than in the pivotal companies. Not once in the seventeenth or eighteenth century did the first presidency of the Parlement of Paris pass from father to son, though such families as Harlay, Potier de Novion, and Le Peletier each provided two or more premiers for non-consecutive terms during that period.

[28] Bastard d'Estang has not overlooked this phenomenon. In his monograph, *Du Parlement de Toulouse et de ses jurisconsultes* (Paris, 1854), 23, he cites a long series of parlementaires who had had such prior experience.

had previously been designated "avocat," either of that court or some other.[29] The same pattern was followed almost as completely in the Chambre des Comptes of Aix[30] and in the Parlement of Provence.[31] The list of those avocats taxed for registration of their coats of arms beginning in 1698 reads like a census of the great robe families.[32]

Just what a future magistrate did with his period at the bar depended, of course, on his character, his ambitions, and his intelligence. The majority doubtless used their positions as avocats to develop their personal contacts in a given palais de justice, when indeed they came near the palais at all. The active avocats so frequently mentioned by Barbier and Marais certainly represented only a fraction of the total number authorized to plead. A list drawn up on this basis of genuine activity reveals a preponderance of lawyers who were of bourgeois rather than high robe families and were devoted to the bar as a lifetime career in itself. There were, however, a certain number of relatively serious sovereign court heirs who went on from a genuine apprenticeship to form the working cadres of judicial companies.[33]

I have stressed the exceptional cases of the first presidents and the gens du roi, as well as the possibilities offered by service at the bar, because without some recognition of these factors the reader might reasonably expect to find the sovereign courts of the eighteenth century existing as nothing but the gathering places for idiocy and hemophilia. No such bizarre conclusion is justified. But the general impression remains one of serious deterioration in the high robe's capacity to fulfill its institutional task: the administration of sovereign justice. Little wonder that the system by which the courts were staffed should have become a subject of increasingly acrimonious debate.

[29] A.D. Isère, B. 2271-2275.

[30] Bib. Méjanes, Ms. 730 (826).

[31] Bib. Méjanes, Ms. 947 (902).

[32] A.N., Q^3.94.

[33] See above, 47, n.24, for evidence of such cores in the chambers of the Parlement of Paris.

5

The criticism leveled against venality in the early eighteenth century must be separated into two distinct lines of argument. The first was conservative, in that it was directed against the loose creation of new offices to the detriment of the old. The second raised much more fundamental questions about the political and social effects of the whole system, including not only venality but heredity as well.

Within the narrow limits of the first approach, it was perfectly possible for criticism to come from the sovereign courts themselves; and in a remonstrance of August 1722, the Parlement of Paris complained that the wholesale commerce in offices during the preceding reign "ne pouvait presque manquer d'exciter la cupidité dans ceux qui servaient l'État."[34] The context of the statement makes clear the Parlement's very special point of view. The court was by no means opposed to venality as it had operated in the past, during the high robe's own period of gradual entrenchment. Still less was it questioning the value of hereditary transmission. What did excite the parlementaires' misgivings was the danger that wide-open sale of newly created offices might endanger their own privileges, as well as their share in the available income to be derived from the totality of public functions. In a later connection, the same court warned that "il est bien difficile que la multiplication des officiers n'attire pas tôt ou tard une augmentation de droits" and pointed to serious results if officers "ne trouvent pas dans la répartition de ceux [i.e., droits or income] qui leur sont actuellement accordés une subsistance propre à les indemniser."[35]

Göhring has well summarized the attacks on venality by such spokesmen of the old aristocracy as Fénelon, Saint-Simon and Boulainvilliers,[36] who condemned it primarily as the mechanism which had raised a new class of wealthy parvenus. The Abbé de Saint-Pierre, on the other hand, criticized the system for its ruinous effects on the French army, as contrasted with the already impressive machine of the Prussian monarchy.[37] The most thoroughgoing

[34] Flammermont, *Remontrances*, I, 158.

[35] Flammermont, *Remontrances*, I, 227.

[36] *Ämterkäuflichkeit*, 301-304.

[37] *Ouvrages politiques* (Rotterdam, 1734), VIII, 268.

among the early eighteenth-century condemnations of the entire structure, however, came from the Marquis d'Argenson, who here foreshadows the critique which the Physiocrats and the liberal *philosophes* were later to bring to bear on venality. In a passage from his *Considérations sur le gouvernement ancien et présent de la France*, written in the 1730's but not published until two decades later, d'Argenson stated his judgment in unequivocal terms:

> All that I have said of the evil done by usurpation of fiefs is nothing in comparison with the bad effects of venality of offices. It has prevented that happy progress of democracy which we have just been admiring . . .
>
> By spreading ever wider under the reigns which followed Francis I until the present, like a principle of corruption which infects the blood stream, it has destroyed in France all idea of popular government . . .
>
> Thereby, the King has alienated forever the fairest of his prerogatives, which is the choice of his officers . . . Thereby, few faults are punished, few defects put right, although the misdemeanors of those who should serve as examples are felonies [when judged] by their consequences for Society . . . Thereby, one sees on all sides negligence and disloyalty in public service, in a word, all the ill effects which derive from property mis-acquired in its origins and in its institution.[38]

As striking as is this attitude, it is perhaps equally striking that the number of such radical strictures composed during the first half of the eighteenth century was not larger. During this period, however, both liberal and absolutist criticism seems to have been stirring, at least in conversation and in scattered correspondence; for it is unlikely that defensive writings, which were appearing in some volume, could have been inspired by universal applause. One flurry occurred between 1718 and 1720, when John Law is alleged to have more than once urged the Regent to buy out all parlementary charges at Paris and replace them with commissions. Naturally a président à mortier such as Hénault reported this project with horror.[39] It is more surprising to find the robe's position supported in this instance by its old enemy, Saint-Simon, on the grounds that venality had permitted the Parlement to become the only corps

[38] *Op. Cit.* (Paris, 1752), 155-156.
[39] *Mémoires*, 292 ff.; Saint-Simon, *Mémoires*, XXXVI, 301-312.

capable of resisting capricious despotism on the part of the king or the pope.[40] The reference to Rome suggests that Saint-Simon's dislike of ultramontane policies had momentarily outweighed his enmity toward the robins.

The most complete statement I have found in favor of offices as property and at the same time the best indirect evidence of mounting criticism is a manuscript at the Bibliothèque Nationale entitled *Vénalité des charges*.[41] The pamphlet is anonymous and bears no date; but the orthography, style, and content all suggest composition in the second quarter of the eighteenth century. The author had clearly either read d'Argenson's outburst or at least heard it discussed, for he refers to several of its main points, including what he considers the unfair stigma attached to Francis I for having allegedly been venality's chief architect. The standard lines of defense are all here: that venality encourages trade by ensuring honorific rewards for success in business, that it permits the government to use money-making success in private life as a guide to able officials, that it ensures continuity and independence in the magistracy. And yet, of all these arguments, it will be noted that only the last could really be said to apply to eighteenth century conditions at the sovereign court level.

The pamphleteer admits, it is true, that many of his contemporaries have made telling points concerning the bad effects of venality on the quality of some officers and on the crown's administrative freedom. He gives a fairly candid report of these objections. But, he insists, "I return to venality and I conclude that if it is in fact an evil, it is one of those which must be allowed in order to escape still more dangerous consequences."[42] He argues that the kingdom could not finance the redemption of all existing charges; and even if it could, the results would disrupt society by creating resentment in the ensuing scramble to restaff such agencies as the courts, while countless great and presumably valuable families would be ruined in the process. The claims of vested privilege could scarcely have been more neatly packaged.

One more defense of venality, by far the most famous though by

[40] *Mémoires*, XXXVI, 308. [41] B.N., Ms. fr. 7012, fol. 481-497.
[42] B.N., Ms. fr. 7012, fol. 495 verso.

no means the most complete, is that which Montesquieu inserted in his *Esprit des lois*.[43] To the question: "Should public employments be sold?" he replies that in a despotism they should not, since the prince must be free to place and displace his officers at will. Continuing within the framework of his famous trichotomy, he cites Plato's condemnation in Book VIII of the *Republic*, as proof that the principle is equally unsound in a government which depends on virtue. But when one turns to true, that is, aristocratic monarchy, with its central principle of honor, "this custom is not at all improper, by reason it is an inducement to engage in that as a family employment which would not be undertaken through a motive of virtue; it fixes likewise everyone in his duty, and renders the several orders of the Kingdom more permanent." He also avers that pure chance would make better selections than would the choice of the prince and adds the familiar claim that venality offers a noble incentive to commerce and industry.

The real crux of Montesquieu's position was unquestionably the role of venality and heredity in solidifying his beloved *corps intermédiaires*, placing them beyond the reach of either despotic rulers or irresponsible democrats. The doctrine of intermediate powers is too fundamental to the whole structure of Montesquieu's thought to be dismissed as merely the product of his own magistral background. His attitude toward ownership of office is consistent with his conception of a sound society. When all that is admitted, however, there remains the uneasy feeling that nowhere did the philosopher's ideology carry him further from reality; for he passes over abuses so fundamental as to reflect on the principle itself. To modern ears, the explosive reaction of Voltaire rings true: "La fonction divine de rendre justice, de disposer de la fortune et de la vie des hommes, un métier de famille!"[44]

[43] Book V, ch. 19. For the French text, I have used the edition of Gonzague Truc (Paris, 1944-1945), 2 vols.; the English translation is by Thomas Nugent, most recently published with an introduction by Franz Neumann (New York, 1949).

[44] "Commentaire sur *l'Esprit des lois*" (*Oeuvres*, ed. Moland, Paris, 1877-1885), XXX, 425.

Chapter Seven

The Robe Family

1

One of the aspects of the late *ancien régime* most familiar to modern students of French history is the existence of powerful official families, boasting generations and in some cases centuries of past honors in lineal descent. Thus when one reads of old Jean Bouhier, councilor in the Parlement of Burgundy in 1512, one is struck perhaps but scarcely amazed at the list of présidents à mortier among his descendants: Bénigne Bouhier (received in 1665), Jean (1691), Jean (1704), Jean (1716).[1] And the beholder is apt to be more impressed by the calligraphic beauty than startled by the implications of the great genealogical chart of 64 quarterings for President Louis-Augustin de Harlay which is displayed under glass at the Archives Nationales.[2]

This phenomenon of family power, however, has a special importance for the present problem which calls for some further analysis. Even in its simplest form, it can be discusssd in two separate contexts, one relating to the robe dynasties themselves in their characteristic eighteenth-century stage of development, the other centering around their grip on the courts as institutions. Beyond this dual approach, social and institutional, is the question of the robe families' infiltration of other social groups, especially other portions of the noblesse. And closely connected with that problem in turn is the pattern of marriages as a factor in shaping the high robe's interests and status under Louis XV.

[1] Pierre Palliot, *Le Parlement de Bourgongne* (Dijon, 1649), 167; François Petitot, *Continuation de l'histoire du Parlement de Bourgogne* (Dijon, 1733), *passim*.

[2] Case A-16.

For the above purposes, there exist the official records of receptions and armorials of various courts. All of the former and many of the latter are available only in manuscript. Some items, such as Michel's *Biographie du Parlement de Metz*[3] and d'Arbaumont's *Armorial de la Chambre des Comptes de Dijon*,[4] have received ordinary publication; while Mademoiselle Denys' subsidized armorial of the Chambres des Comptes of Paris appeared in a luxurious limited edition. Aside from these listings by offices, there are also numerous genealogical studies composed by eighteenth-century antiquarians either from curiosity or by commission. In this category must be cited especially the section on robe nobles in the Bibliothèque Nationale's Cabinet des Titres.[5] Finally, in all departmental archives family papers are assembled under Series E, while a wealth of incidental data resides in the notarial archives and registers of *insinuations*, even though the chief value of the latter two types of sources lies in the economic sphere.

Confronted with this mass of material, the researcher inevitably finds himself beset by numerous problems of evaluation and emphasis, several of which will become apparent in the course of the present chapter. Underlying the other problems is that of direct conflicts of testimony, here encountered in the form of contradictions between different membership lists for a given court or rival genealogies of the same family. Some of the documents, when read in the light of other evidence, stand revealed as pure fabrications. The Baron de Roure reports with considerable indignation that after having accepted the claims of the Marquis de Brue et Saint-Martin to a family background of nobility since before 1350, he discovered in reception records that the Marquis' bourgeois ancestor, Pierre Laurens, had bought a councilorship in the Parlement of Provence in 1623.[6] D'Hozier uncovered many other such delusions and forgeries, of course, in preparing the Armorial Général.[7]

No degree of care, I am convinced, can wholly eliminate the possi-

[3] (Paris, 1853). [4] (Dijon, 1881). [5] B.N., Mss. fr. 32138-32145.

[6] *Les recherches de noblesse en Provence sous Louis XIV et Louis XV* (Paris, 1910), 17.

[7] A.N., MM. 818[1], Mémoire contenant les veritables origines de Messieurs du Parlement, Chambre des Comptes, Cour des Aydes, etc. de Paris, dated 1706 and signed by d'Hozier, dismisses as fraudulent the published genealogies of many high robe families still to be seen in French collections.

bility of error when dealing with problems of this sort. All that can be claimed for the conclusions set forth in the next few pages is that they have been formulated with a full awareness of the dangers involved and after a genuine effort to minimize those dangers.

2

Nowhere is the difficulty of generalization more apparent than in the attempt to portray the typical high robe family of the early eighteenth century. In each of the sovereign courts, even at that late date, there were certain cases of officers who represented the first generation at their particular levels of dignity and whose nobility had begun only with their own receptions. It will be recalled that even for Brittany, Saulnier found three new officers after 1671 who had entered the Parlement as non-nobles.[8] At Grenoble in 1707, one "Etienne Brunet, bourgeois," was received as maître des comptes in the Chambre des Comptes and in 1748 passed his office on to his son, Ennemond-Etienne, who was still on the rolls when the court was abolished in 1790.[9] A similar case in the same court was that of François Mérindol, received in 1703, and his son, François *de* Mérindol de Vaux, who succeeded in 1741 and was by 1790 dean of the maîtres des comptes.[10] Many similar examples of comparatively recent arrivals may be cited: a Gaspard de Gueidan in the Parlement of Provence;[11] a Jacques-Claude Blanche or a François Maublanc in the Parlement of Burgundy;[12] a Jacques Hericart in the Paris Cour des Aides;[13] a François-Paul Roualle in the Grand Conseil;[14] not to

[8] See above, 74.

[9] A.D. Isère, *Catalogue*, Série B, II, 94-95. A.D. Isère, E. 180, contains a short dossier on this family in the eighteenth century.

[10] A.D. Isère, *Catalogue*, Série B, II, 93, 94, 95.

[11] Bib. Méjanes, Ms. 947 (902), Histoire du Parlement de Provence, by Jean Louis Honoré d'Esmivi and continuators.

[12] Bib. Dijon, Ms. 1330 (19), Tableau des officiers du Parlement de Bourgogne, suivant l'ordre de création de chacun des offices.

[13] B.N., Ms. fr. 7723, Tableau chronologique de tous les officiers de la Cour des Aydes de Paris, depuis son établissement.

[14] B.N., Ms. fr. 14015, Genuit des conseillers du Grand Conseil, depuis l'an 1483 jusques à present (1756).

mention the special case of practically all the officers of the newly established Cour des Monnaies of Lyon.[15]

At the other extreme there were some robe houses which could produce evidence of dignities five to six centuries old. Imagine the pride of Councilor de Chaponay at Grenoble, whose family archives contained a "Concordia matrimonialis aequitas Caroli de Chaponay, cancelarii Delphinatus et D. Ceciliae de Cassenatico, 2 nonas feb. 1134."[16] The Berthiers at Toulouse were one of the greatest chivalric houses of late medieval Languedoc;[17] while the widely distributed Verthamons could trace their lineage to fourteenth century Limousin.[18] At Bordeaux the d'Albessards had occupied offices in the Parlement of Guienne for over two-and-a-half centuries when Louis XV came to the throne—in other words, since the end of the Hundred Years' War.[19]

But with all due regard for such cases, there remains a definite pattern of high robe family backgrounds which, with certain regional variations, deserves to be called characteristic and which is for that reason worth having clearly in mind. What this pattern was, in the case of the Parlement of Paris, emerges most clearly from a survey of that court submitted to Louis XIV by the Juge d'Armes, d'Hozier, in 1707, that is to say, close enough to 1715 to contain most of the names which were to be important during Louis XV's early decades.[20] D'Hozier notes the peculiar cases, such as President de Harlay, whose family had been ennobled in 1465 for military services, and Councilor Savonnières, sprung from the noblesse de race of Anjou, on the one hand, and Councilor Bruneau, son of a notary, on the other. But the dominant theme of the report will emerge from a few examples:

Président à mortier Potier de Novion: Documents dated 1443 and 1479 show family engaged in successful fur business at Paris; Nicolas de Novion

[15] Bib. Méjanes, Ms. 565 (39), section on this court in Notices sur les membres du Parlement de Paris, de Grenoble, de Toulouse, etc.

[16] Bib. Grenoble, Fonds dauphinois, Ms. 1431 (R. 80).

[17] J. Villain, *La France moderne généaologique: III, Haute-Garonne et Ariège* (Montpellier, 1911-1913), 39 ff.

[18] Pierre Meller, *Les anciennes familles dans la Gironde* (Bordeaux, 1895-1896), I, 48-50.

[19] Gabriel O'Gilvy and Pierre-Jules Bourrousse de Laffore, *Nobiliaire de Guienne et de Gascogne* (Bordeaux, 1856-1883), II, 15-17.

[20] A.N., MM. 818^1.

was Général des Monnoyes of Louis XI in 1475; his grandson, Nicolas, great-great-grandfather of subject, began unbroken series of parlementary presidencies in 1545.

Councilor Mérault de Boinville: Great-grandfather was rich merchant and *échevin* of Paris; grandfather bought charge in Cour des Aides.

Councilor L'Escalopier: Great-great-grandfather was "bourgeois de Paris" in 1563; great-grandfather entered Parlement as councilor; grandfather was président à mortier.

Councilor de Forêts: Grandfather was bailli of small town in Auvergne; father was councilor in Cour des Aides.

Councilor de Vienne: Great-grandfather and grandfather were councilors in présidial at Troyes; father was *lieutenant particulier* at Châtelet.

Président des Enquêtes de Maupeou: Great-grandfather was a president in the Paris Cour des Aides; father held and bequeathed presidency of Enquêtes in Parlement.

Président des Requêtes Vallier: Great-grandfather was merchant in Saumur; grandfather was secrétaire du roy; father was *commissaire général des camps et armées du roy.*

These specimens illustrate the principle features of more than 90 percent of d'Hozier's cases.[21] The pattern is not wholly unitary, for the reader will note the existence of two recurrent types of family background which are different though related. One reveals the more or less direct crossover from big business to high robe offices during the sixteenth or seventeenth century (e.g., Potier de Novion, Mérault de Boinville, L'Escalopier). The other also begins with some degree of business success but proceeds by a more gradual rise through the official hierarchy, beginning with bailliage positions or local secretaryships and arriving only late in the seventeenth century at the sovereign court level (de Forêts, de Vienne, Vallier).

All through the Paris list, however, runs the constant emphasis on gains made by the third and fourth generations preceding the incumbents, in other words, on the late sixteenth and early seventeenth centuries—the age of Paulet and Loyseau—as the period in

[21] Corroborating genealogical evidence concerning the high robe of Paris exists in A.N., M. 257-607 and MM. 821; B.N., Mss. fr. 32138-9 (volumes du Cabin et des Titres); Bib. Méjanes, Ms. 730 (826).

B.N., Cabinet des Estampes

A *lit de justice*
(Louis XV at the Parlement of Paris on September 12, 1715)

B.N., Cabinet des Estampes

A pro-parlementary print of the 1730's

which the majority of eighteenth-century high robe families had fastened their grip on their first offices and had staked their claims to magistral nobility. Nor is there any need to limit this formulation to the Parlement of Paris. If one looks at Bordeaux, one finds the same dominant pattern: the Baritaults had descended from a fifteenth-century merchant of Poitou and had been noble since 1635, with a solid record of offices in both Cour des Aides and Parlement;[22] while the Secondats de Montesquieu had originated in Berry and begun their official rise after moving to Guienne about 1500[23] In Languedoc, the record bristles with such cases as that of the d'Assézat family, which had moved in from Rouergue in the early sixteenth century, succeeded in commerce at Toulouse, and by 1568 had already placed one Bernard d'Assézat as councilor in the Parlement.[24] Turning to Rouen, Metz, Dijon, Besançon, Grenoble, Aix, one finds countless genealogies of the same type.[25] If examples are needed for other types of sovereign courts, they are plentiful in such documents as the "Noms de tous les officiers de la Chambre des Comptes,"[26] or the records of the Paris Cour des Aides, with its two-century-old robe houses: Le Camus, Lotin de Charny, Pajot, etc.[27]

There is one other incidental but nonetheless significant feature of these family histories which should be placed beside their age and characteristic form of advancement. This is the evolution of titles. Except in the scattered cases of "pre-robe" noblesse, where such titles as "chevalier," "baron," or "comte" already adorned the

[22] Meller, *Anciennes familles*, nouvelle série, 32-33. Also A.D. Gironde, Série E, "Baritault."

[23] Meller, *Anciennes familles*, I, 78-80. The family archives are in Montesquieu's magnificent château, La Brède, just south of Bordeaux.

[24] Villain, *La France moderne généalogique*, Part III, 1583. Also A.D., Haute-Garonne, E, "D'Assézat."

[25] B.N., Ms. fr. 32318 (volumes du Cabinet des Titres), Mémoires pour servir à l'histoire du Parlement de Rouen, by François de Vigneul; and Ms. fr. 11924, Recherche sur quelques familles parlementaires attachées au parlement de Normandie; Michel, *Biographie du Parlement de Metz;* Bib. Dijon, Mss. 1331-1371 (20). Titres généalogiques, Juigné collection; A.D., Côte d'Or, Série E; A. Estignard, *Le Parlement de Franche-Comté* (Paris-Besançon, 1892), I, 137-138; Bib. Grenoble, Ms. 1074 (U. 474) Mélanges de Guy Allard, and various dossiers by name in Fonds dauphinois, especially R. 80; A.D. Isère, Série II, E; Bib. Méjanes, Ms. 730 (806) and Ms. 947 (902), Histoire du Parlement de Provence, by Esmivi.

[26] A.N., KK. 888.

[27] B.N., Ms. fr. 32991 (volumes du Cabinet des Titres).

family names before their first appearance on sovereign court rolls, it is customary to find a distinct progression. The president, councilor or maître des comptes of 1715 had most likely had a great-grandfather who had styled himself by his office and had perhaps added "Bourgeois de Paris" or "Noble homme d'Aix." The grandfather and father, on the other hand, might well have acquired a "de" between surname and patronymic, or between patronymic and fief name. They had probably also begun to add "Écuyer" or "Sieur" to their signatures. But consider the formidable battery of distinctions written into a high robe signature of the eighteenth century: Joseph-Gaspard, chevalier, Marquis de Maniban, received président à mortier in the Parlement of Languedoc in 1714;[28] Charles de Lombard, Marquis de Montauroux, councilor in the Parlement of Provence in 1718;[29] Jean-François de Bazemont, Baron de Chandieu, seigneur de Saint-Egrève, Proveyzieux, Mont-Saint-Martin, second president in the Parlement of Dauphiné.[30] The verbal trappings of self-conscious aristocracy were practically complete.

The relative age and distinction of high robe families—relative, that is, to other groups within the nobility—varied considerably from one section of France to another. At one extreme, of course, is encountered that dependable exception, Brittany. The Parlement at Rennes and the Chambre des Comptes at Nantes contained many officers whose backgrounds fitted into the general pattern described above. But so many others had entered the high robe from the old nobility, and so many Breton families of nobles d'épée had issued fairly recently from interludes in the magistracy that, in terms solely of family origins, one can scarcely assign the sovereign courts' personnel a separate place in the genealogical history of the province.[31]

In Dauphiné the situation was more ambiguous. Guy Allard, writing in 1700, listed 67 noble houses with *filiations* dating from the delphinal period, that is, from before the mid-fourteenth century incorporation into France.[32] Here is clear proof of a section of the

[28] Bib. Toulouse, Ms. 692.

[29] Bib. Méjanes, Ms. 947 (902).

[30] A.D. Isère, H (Supplement), B. 7.

[31] *Liste générale de Nosseigneurs du Parlement de Bretagne depuis son Erection en 1554* (Rennes, 1725).

[32] Bib. Grenoble, Ms. 1074 (U. 474), fol. 229.

nobility which antedated most of the high robe families. At the same time, among these 67 old houses there were a dozen or more, Bardonnenche, Bocsozel, La Poype, Ponnat, et al., which held offices in the Parlement or the Chambre des Comptes of Grenoble during the early eighteenth century. These were obviously atypical cases among the more commonly one- to two-century-old nobility of robe families; but just as obviously the magistrates as a group could boast of considerable prestige at Grenoble. This was the most general situation, applicable to at least three-fourths of the sovereign court localities, including Paris. Only a few robe houses could be included among the bona fide medieval lines; but fewer still could be denied a relatively high status in a society accustomed to think in terms of families and the age of families.[33]

Almost as far removed from this position in one direction as Brittany was in the other, were the special cases of Dijon and Bordeaux. In these urban centers the high robe had not been penetrated by the older aristocracy. It had not taken a place beside or below it. It had to a very large extent replaced it. In each case the process had begun with conquest by the French crown. As early as 1600, that is to say, only 150 years after the French period began at Bordeaux, the pre-1450 noble families of Guienne had practically vanished from sight. Economic changes and the political backlash from a too nostalgic attitude toward English rule had wiped them out in six generations. Only the great house of the Captaux de Buch survived, in female succession by alliance with the Toulousain d'Épernons. The parlementaires of Bordeaux, including the Cour des Aides officers, had moved in with their wealth to take over titles, mansions, châteaux, and social status.[34]

No less striking was the situation in Dijon, which has to this day retained the flavor of *la ville parlementaire* par excellence. Here again, as Gaston Roupnel has brilliantly demonstrated,[35] the break had come in the late fifteenth century; though not until the eighteenth can one speak of a closed robe caste. Here again the chief

[33] This relative position is well illustrated in a composite eighteenth-century summary of Parisian genealogies, A.N., M. 609.

[34] Camille Jullian, *Histoire de Bordeaux* (Bordeaux, 1895), 423 ff.

[35] *La ville et la campagne au XVIIe siècle* (Paris, 1922), 158 ff.

agent of change had been Louis XI, who had smashed the followers of Charles the Bold so thoroughly that their names had disappeared from prominence except in those cases where descendants had succeeded in worming their way back upward by service in the Parlement or the Chambre des Comptes. In the Burgundian hinterland, it is true, certain old houses had managed to cling to their lands and titles. In the high society of Dijon, however, the magistrates reigned unchallenged.

But returning to the more general pattern of Paris and Rouen, Grenoble and Aix, Toulouse and Pau and Montauban, it may be of some interest to consider for a moment what the average age of parlementary families meant within the outer limits of the aristocracy. I have been speaking primarily from the standpoint of 1700-1715, because at that period the progression of family development can be shown most clearly in terms of successive generations. It is worth remembering, however, that by 1748, at least one and in many cases two additional generations had been laid on top of the development from new wealth and new offices in the sixteenth century, through nobility in the seventeenth, to titled dignity in the early eighteenth. From such figures as I have been able to obtain, I should set the average age of a high robe dynasty in 1748 at something over five generations in terms of offices and about four in terms of recognized nobility. This, be it remembered, takes into account families of more recent ascent and others which were much older.

Unfortunately, there is no reliable way in which to set an average for the noblesse d'épée as a whole, since it included thirteenth-century houses intermingled with ennobled army officers of Louis XIV's last wars, and since its records, though voluminous, are still fragmentary.[36] An interesting mid-eighteenth century manuscript at Aix-en-Provence insists that the high robe of France, taken as a whole, was as noble as any similarly large section of the king's sub-

[36] There are no fewer than 5,292 volumes in the Cabinet des Titres proper (B.N., Mss. fr. 26485-31776), while all additional numbers up to and including Ms. fr. 33264 are listed as "Volumes du Cabinet des Titres," a supplementary series. The 3,061 volumes of "pièces originales" alone contain 68,460 genealogical dossiers, and the "Cabinet d'Hozier," bequeathed to the crown in 1717, contains another 9,739 dossiers in 344 volumes. Yet all this mountain of documentation, whatever its value to genealogists of individual families, is too incoherent and uneven to provide a basis for statistical analysis.

jects.[37] Even so revered a family of the sword as that of Riqueti in Provence had been only *écuyers* until 1685, when its lands were finally erected under a name destined to be one of the most famous in French history: the marquisate of Mirabeau.[38] The peerage of Saint-Simon's time was itself primarily composed of houses raised to that level of honor since 1600.[39]

The fact remains that there exist no statistical sources for the French nobility as a whole over any long period. For this reason one can only turn to a comparative standard, that of Sweden, where the meticulously organized genealogical records of the *Riddarhus* provide a unique set of data covering more than three centuries. A Swedish sociologist, P. E. Fahlbeck, has shown that of 1,547 noble families originally registered when the institution was established in 1626, only two lasted nine generations in direct male succession and eighty-four percent were actually interrupted or survived only through the marriages of daughters by the *third* generation![40] In other words, only sixteen percent of the Swedish noble houses of the eighteenth century were as old as the average French robe dynasty of the 1740's. The three generations after 1626 admittedly saw Sweden involved in almost continuous and extremely bloody warfare; but during the same period the French fighting caste too was undergoing decimation by battle. After making a broad allowance for national differences, the reader will still see in these figures some suggestion of why the high French magistracy appeared increasingly aristocratic, even when compared with non-robe nobles who boasted medieval traditions but could seldom claim medieval origins.

3

If the emphasis is now reversed, one can make use of most of the archival materials employed above for an idea of the robe situation viewed in terms not of families but of corporate institutions. In

[37] Bib. Méjanes, Ms. 730 (826).

[38] Louis de Loménie, *Les Mirabeaux* (Paris, 1879), I, 53.

[39] See below, 175.

[40] "La noblesse de Suède: étude démographique," *Bulletin de l'institut international de statistique* (Kristiana, 1900), XII, 169-181.

other words, instead of seeking only to portray lineal backgrounds, there is need to examine the grip of hereditary transmission on the sovereign courts, as revealed between 1715 and 1748.

Here there are several methodological problems. One is the confusion of names which resulted from that growing use of titles to which I have already referred. The eighteenth-century robe official loved to designate himself by his fairest fief or seigneury, instead of by his patronymic. Thus at Paris, Councilors de Montsabert and de Baillé, as given in the printed rosters issued each Easter by the Parlement,[41] were in fact both sons of Councilor Goislard; and at Grenoble, what at first appears to have been the commercial transfer of a parlementary office from the Sieur de Comiers to the Seigneur de Miribel in 1743 was actually a testamentary bequest from François de Copin to his son, André.[42]

Another problem is that of following family continuity beyond its most obvious aspect, that of father-to-son successions in the same offices. Such successions are clearly shown in reception registers and in the armorials, which list the charges separately by title and under each title by date of creation, then list the names of consecutive holders under each. These compilations are valuable in themselves. They reveal, for example, that in the Parlement of Provence, 10 of the 21 présidents à mortier who served at various times between 1715 and 1748 had been received as close relatives of their immediate predecessors, while the 72 councilors included 40 who were designated sons, grandsons, nephews, brothers or first cousins of the previous incumbents.[43] Among the 103 presidents and maîtres of the Paris Chambre des Comptes received between 1715 and 1748, 41 were sons or nephews of their predecessors.[44] Taken alone, however, such figures constitute only a partial index of family power. For almost as common as the direct survivance in one office was the procedure under which a magistrate could sell his own charge when so inclined, then later buy a different one for his heir. Montesquieu, to cite a famous case, received his presidency at Bordeaux directly from his

[41] B.N., Lf[25].31, *Listes des membres du Parlement* (printed, various dates).

[42] A.D., Isère, *Catalogue*, Série B, II, 46.

[43] Bib. Méjanes, Ms. 947 (902).

[44] Denys, *Armorial de la Chambre des Comptes*, I, 5-85.

uncle in 1716, but sold it in 1726 and in 1736 bought a councilorship for his son.[45]

Hence, the search for an accurate picture of robe dynastic power demands a larger unit than the individual office. It is only when one considers an entire court, or better still, all the sovereign courts in a locality having more than one, that the full pattern becomes discernible. Only then does one perceive the intricate relationships—a father risen to président à mortier in the Parlement of Guienne, after having surrendered to his son his former, inherited charge in the Bordeaux Cour des Aides; another son installed in a newly purchased office of conseiller des enquêtes and destined later to move up to his parent's presidency; a son-in-law waiting in an office at the local présidial for the vacancy in Enquêtes which will then be his.

Now this characteristic pattern produced one curious effect as regards the roster of a given court at any one date, an effect which at first glance appears to refute the whole idea of family power. I have pointed out that dispensations for parenté were extremely common, and it would seem natural to expect a marked concentration of certain names on every attendance roll. Actually this is not the case. The 163 robe officers of the Paris Parlement who attended the great lit de justice at the Tuileries in 1718 represented no fewer than 134 different patronymics; and of the 26 names which are repeated, only Feydeau, Lamoignon and Pajot appear three times.[46] In 1732, for a similar assembly at Versailles, the ratio was 139 family names to 156 officers, with only La Guillaumie appearing three times in this case.[47] The distribution was somewhat less scattered in the provinces; but at Dijon in 1748, though the Parlement at that date contained 5 Bouhiers, 4 Fijans, and 4 Perreneys, there were no fewer than 65 patronymics among the 92 active officers, exclusive of the non-robe chevaliers d'honneur.[48]

Does all this indicate a weakening of family power? Not in the least. Look again for an instant at the hypothetical example of the

[45] See above, 106.

[46] A.N., K. 696, no. 41 and no. 54[1]. It is true that shortly afterward, during the exile to Pontoise of 1720, Delisle recorded that President Gilbert had secured a house for himself and for his two sons, one of whom was avocat-général, the other, greffier-en-chef. A.N., U. 747.

[47] A.N., K. 698, no. 10 *bis*.

[48] Bib. Dijon, Ms. 1330 (19).

Bordeaux family. It will be noted that four close relatives are involved in present or future offices at the sovereign court level. At the moment selected, however, *only two* would be listed in a roster of the Parlement of Guienne and even those two only for the overlap period before the father gave up his presidency, after which there would be two brothers-in-law and hence two separate patronymics. I submit that most of the duplications of names that appear in any given attendance list reflect short overlaps of this kind, that the duplications shifted constantly from one family to another, and that for these reasons even a whole court is an inadequate unit for analysis if examined during too short a period.

I have discussed these insufficient types of approach in order to illustrate the absolute necessity of looking sideways beyond the narrow limits of individual offices and lengthwise over a substantial time span. The only reliable basis for generalization lies in a series of lists, arranged alphabetically by patronymics and each composed of all persons who were occupying high robe offices in a given locality when Louis XV ascended the throne or were received between then and 1748. For Rennes, Rouen, Colmar, and Metz, I have been able to compile such lists from printed materials; for Toulouse, Bordeaux, Dijon, and Aix-en-Provence, from documentary sources; for Paris, Grenoble, and Besançon, from a combination of both. There would be little value in reproducing all these compilations, but the main points which emerge from them can be briefly illustrated.

At the Parlement of Dauphiné and the Chambre des Comptes of Grenoble, a total of 261 individuals were either presidents, councilors, maîtres, *correcteurs*, auditeurs, gens du roi or greffiers-en-chef at some time between 1715 and 1748. They may be grouped under 172 family names, of which 37 appear twice, 15 three times, 2 four times, and those of Gratet and Pourroy, five times each.[49] And even this, be it noted, does not take into account the many relationships by marriage. At Dijon, the combined turnover of the Parlement and the Chambre des Comptes in the same period came to 254, representing only 140 family names, with Bouhier repeated ten times, Joly seven times, Rigoley six times, and Espiard, Fyot, Quarré,

[49] A.D. Isère, *Catalogue*, Série B, II, 1-105, *passim*.

and Richard five times each.[50] Even in the seething commercial atmosphere of Bordeaux, where circulation seems to have remained more than ordinarily active well into the eighteenth century, the 173 parlementary councilors received between 1700 and 1748 may be grouped under 118 patronymics, though only that of Paty appears four times.[51] In aristocratic Brittany, on the other hand, the ratio was higher than two officers per name.[52] The remaining centers fall within this general range.

The situation at Paris was more complex than most, because the high robe families of the capital, instead of clinging to sovereign court positions as their one insurance of prestige, were constantly being diverted into administrative offices or moving to the provinces when commissioned to first presidencies of outlying courts. Conversely, the steady stream of recruitment from the greatest magistral houses of provincial origin—Joly from Dijon, Turgot from Rouen, Berthelot from Metz—swelled the total of new names, though it still implied continuity within the high robe as defined in nationwide terms. But even in Paris, where some 1,200 persons held offices in Parlement, Chambre des Comptes, Cour des Aides, Grand Conseil, or Cour des Monnaies during these thirty-three years, one finds fewer than 850 separate names, with about 150 recurring with notable frequency. Furthermore, in considering these large numbers it is important not to lose sight of the relatively few great houses—Amelot, Lamoignon, Feydeau, Joly de Fleury, Le Peletier, Nicolay, Verthamon, Le Camus—whose members figured in more than one court at once, initiating and directing political action and at the same time moving in the highest circles of church, army, and administration. For the importance of their caste had long since ceased to be confined within the walls of the palais de justice.

[50] Bib. Dijon, Ms. 1330 (19), Tableau des officiers du Parlement de Bourgogne; and Ms. 655 (453), Tableau des officiers de la Chambre des Comptes de Dijon.

[51] Bib. Bordeaux, Ms. 369; A.D. Gironde, C. 2636, 2701, 2719, 2752. See also Dast Le Vacher de Boisville, "Liste générale et alphabétique des membres du Parlement de Bordeaux, 1462-1790," *Archives historiques du Département de la Gironde* (Bordeaux, 1896), XXXI, 1-62.

[52] *Liste générale de Nosseigneurs du Parlement de Bretagne.*

4

In all my emphasis on professional dynasties, I have as yet taken little notice of the other callings, noble but not judicial, into which the eighteenth century saw a remarkable movement by younger sons and in some cases even the principal heirs of sovereign court families. The invasion of the army was most striking. Here was a source both of income and of honors, not of solemn justice but of chivalry itself, in all its twilight splendor. The visitor to the château of La Brède cannot fail to be struck by the series of portraits which decorate the walls of Montesquieu's salon. After the heavy, square countenances of earlier Secondats comes Montesquieu's uncle, resplendent in presidential ermine, then the delicate features of the philosopher himself, and finally, bespeaking a shift in the values and aspirations of one whole segment of the class, his grandson in the uniform of an aide-de-camp in the armies of the king, a deputy to Rochambeau in America.

The aristocratization of the French army after Louis XIV presented no problem to families whose noblesse rested on more than enough generations of office to guarantee the requisite degrees and quarterings. By mid-century one observer in Provence wrote matter-of-factly:

> The majority of these [robe] houses have embraced the sword and have risen at court and distinguished themselves at war by their gallantry and their services. More than half of the *Capitaines aux Gardes* are children of parlement.[53]

The testimony of private documents may be illustrated by an inventory of household furnishings involved in a testamentary dispute over the estate of Bénigne Bouhier at Dijon between his widow and his three sons—Jean, président à mortier; Claude, prior of Pontailler; Bénigne, colonel in the infantry.[54] A similar example from Dauphiné appears in a recognition of indebtedness enacted before a Grenoble notary in 1748 by Maître des Comptes Etienne Brunet de Vence, on behalf of himself and Thomas Brunet de Portemant, "officier de cavalerie au Regiment de Rohan," in favor

[53] Bib. Méjanes, Ms. 730 (826). [54] A.D. Côte d'Or, E. 104.

of their brother, Jean Claude Brunet du Vivier, "chanoine honoraire en l'Eglise cathedrale de cette ville."[55]

The appearance of clergymen in both these cases reveals another, albeit older, ramification of robe family power. As in the seventeenth century, the sons of magistrates were everywhere pressing into high ecclesiastical positions. At Paris, the celebrated *conseiller clerc*, Abbé Pucelle, was the descendant of an old magistral house, his grandfather having been first president of the Parlement of Dauphiné.[56] He was typical of the many ecclesiastical councilors who had simply taken the tonsure while remaining in their fathers' profession. Aside from parlementary clergymen, there were numerous prelates with robe backgrounds, such as Jean Bouhier, first bishop of Dijon; Antoine-François de Berthier, bishop of Rieux in Languedoc; Jean d'Yse de Salion (Dauphinois parlementary house), "primat des primats," archbishop-count of Vienne.[57] From such evidence there emerges a plausible picture of the growing solidarity of privileged groups not simply in terms of common interests but actually in terms of direct interrelationship.

The movement from sovereign court offices into administrative posts in the royal government is well established and needs little illustration beyond the mention of such names as Le Peletier, d'Aguesseau, Chauvelin, Dodun, Le Febvre d'Ormesson, and later, of course, Turgot and Maupeou. This tendency, however, had a different effect than did others discussed here; for as I have remarked in an earlier connection,[58] the robe families whose representatives became ministers or even intendants tended to change their attitude toward the crown, to become more dependent on it and identified with it. They and their descendants were for the most part lost to the regular aristocracy.[59] To see this process at work, one has only to read the

[55] A.D. Isère, III. E. 1181[22], fol. 378-379.

[56] B.N., Ms. fr. 32139, Généalogies de messieurs les . . . présidents et conseillers au Parlement, etc.

[57] A.D. Isère, III.E.1181[22], contains a record of a notary's having been summoned to Vienne in 1748 to receive a legal act appointing a procureur for the archbishop's family interests in Grenoble.

[58] See above, 34.

[59] A sample biography of this type may be worth summarizing here: François-Victor Le Tonnelier de Breteuil, Marquis de Fontenay-Trésigny, received councilor in Parlement of Paris, 1705; named maître des requêtes and intendant of Limoges, 1718; secretary of

criticism of privileged groups contained in the instructions sent to Tourny, intendant of Bordeaux in the 1740's, by more than two dozen ministers, many of them bearing old robe names.[60]

Aside from the lower court offices, experience in which sometimes replaced service at the bar as apprenticeship for heirs of magistral titles,[61] there is one other type of overlap which calls for mention. This is the relationship between sovereign court and high municipal offices—between the "robe" and the "cloche." The situation here is by no means simple, for it displays two separate and to some extent conflicting tendencies. On the one hand, one finds well-established parlementaires gladly accepting royal appointment to the upper level of town offices filled in that manner. The honorific title of Prévôt des Marchands de Paris generally went to one of the king's conseillers d'état or maîtres des requêtes; but from 1725 to 1740 it was held by two successive members of the Parlement: Nicolas Lambert and Michel Etienne Turgot, both présidents des requêtes.[62] President Dugas of the Cour des Monnaies at Lyon was at the same time Prévôt des Marchands of that city, as his presidential predecessor, Ravat, had been prior to 1716.[63] The list of maires of Dijon between 1700 and 1750 reads as follows:

1694–1703—François Baudot, maître des comptes in the Chambre des Comptes of Dijon.

1703–1711—Julien Clopin, councilor in the Parlement of Burgundy.

1711–1714—Nicolas Labotte, trésorier de France in the Bureau des Finances at Dijon.

1714–1729—Etienne Baudevat, procureur du roi in the Bureau des Finances.

---

state for war, 1723-1726 and 1740 until his death in 1743. Hénault, *Mémoires*, 55, note 2. The cursus honorum of the seventeenth- and eighteen-century minister generally included a period on the bench of a sovereign court prior to his becoming a maître de requêtes, the first step in his administrative career per se.

[60] A. D. Gironde, C. 187.

[61] In 1727, for example, the president of the présidial at Bordeaux was of the parlementary house of d'Albessard (A.D. Gironde, C. 2752), and sons of the d'Argouges family at Paris regularly served as *lieutenants-civils* in the Châtelet. There are countless othei such instances scattered through the records of subordinate jurisdictions in sovereign court centers.

[62] B.N., Ms. fr. 32986, "Chasot de Nantigny," Tablettes de Thémis.

[63] *Ibid.*

1729–1731—Philippe Baudot, maître des comptes.

1731–1750—Jean-Pierre Burteur, councilor in the Parlement.[64]

Councilors at Colmar also served as *préteurs royaux* of that city and of Sélestat, while one, Jean Baptiste de Klinglin, became préteur royal of Strasbourg in 1725.

This duplication of functions is interesting, but it was by no means universal. At Bordeaux, after a royal order in council of November 5, 1715, the municipal *jurats* could assemble only with permission of the Parlement of Guienne and in the presence of two of its councilors.[65] During the eighteenth century this difference of rank was reflected in the attitude of parlementary families; for the *jurade*, which in the sixteenth and seventeenth centuries had been eagerly sought by such powerful clans as Le Berthon, Secondat, Alesme, and Barbot, in this later period was clearly a lower order of dignity, from which the parlementary heirs held stiffly aloof.[66] To a lesser degree the same was true in Languedoc. The prestige of the Capitol at Toulouse remained high, when compared with that of other town councils since the decline of municipalities. But even the capitouls, whose offices had once brought noblesse to countless southern families, had become a separate group distinctly below the Parlement and carefully kept in its place by the latter.[67]

What emerges from the evidence is a picture of a relatively small group of powerful robe families which placed clusters of their members in the sovereign courts from 1715 to 1748, another group which placed only one before dropping out of magistral pursuits, and a middle group, the largest of all, made up of houses each of which at least maintained a single file of succession. All of the chief dynasties and most of the lesser ones were sending ever more powerful and intricate tentacles into army and church, occasionally defecting in

[64] Bib. Dijon, Ms. 744 (448^3).

[65] A.D. Gironde, C. 3622.

[66] Cf. Dast Le Vacher de Boisville, "Liste alphabétique des sous-maires, lieutenants de maire, prévôts, jurats, clercs de ville, procureurs-syndics et leurs substituts et trésoriers de la ville de Bordeaux, de 1208 à 1790," *Archives historiques du Département de la Gironde* (Bordeaux, 1899), XXXIV, 212-250.

[67] Bib. Toulouse, Ms. 699, 105, is an account by Pierre Barthès of the capitouls' being forced to withdraw from a religious procession and assembly in 1742 because they had sought to share the Parlement's place of honor.

favor of appointive royal functions, clinging to municipal titles which still carried honor, shunning those which they felt did not. But one other factor deserves some attention in connection with the high robe's family power: the effect of alliances by marriage.

5

In the early eighteenth century the characteristic pattern of high robe marriages comprised at least three separate elements, one old and familiar, the others relatively new and extremely important for the caste's social standing under Louis XV.

The older tendency, which had for two centuries served the building of magistral solidarity, was that of intra-robe alliances. Here it is worth returning for a moment to the 64 quarterings of President de Harlay, which was mentioned at the beginning of the present chapter. This magistrate was the son of a conseiller d'État, whose father had also served in that capacity, and whose great-grandfather had been a président à mortier in the Parlement of Paris. But the paternal succession did not constitute de Harlay's entire pedigree, for on his mother's side he was the grandson of a chancellor of France and great-grandson of a dean of maîtres in the Paris Chambre des Comptes. He was descended at the sixth generation from no fewer than nine officers in the Parlements of Paris and Dauphiné and the Paris Cour des Monnaies.[68]

In the eighteenth century such intermarriage was still an essential feature of robe solidarity. Social contacts among sovereign court families were so frequent that the attractive daughter of a councilor at a cour des aides might reasonably expect to catch the eye of a parlementary président à mortier's son and prospective heir. But marriages of love, in which the bride's beauty or personality made any difference, were scarcely the rule in the society to which the high robe aspired. Much more in keeping with that society's view of parental authority and its distaste for husbandly infatuation were the pre-arranged marriages such as the union of Lamoignon and a Nicolay, children of great robe families.[69] Many less notable but still important cases are revealed in testaments and contracts.

[68] See above, 124. [69] Barbier, *Journal*, I, 165.

President Jacques-Philippe de Ciron at Toulouse, for example, had been pre-deceased by his wife, daughter of one Councilor Toupignon; so in 1723 he was free to leave to their three daughters a total of 100,000 livres with which to arrange marriages, preferably within the Parlement of Languedoc.[70] At Dijon in 1717 a contract for liquidation and division of a joint bequest was signed between Abraham François Nigieu, councilor in the Parlement of Burgundy, on one side and his sister's husband, Jacques Charles Fevret de Fontette, also a councilor in that court, on the other.[71] The Antoinette de Brion, daughter of a Paris Cour des Aides and Grand Conseil family, who signed her testament in March 1747, is described in the document as "veuve de Charles Amelot, conseiller et ancien président en la 3me Chambre des Enquêtes."[72]

The above handful of illustrations will perhaps suffice to show that the old network of intermarriage within the boundaries of the robe still played its part during the early eighteenth century. At the same time, however, a second dominant tendency was becoming apparent in the form of ever more numerous marriages with families of the noblesse de race. The memoirs of contemporaries refer to such alliances with great frequency but quite without surprise, in itself a good indication of how accepted the idea had become. The chronicler of Toulouse, Pierre Barthès, notes that in November 1741, President de Maniban was welcomed home after a long visit to Paris for the marriage of his daughter and the Marquis de Livry.[73] When in 1718 the daughter of Charles de Ribeyre, First President of the Cour des Aides at Clermont-Ferrand, and of Madeleine de Bérulle of the Dauphinois parlementary family, married Louis-Théodose de Scorailles, Marquis de Roussille, Chevalier de Saint-Louis, she ensured her future children a combination of both magistral and military honors.[74] Here again one finds a wealth of material in archival sources, such as the testament of Dominique Bastard, dean of councilors in the Parlement of Languedoc, which provides

[70] A.D. Haute-Garonne, Testaments séparés, 11822, no. 1968.

[71] Bib. Dijon, Ms. 1354 (20).

[72] A.D. Seine, DC^6.232, fol. 165.

[73] Bib. Toulouse, Ms. 699, 85.

[74] Baron de Scoraille, "Un lieutenant du roi en Haute Auvergne, au XVIIIe," *Revue de la Haute Auvergne* (Aurillac, 1908), X, 368.

for payment of the balance of his daughter's dowry to the Baron de Gendonoussac.[75]

Now these robe-épée marriages must be treated with some reservations if their significance is not to be misunderstood. In the first place, they concerned, on the épée side, primarily the court nobility of Versailles and Paris and the very highest provincial families de race. The *hobereaux*, poor but for that very reason all the more proud, figured relatively little in such alliances, partly, no doubt, because of the tradition of intermarriage among only the oldest families in rural localities. But this is not the full explanation; for even if some hobereau had felt inclined to join his house to one of magistral wealth, the robe's own contempt for the poorer gentry might well have made it impossible. Secondly, there is always the suspicion that even the great families of the sword accepted sovereign court officers only reluctantly, for the financial transfusion the latter brought to depleted fortunes. This view is reinforced by the famous outburst of Saint-Simon on hearing that his brother-in-law, the Duc de Lorge, was to marry the daughter of First President de Mesmes of the Paris Parlement.[76] Nevertheless, it can, I think, be shown that in this as in much else Saint-Simon's attitude was distinctly anachronistic in the eighteenth century. Not only were the robe families marrying into the noblesse d'épée, but their sons were in many cases actually becoming nobles d'épée by profession. The old expression of "manuring one's land with bourgeois gold" appears almost not at all after 1715 with reference to high robe-épée marriages.

Where it does still appear in connection with the magistracy—and this leads to the third point in the present section—is in exactly the opposite type of alliance: that between a sovereign court family and one of middle class finance. The robe family itself, now securely noble but often eager for additional wealth to offset mounting social expenses, had reached the stage of turning not always to professionally advantageous marriages, not always to those which brought added prestige, but sometimes to those which offered a share in the fruits of commerce. Consider for a moment the celebrated

[75] A.D. Haute-Garonne, Testaments séparés, 11811, no. 458. Also Insinuations, register 38, fol. 522.

[76] *Mémoires*, XXXVII, 252-253; XXXVIII, 61-68.

Hôtel Mimeure (Fyot), Dijon

Montesquieu's La Brède, south of Bordeaux

TWO ROBE RESIDENCES

B.N., Cabinet des Estampes

The magistrate as social lion
(From a fashion book of the 1730's)

marriages of the children of Samuel Bernard, the greatest French capitalist of the age. Under the Regency his sons all married daughters of families de race: Saint-Chamans, Boulainvilliers, de la Cosse.[77] A few years later, however, his three grand-daughters married, respectively, President Molé in 1731,[78] President Lamoignon in 1732,[79] and the Marquis de Mirepoix in 1733.[80] It was after this series of events that Barbier reported the following popular verse:

O temps, ô moeurs, ô siècle déréglé!
Où l'on voit déroger les plus nobles familles.
Lamoignon, Mirepoix, Molé,
De Bernard épousent les filles,
Et sont les recéleurs du bien qu'il a volé.[81]

In the poetaster's eyes at least, robe and *épée* alike were manuring their lands.

It has been necessary to touch upon a variety of aspects in order to obtain even a summary analysis of the magistral houses, their roots, their institutionalized power, their ramifications. Age, offices, extension into other callings, alliances by marriage, all went into the total concept of the robe dynasty. But one other factor, though also partly a matter of family, I have left for separate treatment because of its many-sided importance for the rest of my general investigation. This is the question of the high robe's economic position.

NOTE. In a recent article, "L'aristocratie parlementaire française à la fin de l'Ancien Régime,"[82] Professor Jean Egret warns against exaggerating the exclusiveness of the high robe, even as late as 1774-1789. To support his argument, he cites the fact that of the 943 parlementaires received during those years and still in office in 1790, no fewer than 394 were former roturiers who became noble by virtue of their entry into the sovereign court magistracy.[83] He

[77] Marais, *Journal et mémoires*, I, 375-376. Cf. E. de Clermont-Tonnerre, *Histoire de Samuel Bernard et de ses enfants* (Paris, 1914).

[78] *Ibid.*, IV, 218. [79] *Ibid.*, IV, 410. [80] *Ibid.*, IV, 516. [81] *Journal*, II, 28.

[82] *Revue historique* (Paris, July-September 1952), 1-15.

[83] Using material from A. de Roton, J. de La Trollière, and R. de Montmort, *Les Arrêts du Grand Conseil portant dispense du marc d'or de noblesse, 1771-1789* (Paris, 1951). As Egret points out, "Grand Conseil" is a misnomer, as used in the title.

concludes that, save in Brittany, this magistracy was not closed to new men, down to the Revolution itself.

An analysis of such a problem by a recognized French authority is obviously both welcome and important from the point of view of the present study. However, even if Egret's essay had appeared while this book was still in manuscript, I do not believe that it would have occasioned any major change in my conclusions—the latter, incidentally, having been strongly influenced by Egret's own remarks in his earlier work on the Parlement of Dauphiné.

There are three points to be made here, it seems to me. First, the concept of a closed caste, as applied to eighteenth-century France, is necessarily relative, both to earlier conditions and to the increasing pressure for more circulation. Second, it is a question of emphasis whether one is more impressed by the 42 per cent of the new parlementaires who became noblemen on reception or by the 58 per cent who were noble by birth. Third, the political record of the last decades of the old regime shows that the "new men" either could not change the direction of high robe activities or, much more probably, assimilated the aristocratic views of their colleagues.

These are qualifications which Professor Egret has provided for in his article, but which need to be made explicit in the present context.

Chapter Eight

The Robe Fortune

1

THE FRENCH NOBILITY, a unified class in legal terms by the end of the seventeenth century, never ceased to be criss-crossed by a host of internal subdivisions. The eighteenth century did not wholly eradicate any of these various lines of differentiation, but it did see a notable shift of relative importance among them. There remained, to be sure, all the old differences of title, family origin, profession, special honors. In its significance for the social and political configuration of the class, however, not one of these criteria could any longer be compared with a scale which Funck-Brentano calls "la plus moderne, la plus crue et la plus brutale,"[1] that of wealth.

The capitation schedule of 1695 has already provided an idea of the high robe's place on this scale late in the reign of Louis XIV.[2] This tax was renewed on various occasions after 1715, each time with the privileged classes relieved of part of the share which they had borne in the original project, but with the sovereign court officers always high on the tariff of rates. In 1739 and again in 1748, the first president of the Parlement of Burgundy was assessed 1,275 livres; each of the présidents à mortier, 382 livres 10 sous; the councilors and gens du roi, 191 livres 5 sous apiece; and the greffier-en-chef, 102 livres.[3] At Bordeaux, in 1727, the présidents à mortier of

[1] *L'Ancien régime* (Paris, 1926), 164.

[2] See above, 32-33.

[3] A.D. Côte d'Or, B. 12155 and C. 5646. For the Chambre des Comptes of Dijon the individual rates in 1748 were: first president, 540 livres; presidents, 312 livres 18 sous 4 deniers; maîtres des comptes and gens du roi, 187 livres 18 sous 4 deniers; correcteurs and auditeurs, 125 livres 8 sous 4 deniers; and greffiers-en-chef, 62 livres 18 sous 4 deniers.

the Parlement of Guienne paid 450 livres apiece and the councilors, 225; whereas the rating of non-robe nobles seldom went over 100 livres.[4]

The personal fortune of a sovereign court officer had even before the accession of Louis XV come to comprise at least three separate elements. One was the capital value of his office and the professional income he derived from it. Another was his combination of peculiarly urban holdings, including his town house, his investments in commercial enterprises, his loans to private parties, and his *rentes* on the royal government or municipalities. The third was his land, perhaps only a modest country place but just as possibly a series of major fiefs and seigneuries, at least one of them titled. Not every magistrate possessed all three types of wealth, of course; but by the early eighteenth century the overwhelming majority did. It was the combination and interdependence of offices, urban investments, and land which explained the power of the high robe's economic position, even as it dramatized the fusion of relatively recent noble characteristics with the bourgeois past.

2

The cash value of a high robe office varied with its rank, the type and location of the sovereign court, and the state of the market. Much has been written about the decline in the level of prices after 1715. It is unquestionably true that offices attracted fewer avid buyers during this era of the courts' waxing prestige and influence than they had during the political eclipse under Louis XIV. No simple explanation will account for this outwardly paradoxical phenomenon. To some extent, of course, it reflected changing conditions in the national economy as a whole, for the wealthy bourgeois who had once been willing to buy an office at almost any price now saw tempting alternatives for investment in the rapidly expanding industry and commerce of France.[5] Doubtless the un-

[4] A.D. Gironde, C. 2719 and C. 2752. Following are some examples of non-robe noble assessments in 1727; the Marquis de Beynac, 150 livres; Monsieur de la Roussie, 43 livres; the Sieur de Brona, 11 livres 10 sous; the Demoiselle de Saint-Quentin, 5 livres; and the Sieur de Laborie de l'Aussel, 2 livres.

[5] Sagnac, *Formation de la société française*, II, 55.

pleasant recollection of Louis XIV's bad faith in revoking provisions and his extortionate treatment of his functionaries had also contributed to making public charges less attractive, though this applied less to the sovereign courts than to the much-abused lower offices.[6]

These strictly economic factors, however, do not alone suffice to explain the decline in cash value of high robe charges. One must also, I think, take into account the effects of family solidarity and exclusivism, which were making the sovereign courts increasingly difficult for parvenus to enter. Even after having bought a charge, the newcomer might well find himself excluded from office by the company's own refusal to approve his reception. He could still resell his claim to a more acceptable candidate, of course; but the prospect of such a fiasco must have made investment in an office decreasingly attractive. It is impossible to fix the number of rejections of this type; for the majority would have occurred at the time of the aspirant's first, informal application to the screening committee of senior magistrates, after he had bought a *resignatio in favorem* but before he had left any trace on royal records by a demand for letters of provision. Nevertheless, contemporary references to the courts' admission barriers are frequent enough to make this element appear significant in the general trend.

In spite of its apparent importance, however, the fall in the price level of offices should not be exaggerated with respect to the sovereign courts, where until the latter half of the eighteenth century it was much less marked than in the présidiaux, élections, *maréchaussées* and similar subordinate institutions.[7] True, the crown could no longer count on selling two charges of président à mortier in the Paris Parlement for 450,000 livres apiece, as it had done at the peak in 1690.[8] Levels had almost everywhere fallen below the general range of the 1660's and 1670's, when presidencies had sold for any-

[6] See above, 111-112.

[7] The much more extreme revulsion in the case of lower robe offices is illustrated in a letter written by Chancellor d'Aguesseau concerning the sénéchaussées in 1740: "Un degoût presque général pour les charges de judicature semble avoir succédé à cette avidité presque incroyable avec laquelle nous les avons vu rechercher pendant longtemps." A.D. Ille-et-Vilaine, C. 1818, quoted by A. E. Giffard, *Les justices seigneuriales en Bretagne* (Paris, 1903), 214. Nothing this strong could have been said of the sovereign courts.

[8] Dangeau, *Journal*, III, 248. The buyers were Talon and de Menars.

where from 60,000 livres in the Parlement of Navarre to 150,000 in the Parlement of Normandy, 200,000 in the Paris Chambre des Comptes and as high as 400,000 in the Parlement of Paris; advocate-generalcies for 100,000 in Toulouse, 110,000 in the Paris Cour des Aides, 150,000 to 300,000 in the Parlement of Paris; councilorships for 48,000 to 70,000 in Bordeaux, 60,000 in Metz, 80,000 to 150,000 in Paris.[9]

Nevertheless, the drop was not yet as notable as it became in the years after Maupeou's abortive suppression of the parlements in 1771.[10] There were still transactions involving huge sums, as when the future minister, Chauvelin, bought a Paris presidency à mortier from Le Bailleul for 650,000 livres during the 1718 inflation.[11] Even leaving aside such geographically or chronologically atypical cases, it can safely be said that high robe offices in the period 1715 to 1748 represented substantial blocks of capital. A councilorship at Bordeaux might cost Montesquieu only 27,000 livres in 1736;[12] but the same grade of office at Dijon had cost Chartraire de Loppin 60,000 only seven years earlier,[13] and Councilor Deburge at Douai set his office at 48,000 in his testamentary division of 1746.[14] In spite of almost infinite variations, one can, I think, take the following ranges as typical for office values in the provincial parlements during the period 1715-1748: 25,000 to 50,000 livres for councilorships, 60,000 to 80,000 for presidencies of requêtes or enquêtes, and 70,000 to 100,000 for presidencies à mortier, as well as for positions in the parquet. In provincial sovereign courts other than parlements the levels for equivalent charges were perhaps 20 percent lower. In Paris the prices still were as much as 50 percent higher than the provincial averages, and in the case of the Parlement, not infrequently doubled them.

These prices appear less shrunken when placed in the context of generally declining prices. D'Avenel set the decline in land values from 1675 to 1725 at just under 45 percent in terms of equivalent

[9] Bastard d'Estang, *Les parlements*, I, 114, note 1; Michel, *Histoire du Parlement de Metz*, 274; Eugène La Pierre, *Le Parlement de Toulouse* (Paris, 1875), 35.

[10] Carré, *La fin des parlements*, 6-7. [11] Hénault, *Mémoires*, 299.

[12] See above, 106. [13] Bib. Dijon, Ms. 1340 (20).

[14] Pillot, *Parlement de Flandres*, I, 8.

buying power.[15] The price of an office would probably have bought nearly as many *charrues*, or one-plow units, in the 1720's or 1730's as the higher price of the same office would have bought a half-century earlier. Other prices were less deflated than those of land and offices, but the 1720's, '30's and '40's were a time of relatively dear money and general prosperity for groups with assured incomes.[16] When a bottle of red wine cost one-third of a livre, a large loaf of the best bread, less than one-fifteenth of a livre, and a modern kilogram of beef, only one-tenth of a livre, as they did at Bordeaux in the late 1720's,[17] the holder of a 30,000-livre councilorship was obviously a man of substance.

The financial importance of a high robe office did not, of course, lie solely in its capital value. It also represented a combination of regular income and periodic expenses to its possessor. The outlay which was involved had been considerably reduced by the sovereign courts' escape from the Paulette taxes before Louis XV's reign had even opened.[18] Most of the remaining expenses were concentrated at the beginning of a magistrate's time in office. Before issuing provisions, the crown still demanded the marc d'or, generally about one-fourth of the finance for which the office had originally been sold by the Parties Casuelles. A special *droit de survivance* might also be required of the new magistrate, ranging from one-fourth to one-sixth of the marc d'or. The chambre des comptes which registered the letters of provision had to be paid a *droit de sceau*. But by far the most complicated set of payments were those made to the receiving court itself, be it parlement, chambre des comptes, cour des aides, cour des monnaies or Grand Conseil. To the officer who presided at the reception ceremony the newcomer must give *étoffes* (in the eighteenth century a set fee in cash) and to the corps as a whole, *épices honnêtes et moderées*, plus a *repas de confraternité*, ori-

[15] *Histoire économique de la propriété, des salaires, des denrées et de tous les prix en général depuis l'an 1200 jusqu'en 1800* (Paris, 1894-1912), I, 387-388 and *passim.*

[16] Georges d'Avenel, *Histoire de la fortune française* (Paris, 1927), 30.

[17] J.-A. Brutails, "Tableau de prix, 1434 à l'An IV," in *Inventaire sommaire des Archives départementales, Gironde* (Bordeaux, Série E, 1908), Supplement, IV, x-li. Prices are given in terms of the franc of 1908, which must be translated into one-third of a livre at the latter's mean value from 1725-1750.

[18] See above, 112.

ginally a banquet but long since commuted to as much as 1,200 livres. In some courts there was a *droit d'entrée*, running to as high as 1,500 livres, and in others a contribution of perhaps 1,000 livres to the common debts of the company. The Parlement of Metz exacted a peculiar *droit de bonnet*, which cost the entrant 12 livres to be paid to each président à mortier, 3 to each councilor. The variety of such expenses was practically limitless, but their total effect was everywhere to impose a substantial element of economic selection.[19]

Once these expenses had been met, however, the magistrate could look forward to a steady yield, which, notwithstanding many complaints by both the eighteenth-century robe and its modern admirers, was by no means negligible. Aside from the special pensions which certain officers enjoyed,[20] there were two basic types of official income for the sovereign courts. One lay in gages, theoretically the interest on original finances and subsequent *augmentations* paid to the crown. The other lay in épices, which were paid to any court by litigants who came before it.

The gages, which in 1716 totaled almost 2,000,000 livres for the sovereign courts of Paris alone,[21] were the subject of constant altercation between the courts and the crown. For one thing, the interest rate on the basis of which they were computed was forever being manipulated by the government: set at over 5½ percent (denier 18) in the seventeenth century, it had been cut to 5 percent in 1700, raised once more, cut to 4 percent in 1716. Even this reduced amount was frequently in arrears; in 1730 the Parlement of Navarre was still demanding its members' gages for the years 1717, 1718, and 1719.[22] A distinctly apologetic royal declaration of July, 1717, promising more regular payments in the future, provides further evidence of general laxity.[23] The *payeur des gages*, who was appointed for each

[19] Bastard d'Estang, *Les parlements*, I, 110, note 1.

[20] In a list which appears to be for 1717, B.N., Ms. fr. 7547, fol. 20-26, we find First President de Mesmes of the Paris Parlement mentioned as entitled to 15,000 livres in pensions and *appointements*, and Président à mortier de Maisons, 4,500. In 1736, President Portail's son was receiving his old pension of 6,000 livres per year. See Luynes, *Mémoires*, I, 83.

[21] B.N., Ms. fr. 7547.

[22] Pierre Delmas, *Du Parlement de Navarre* (Pau, 1898), 153.

[23] A.N., K. 137, 6 *bis*.

sovereign court by the king, was supposed to ensure the delivery of proper funds out of the income from the gabelle; but an interesting correspondence of 1724, concerning the payeur at Bordeaux, shows him as the creature of the intendant and the target for strong parlementary resentment.[24]

In spite of interruptions and periodic reductions, however, a magistrate's gages and appointments were normally an important part of his income. At Paris, for a parlementary président à mortier they were set at 2,000 livres per year and the same for presidents of the Chambre des Comptes and Cour des Aides;[25] for the procureur-général of the Grand Conseil, 1,950;[26] for a councilor in the Cour des Aides, 1,400 to 1,450;[27] for a councilor in the Cour des Monnaies, up to 2,000.[28] There was a wide variation in the provinces, where a councilor at Grenoble during this period received about 900 livres in gages,[29] an avocat-général at Colmar, 900,[30] a lay councilor at Dijon, 700 to 750,[31] and a procureur-général at Besançon, as little as 292,[32] while the well-paid councilors of the Chambre des Comptes at Aix received 1,311 apiece[33] and those of the Parlement of Brittany, 900 to 1200.[34]

What these gages represented in terms of interest can be computed in either of two ways. The more realistic standard, no doubt, is that based on their relation to the realizable sale value of a particular office at any given time, in other words, how they compared with what an officer could expect as yield from the same amount of capital, otherwise invested. Figured on that basis, gages never represented more than a modest return during the eighteenth century, seldom

[24] A.D. Gironde, C. 852.

[25] B.N., Ms. fr. 7547, fol. 20 ff., A.N., G^7.919.

[26] A.N., G^7.919.

[27] B.N., Ms. fr. nouv. acq. 1643, fol. 424 ff.

[28] *Ibid.* The offices in this court had in many instances been created late and sold at high finances, hence the higher *gages.*

[29] Pilot-Dethorey, "Notice sur les Séries A et B des Archives départementales de l'Isère," *Inventaire-sommaire des Archives départmentales de l'Isère* (Grenoble, 1864), I, 16.

[30] G.-M.-L. Pillot and de Neyremand, *Histoire du Conseil souverain d'Alsace* (Paris, 1860), 230.

[31] B.N., Ms. fr. 16819, fol. 83.

[32] Estignard, *Parlement de Franche-Comté*, I, 106.

[33] Bib. Méjanes, Ms. 730 (826).

[34] Le Moy, *Parlement de Bretagne*, 30.

higher than 4 percent, often as low as 1 to 1½ percent, while the legal rate on private loans averaged about 5 percent.

But if this seems to point to financial sacrifice by high robe officers, it should also be borne in mind that gages were in the majority of cases the return from old investments, which were much smaller than the market values of early eighteenth-century offices. That is to say, if one views the real price of an office as the original finance plus whatever augmentations the crown might subsequently have exacted, he arrives at a somewhat different idea of the value of gages. At the Dijon Chambre des Comptes, according to a document preserved in that city's library, the presidencies had cost their late seventeenth-century purchasers as much as 100,000 livres (the price set by Colbert's edict of 1665); but to the family of at least one incumbent under Louis XV, a presidency represented a total of only 19,128 livres in early seventeenth-century finances and later augmentations. Thus the gages of 2,050 to 2,605 livres represented anywhere from 2 to 10 percent of the original cost, depending upon which office is being discussed. The charges of conseillers maîtres des comptes at Dijon, yielding 1,213 to 1,490 livres in annual gages, had cost the possessing families from as little as 12,538 livres to as much as 50,000—again a high of around 10 percent return in certain instances.[35] In order to arrive at complete mathematical precision, one would have to include an additional factor, the change in money values over the period since the first finances had been paid; but the figures given above will at least suffice to illustrate one of the most important characteristics of high robe gages: the extreme variability of their relationship to different family fortunes.

The other type of official income, the épices, had developed out of earlier informal gifts of spices, jewelry or fine cloth offered by both parties in a suit to the particular judges before whom it was to be tried. By the eighteenth century they had been institutionalized in the form of set fees, paid by litigants into a common fund for an entire court and then distributed to all members of that court by the *receveur des épices*. At Rennes in 1723, for example, the schedule

[35] Bib. Dijon, Ms. 755 (453), Tableau des officiers de la Chambre des Comptes de Dijon, suivant l'ordre de création des offices, et état des finances, gages et augmentations de gages attribuës auxdits officiers.

of shares exhibited a typical range of variation: each councilor received 143 livres for February, 133 for March, 140 for April, 85 for May, 84 for June.[36] At the same parlement Councilor Marnier of the Grand' Chambre received 1,043 livres of épices for the judicial year, 1743-1744.[37] One characteristic of payment in the parlements had definite political significance: the largest amounts seem everywhere to have gone to the présidents à mortier and councilors of the respective grand' chambres, a fact which helps to explain the greater readiness of officers of enquêtes and requêtes to interrupt court services for political reasons.

The non-parlementary sovereign courts also had considerable sums to parcel out. The Paris Chambre des Comptes received a total of 39,418 livres 15 sous for just the first two months of 1696. Out of this lump sum each president was paid 360 livres, each maître, 240, each correcteur, 168¾, and each auditeur, 150.[38] Eighteenth century figures for this court are less detailed; but what there are indicate that the above figures remained typical.

Even the regularly distributed amounts fail to reveal the full importance of épices in the budget of an active magistrate. For if he sat in the chambre des vacations of his court, he received additional income; and the special fees paid directly to any judge who went outside the palais to conduct hearings might run to as high as 31 livres per hour.[39] It was the composite of such fees that constituted the *ancien régime's* conception of return for professional services, as distinguished from the gages as mere interest on finances. Taken together, gages, épices and sale value combined to determine the place of an office in its holder's total fortune.

3

In the older neighborhoods of any of a score of modern French cities there stand the architectural monuments of a departed aris-

[36] A.D. Ille-et-Vilaine, B. Registres des Épices, 1723, quoted by Le Moy, *Parlement de Bretagne*, 34.

[37] *Ibid.*

[38] Bib. Toulouse, Ms. 581, Chambre des Comptes de Paris, fol. 55. The original division had given the presidents 450 livres each and the maîtres only 225, but it had been revised after protests by the latter.

[39] Le Moy, *Parlement de Bretagne*, 34, cites "vacations" set at this figure.

tocracy: the *hôtels parlementaires*. At Paris, scattered through the Saint-Sulpice and Saint-Germain-des-Prés neighborhoods, squeezed among busy shops and warehouses in the Marais, clinging to beleaguered plots in the Faubourg Saint-Honoré, are still to be seen the massive homes of some of the capital's proudest robe families: Amelot, Nicolay, Fieubet, Lamoignon, Le Peletier, Berthier de Sauvigny. Others like them stand along the Cours du Chapeau Rouge at Bordeaux, the Rue Saint-Rome at Toulouse, the Place Bossuet at Dijon, the Cours Mirabeau at Aix. Many are at least partly vacant now—great, gray shells whose gates open into courtyards paved with buckling cobblestones and encircled by barely translucent windows. Yet they still bring to mind the picture of a proud and opulent class of proprietors.

In most old sovereign court localities, the distribution of high robe dwellings was much wider in the early eighteenth century than surviving hotels might indicate. The much-prized dwellings on the Île de la Cité have been swept away by new buildings in that administrative heart of Paris. Only with difficulty can one find traces of the magistracy in some of its other favored sections, from the Rue Vielle du Temple to the Rue de Richelieu or across the river on countless streets around the Rue du Bac.[40] The homes which have survived at Dijon give only a suggestion of the widely scattered parlementary mansions which, when Louis XV ascended the throne, rose like bastions of stone in a city of wood.[41] The members of the Bordeaux courts were more inclined to crowd into the heart of town; but, even so, they covered the parishes of Saint-Maixent, Saint-Siméon, Saint-Pierre, and Saint-Rémi, where street names such as "du Mulet" and "de Mérignac" recall their presence.[42] And at Toulouse, the robe hotels dotted the whole area from the Capitol to the Palais on the Place du Salin.

Not all, of course, matched the size and splendor of those which by their very massiveness have tended most often to endure. The

[40] B.N., Lf[25].31, printed lists of members of the Paris Parlement at various dates, includes several surveys of their home addresses.

[41] Roupnel, *La ville et la campagne*, 114; Albert Colombet, *Les parlementaires bourguignons à la fin du XVIIIe siècle* (Dijon, 1937), 82-93; Pierre Perrenet, *Le Palais de Justice de Dijon* (Rennes, 1936), 112 ff.

[42] Jullian, *Histoire de Bordeaux*, 412.

majority of officers below presidential rank occupied homes which though solid enough were not to be compared with the palatial dwellings of their more exalted colleagues. In general, however, though the value of a parlementaire's home was considerably below that of his office, it represented more capital than most of his fellow citizens possessed in any form. In 1736, for example, Jules de Borie, former councilor at the Parlement of Guienne, sold to Étienne de Baritault, avocat-général of the Bordeaux Cour des Aides, a two-story house on the Rue Sainte-Colombe for 11,500 livres, payable in silver *écus* of 6 livres each.[43] A few years later, at Toulouse, Dominique Simon de Bastard bought from one Richard de Saint-Loup a house three blocks from the Palais for 8,150 livres.[44] Councilor Jehannin of the Parlement of Burgundy seems to have valued his home at about this same price; for in 1719 he left 50,000 livres to his eldest son, his own office to his third son, and another (junior) charge of councilor plus the house to the second.[45] Paris prices made house values higher, and even in the provinces President de Berbisey could pay as much as 26,000 livres for a mansion at Dijon;[46] but for most of France 8,000 to 12,000 livres represented a fair average during this period.

The household expenses of sovereign court officers covered a range commensurate with the capital values of their homes. At one extreme were the large staffs of servants such as First President Albertas of the Parlement of Provence maintained in the 1740's: a cook at 600 livres per year, an assistant cook at 200, a nurse for the children at 480, a firetender at 200, two porters at 20 sous per day, plus a succession of butlers, valets, maids and lackeys.[47] In 1715 each of the presidents at Bordeaux (in both Parlement and Cour des Aides) had at least a cook, a coachman, a valet, two lackeys and several maids. First President de La Caze of the Parlement employed a staff of twenty, ranging from his secretary and his maître d'hôtel to a postilion and six lackeys.[48]

The average robe household staff, as revealed in testamentary

[43] A.D. Gironde, Notariales: Roberdeau, 27 August 1736.
[44] A.D. Haute-Garonne, E. 14, date: 1747.
[45] A.D. Côte d'Or, E. 1001.
[46] Bib. Dijon, Ms. 1332 (20), Titres généalogiques, Juigny collection.
[47] B.N., Ms. fr. nouv. acq. 1421.
[48] A.D. Gironde, C. 2694, capitation list of servants.

bequests to servants, was built around a cook, a coachman, one or two maids and perhaps a nurse or a tutor. A councilor might feel that he could permit himself more help than this; but unless he had stripped his fortune in order to buy his office, he could scarcely accept the social implications of doing with less.

The level of luxury maintained by a high official under Louis XV is well portrayed in the various accounts of First President de Mesmes' household at Pontoise during the exile of the Paris Parlement in 1720: dinners each day for fifty or more guests, balls and concerts, finally a wedding celebration of almost regal splendor.[49] The bon vivant might order liqueurs and brandies by the crate from distant cities; upholstering for the furniture of a single room might cost as much as 750 livres; and the receipt has survived from a purchase of 144 napkins at 20 livres per dozen by Madame Le Peletier in 1723.[50] The less opulent magistrate might prefer to dispense his available cash for books and travel instead of perfumes and tapestries; but the fact remains that an early eighteenth-century noble of the sword who was received in the home of a parlementaire had cause to envy the house, the meals, the servant staff, and the level of comfort, even if he could not appreciate the library.

4

These indications of urban prosperity are matched by evidence of investments, bequests and money gifts. A magistrate's philanthropic donations might run into large figures, as when President Berthier left 2,000 livres to two hospitals in Toulouse,[51] or President de La Chabane, 6,000 to three others at Bordeaux,[52] At Grenoble, the *Hôpital Général* received 6,000 livres from Dean of Councilors de Béesgue in 1718, 10,000 from First President de Valbonnais of the

[49] A.N., U. 747, Jean-Gilbert Delisle's Journal du Parlement séant à Pontoise; Barbier, *Journal*, I, 44, 52.

[50] B.N., Ms. fr. nouv. acq. 3515. This Le Peletier was in the governmental administration by 1715, but his accounts are nonetheless revealing as those of a typical robe nobleman of one of the richer families. In 1714 alone, he received a bill of 522 livres for deliveries by one dealer in liqueurs, including an item for 288 bottles of *ratafia*.

[51] A.D. Haute Garonne, Testaments séparés, 11813, no. 718.

[52] A.D. Gironde, Notariales: Roberdeau, August 1736.

Chambre des Comptes in 1728; 300 from Président à mortier de Bazemont in 1737; and 10,000 from Gabriel Amat, retired greffier-en-chef of the Parlement, in 1739.[53] Pious bequests to churches and religious orders could also run into thousands of livres, usually with stipulations for masses to be said for the dead magistrate's soul. Charles Pinon, a former president in the Grand Conseil, left 7,500 livres in this form, 4,000 to be given to the poor in his parish of Saint-Louis.[54]

Testamentary gifts to servants might be in the form of lump sums for distribution (Président à mortier Caulet of Toulouse left 1,200 livres for this purpose in 1747)[55] or in life rentes, of which Councilor de Gazeau of the Parlement of Paris left provisions for 1,050 livres per year.[56] Cash bequests to relatives, such as Toulouse Councilor Lafont's of 20,000 livres to his eldest daughter (wife of another councilor) in 1720[57] or Grenoble Councilor du Sozey's of 90,000 to a son in 1746,[58] complete an impression of financial strength.

In most cases, these bequests were at least partly in securities. The examples which can be documented furnish a precious insight into this aspect of the high robe's economic status. In 1726, for example, First President de Berbisey of the Parlement of Burgundy left to his children, among other assets, the sum of 40,000 livres in the form of four rente contracts of 10,000 livres each on the Hôtel de Ville of Paris.[59] A former councilor of the same court left a 6,000-livre bond on the Estates of Burgundy in 1747.[60] Half of Pierre du Sozey's bequest of 90,000 livres to his son at Grenoble was in Paris Hôtel de Ville bonds.

In spite of numerous bits of data in notarial archives, however, much less comprehensive information is available about high robe investments than about most other aspects of my problem. Perhaps the most tantalizing lacuna of all is that which pertains to the

[53] A.D. Isère, H (Supplément), B.5 and B.7.

[54] A.D. Seine, DC^{6}.215, fol. 128. Pinon also left the staggering sum of 250,000 livres to his son.

[55] A.D. Haute-Garonne, Testaments séparés, 11820, no. 1731.

[56] A.D. Seine, DC^{6}.255, fol. 70.

[57] A.D. Haute-Garonne, Testaments séparés, 11842, no. 4850.

[58] Bib. Grenoble, o.17872, printed.

[59] Bib. Dijon, Ms. 1332 (20).

[60] Bib. Dijon, Ms. 1340 (20).

magistracy's role in the great wave of speculation under John Law from 1716 to 1720. In attempting to secure adequate documentation on this question, I have, I must confess, encountered an almost completely blank wall. The explanation lies in the methods employed in the great "Visa" by which the government sought to liquidate the Système after Law's flight. Not only did the brothers Pâris suppress much information in the few reports which did appear in print or circulate in manuscript, they also destroyed, in a ceremonial bonfire, all the canceled shares in the Compagnie des Indes and notes on the Banque Générale.[61] The result has been to create a hopeless impasse for modern researchers.

Such sparse data as have survived—and they include the direct allegation of at least one important memoirist[62]—lead one to suspect that the high robe invested heavily in Law's schemes, but without ever shifting the bulk of its holdings enough to alter the older rentier approach which made the sovereign courts hostile to the Scottish financier. In parlementaires' testaments of the 1730's and 1740's there are occasional references to Compagnie des Indes shares, presumably among those certified as valid by the Visa. During the great boom itself, in July of 1720, Président à mortier de Bardonnenche of Grenoble borrowed 6,000 livres in *billets de la Banque* from one Robin de La Picardière for six years at 2 percent.[63] This low interest rate reveals the lender's nervousness about the bank notes' value in the last frenzied months of the Système, but de Bardonnenche must have been hoping even at that late date to profit from their appreciation before 1726.

In Marmont du Hautchamp's *Histoire générale et particulière du visa* there is reproduced a list of 263 "Mississippians" whom the visa had relieved of almost 190,000,000 livres in Système paper.[64] Not a single sovereign court officer is mentioned in this roll. But in the same author's supplementary list of profiteers who were fortunate enough not to be so taxed, there appear a Loubert, a Le Normand, a Godin, a Pasquier, a Boucher, and several other familiar names among those of aristocrats who had succeeded in cashing their

[61] See Lavisse, *Histoire de France*, XVIII, part 2, 44.

[62] Richelieu (Soulavie), *Mémoires*, III, 42-43.

[63] A.D. Isère, III. E. 1415[3].

[64] (The Hague, 1743), II, 153-197.

holdings with impunity. Some of the high robe obviously profited from Law's venture. Others may have had to draw on the remaining portions of their variegated fortunes to cover their losses. Still others saw old investments shrivel in value when their debtors paid off mortgages in the cheap money of the boom.[65] But so far as I have been able to discover none was completely ruined by the Système, and I have no cause to quarrel with Michelet's judgment of the subsequent Visa: "Cette persécution si partiale, qui frappa les riches nouveaux et ménagea les autres, eut l'effet détestable d'une réaction nobiliare."[66]

The involvement of parlementaires in more orthodox business ventures is exhibited at length in such works as Malvezin's *Histoire du commerce de Bordeaux*[67] and *Les grands négociants bordelais au XVIIIe siècle* by Armand Communay,[68] who was also, it is worth pointing out, an historian of the Parlement of Guienne. Bordeaux is especially interesting in this respect; for it offered a wide range of commercial possibilities: shipping, manufacturing for export, wine production, slave trading. In the papers of Ferdinand Hustin concerning plans to make faïence pottery at Bordeaux, for example, there are several letters written in 1719 by President de La Caze, who speaks here as an interested businessman though he also refers to the amount of time he must devote to his lands.[69] The number of such cases is not everywhere so impressive; but in other centers too, individual magistrates, including those of Dijon, who bottled the finest Burgundy for wholesale shipment,[70] and those of Lyon, with their textile interests, had a place in the commercial upsurge of the post-1715 period.

The political importance of the high robe's investments is clear enough when placed beside its "rentier remonstrances" during the

[65] The ease with which many of the landed gentry liquidated their debts after having sold small parcels of their estates at high prices is emphasized in F. Veron de Forbonnais, *Recherches et considérations sur les finances de France* (Basel, 1758), II, 640 ff.

[66] *Histoire de France*, XV, 331.

[67] (Bordeaux, 1892), III.

[68] (Bordeaux, 1888).

[69] Bib. Bordeaux, Ms. 1010.

[70] André Bourrée, "La société dijonnaise vers le milieu du XVIIIe siècle," *Mémoires de l'Académie des Sciences, Arts et Belles-Lettres de Dijon* (Dijon, 1927-1931), 215, cites, among others, Councilors Joly, Lamy, Migieu, Bernard de Sassenay.

Regency and after. These remonstrances concerning interest rates and money values reflected more than the sum of individual holdings within a given court. They were to some extent also the result of the court's corporate holdings, its investments as an institutional entity. In 1715, for example, the royal treasury owed the Parlement of Metz over 500,000 livres at 3 percent, while the Parlement itself was paying higher interest than that to its own creditors. 150,000 livres of this had been invested a full half-century earlier in Compagnie des Indes shares (by a single arrêt in 1654, the court had authorized the borrowing of that amount and its re-investment as demanded by Colbert).[71] The sovereign courts might speak in the phrases of tribunes, but their true reaction to fiscal edicts was not simply the product of dispassionate consideration.

5

The same testaments and contracts which reveal the urban holdings of the high magistracy bear the traces of feudal wealth, most obviously in the testators' own *qualifications:* "Philippe Thomé, chevalier, Seigneur de Rentilly";[72] "Jean François d'Assézat-Toupignon, chevalier, Seigneur de Prezerville et du Cède";[73] "Jean de Berbisey, chevalier, conseiller du Roy en tous ses Conseils, Baron de Vantoux, Seigneur de Belleneuve, Ruffey, Echivey et autres lieux."[74]

From other sources emerge additional proofs of the robe's landed interest. The tax rolls of the 1746 dixième, show that among the 234 seigneuries listed under the bailliage of Dijon alone, the 55 which belonged to officers of the Parlement of Burgundy or the Chambre des Comptes were of such value that they were assessed over 9,500 livres, or 42 percent of the total for all 234.[75] Another index is the record of oaths of homage and fealty to the newly crowned Louis XV, required of each of the king's vassals in 1723. In the *viguerie* of Aix there were 131 such oaths, of which 45 were

[71] Michel, *Histoire du Parlement de Metz*, 307-308.

[72] A.D. Seine, DC^6.236, fol. 24.

[73] A.D. Haute-Garonne, Testaments séparés, 11809, no. 160.

[74] Bib. Dijon, Ms. 1332 (20), Titres généalogiques.

[75] Bib. Dijon, Ms. 1159 (207).

taken by religious institutions and 24 by robe noblemen (this, be it noted, applied only to the relatively few fiefs held directly of the crown). Or again, one may take the *terriers* of seigneurial rights and holdings preserved in notarial archives. The following is typical of such documents: "Terrier et reconnaissance féodale pour messire Michel de Paty, conseiller du Roy au Parlement, seigneur baron de Bellegarde, au duché de Fronsac, habitant de Bordeaux."[76] Finally, at the political level, one cannot overlook a remonstrance such as this one from Metz in 1737, which opens: "Sire, Votre Parlement ne pouvoit se taire sur les objets importants de la mouvance des fiefs et de l'eréction d'une Principauté à Metz," and then proceeds with a violent attack on the Bishop of Metz, whom the king had considered making his sole vassal in the area and hence suzerain of all subordinate fief-holders.[77]

The high robe clearly had a major interest in the feudal land structure. But "feudalism" in its eighteenth-century application must not be thought of as referring any longer to a genuine hierarchy of noble landholdings. What once had been the basic framework for social, economic, and political relationships lived on under the late *ancien régime* as a confused array of misapplied terms and archaic titles. As so often happens when an institution has lost all organic vitality, however, the elaboration of a feudal "system" was going on in the writings of legal theorists at the very time when feudalism, never truly systematic in its era of dominance, was experiencing its reductio ad absurdum. The confusion of medieval concepts and modern real estate phraseology which a feudal purist like Guyot found so lamentable[78] is well illustrated in the following advertisement from a Dijon newspaper:

FOR SALE: Château of Leugny near Auxerre, ten or twelve apartments, of which several are paneled and have parquet floors. With full rights of justice, banalités and tithes. Furniture in good condition. One of the constituent fiefs carries membership in the [chamber of nobility at the] Estates of Burgundy.[79]

[76] A.D. Gironde, Notariales (Terriers), 36: Richard, 1737.

[77] B.N., Ms. fr. nouv. acq. 684.

[78] Germain-Antoine Guyot, *Traité . . . sur plusieurs matières féodales* (Paris, 1738-1751), I, 1.

[79] Quoted by d'Avenel. *Fortune française*, 166.

All this had a double significance for the position of the high robe. One was that in strictly legal terms the magistrates often did not possess true fiefs at all. The domain of Casselardit which, with all its buildings, lands, woods, vineyards, gardens, stables, and dove-cotes, Councilor de Miramont of Toulouse sold to Simon Dominique de Bastard for 19,000 livres in 1738 was entirely allodial, held in fee simple, save for one section held of a Benedictine foundation in feudal tenure.[80] In a great many cases a robe "fief" was nothing but a bundle of small, roturier tenures assembled by detailed purchases over several centuries and now owing a wide range of manorial rather than feudal dues to various seigneurs.[81] The family documents in Series E of various departmental archives contain a wealth of evidence on the piecemeal creation of these holdings through the generations of loans to peasants, followed by foreclosure or purchase, often with the peasant staying on as tenant under one of the several possible *bail* or lease arrangements.

The second aspect of late feudalism when applied to the high robe, however, in a sense negates the importance of technical questions as to whether a magistrate had a fief or a bundle of *tenures censives*, whether he was a vassal or only a composite tenant. For eighteenth-century conditions relegated such problems to the abstract realm of legal theory. Some of the lands of sovereign court officers were true fiefs, those listed for Provence in 1723,[82] for example, or Des Loges, the Breton seigneury which President de Boisgelin purchased in 1730.[83] Others had originally been roturier patchworks but had been erected into titled fiefs by royal letters patent. But even if a seigneury was still just an accumulation of tenures, some noble, some roturier, some allodial, it was no longer subject to the social distinctions which had once made those terms significant of differing levels of prestige. True, robe noblemen were eager to buy

[80] A.D. Haute-Garonne, E. 14.

[81] B.N., Ms. fr. nouv. acq. 3700, contains a fine example of an estate on which 80 tenants held lands, some in fief, some in *tenure censive*, some in *champartage*, i.e., share-cropping. The seigneur, in turn, owed feudal or manorial dues to other suzerains or seigneurs for certain of the plots. Roupnel has shown in his *Ville et campagne* that most robe seigneuries of Burgundy were *rémembrements* of this sort.

[82] See above, 162-163.

[83] Frédéric Saulnier, *Seigneurs et seigneuries* (Rennes, 1886), 22-30.

fiefs en l'air, which brought no land but only some feudal dues, the prestige of being the patron of a parish and perhaps the status of a direct vassal of the king. Nevertheless, the important thing was that a magistrate-seigneur, *any* magistrate-seigneur, felt himself to be part of the feudal class.

The agrarian holdings of the magistracy, when defined in physical terms, measured up to other seigneuries, in fact were often more impressive. The great manor house of the Berthiers' Pinsaguel looked out across vast lands on the Garonne above Toulouse. In the rich green countryside around Dijon, magistrates held the choicest fiefs—Vantoux, Sassenay, Saint-Seine, Vernot, Perigny—while along the sunswept slopes of the Isère's right bank there rose the châteaux of Grenoble's parlementaires, less imposing perhaps than those of Burgundy, but still considerable. In La Brède, just south of Bordeaux, the Secondats de Montesquieu possessed an estate unsurpassed in all Guienne with a château which still stands as a magnificent specimen of thirteenth-century castle architecture. By the late seventeenth century, Parisian magistrates—the Bouchers, the Molés, the Pasquiers, and the Potiers de Novion—had already extended their holdings far into Champagne,[84] as well as over the length and breadth of the Île de France itself. In Provence, Auvergne, Alsace, Flanders, Normandy, Brittany the same pattern is everywhere apparent, with varying degrees of wealth and concentration displayed.

The financial details of the high robe's fiefs and seigneuries cannot here be discussed at length, except to make clear that the magistrates had invested heavily and were exacting substantial returns. The great *livres de raison*, such as that of the de Vachon family for their château of La Murette in Dauphiné,[85] reveal the complexities of accounts for landed estates, expenditures for furnishings, livestock, transport of pay crops, income in rents, shares of produce, seigneurial dues in money, poultry, meat, and grains. A 1741 inventory of the Le Goux' manor house at Saint-Seine reveals an establishment of forty rooms with furniture worth 8,649 livres—the equivalent of

[84] B.N., Ms. fr. nouv. acq. 7881, *Procez verbal de la Recherche de la Noblesse de Champagne* (Châlons, 1673), printed.

[85] A.D. Isère, II. E. 756-757.

about two years of the owner's combined gages and épices as a président à mortier in the Parlement of Burgundy.[86]

If a robe nobleman had several lands, he would normally lease some to one or more persons willing to oversee their production and collect the dues and rents which they yielded. For example, by a contract of 1736 René Alexandre de Bardonnenche of Grenoble farmed his wine and grain estate at Saint-Martin de Vinoux for a term of four years, the *fermier* to pay 420 livres per year plus an annual remittance of 600 bundles of faggots and two "charges de vin du crû de ladite vigne et du meilleur".[87] Something of the toughness which characterized the magistrate as seigneur is revealed in a dispute which arose at Bordeaux between President d'Augeard and the fermier of the estate of Tartaguière for the years 1716 to 1718. The rent had been set at 1,600 livres per year in grain, wine, and cash; but d'Augeard had apparently failed to provide adequate feed for the cattle, which was part of his responsibility, and stubbornly resisted the fermier's claim that the value of such feed should be deducted from the 1,600 livres.[88]

This d'Augeard incident calls to mind the arresting pages of Marc Bloch on the "feudal reaction" of the early modern period as a phenomenon at least partly the result of a change in seigneurial personnel.[89] The economic ruin of the medieval aristocracy had been produced by the failure of the old seigneurs to adjust to changing money values. Having eagerly commuted dues in kind into cash payments during the late middle ages, they had then been caught by the very rigidity of manorial custom, for the converted cens and other payments had shriveled steadily in real value as coinage became more plentiful. It was this development which by the late sixteenth century gave the robe and other bourgeois elements the opportunity to buy lands with fortunes created by urban commerce.[90]

Once installed in their new seigneuries, most of these new lords

[86] A.D. Côte d'Or, E. 1112. [87] A.D. Isère, III. E. 1415[3].

[88] A.D. Gironde, C. 3622.

[89] *Les caractères originaux de l'histoire rurale française* (Oslo-Paris, 1931), 131-154.

[90] De Vaissière, *Les gentilshommes campagnards*, 215 ff., insists that the final decline of the old landed gentry did not, as has often been averred, begin during the Hundred Years' War. The real crisis came after the middle of the sixteenth century, when the influx of precious metals from America began to be significant for western Europe as a whole.

took care to prevent a recurrence of their predecessors' difficulties. Hence the high robe officer of the seventeenth and eighteenth centuries employed the short-term lease instead of rents in perpetuity. He combed the archives of his château for evidence of forgotten dues, establishing with a rigorous precision all the responsibilities of each of his tenants. With his fellow products of the business world, the non-robe bourgeois who had bought lands and entered the noblesse by way of purchased letters patent, he created a general atmosphere of harsh interpretation and exacting collection; for even that portion of the older gentry which had managed to cling to its estates began to imitate as best it could the new and obviously effective methods of exploitation. The feudal reaction was in a sense less a reversion than the application of new business techniques to old relationships. By the eighteenth century the sovereign court magistrate was no longer a bourgeois landowner; but he was part of a landed class whose behavior owed much to the commercial tradition from which he himself had emerged.

It is quite in keeping with the complexity of the high robe's position in the eighteenth century that its members should have added to the original businesslike approach some of the subtler facets of seigneurial attitudes as bequeathed by the old aristocracy. Desiccated and fallen into confusion, manorial relationships nevertheless carried within them the vestiges of their former power as the basis of a closely knit human society. The regularity with which magistrates' testaments contained gifts to their poorer tenants reveals not only pious hopes of heaven but also a genuine sense of *noblesse oblige*. Village philanthropies were far commoner in Louis XV's France than the more resolutely self-satisfied historians of the nineteenth century, flailing an age of agrarian hardship from their own of urban want, were inclined to recognize.

Thus one finds a Monsieur de Chavagnac distributing soup each day to nine hundred drought-ruined peasants at Blesle in Auvergne[91] or a Dame Marie de Kerlech giving her old house at Landeda in Brittany as a hospice for the parish poor.[92] The frequency of such

[91] A.D. Puy-de-Dôme, C. 904, quoted by Jalenques, "La noblesse de la province d'Auvergne," 76-79.

[92] Albert Mousset, *Documents pour servir à l'histoire de la maison de Kergorlay en Bretagne* (Paris, 1921), 396-397.

cases cannot be established with precision, but they deserve to be noted as evidence of a continuing thread of aristocratic responsibility toward "the lower orders," a thread which is to be found in the fabric of more than one robe family history. Hand in hand with cases of interest in the people of the land went increasing interest in the land itself, in agriculture for its own sake. Even before the Physiocrats began their many-sided proselyting endeavors, parlementaires were producing many of the early eighteenth-century memoranda on crops, feed, soils, and fertilizers.[93]

Having abandoned the blacks and whites of post-Revolutionary portraiture of the ancien régime, however, the modern student would, I think, be seriously in error if he were to permit isolated cases of generosity and enlightenment to obscure the wide range of abuses which the aristocratization of the high noblesse de robe tended so strongly to reinforce. It is true that the courts, in part perhaps because of their members' many roturier holdings, discouraged the unlimited extension of old-style seigneurial dues; but by their judicial decisions they did condone great harshness in the exaction of more modern rents and mortgage payments.[94] Nowhere was the problem which was created by having the highest royal courts filled with feudalized gentlemen more apparent than in the matter of seigneurial justice. The rights of "high," "middle" or "low justice" which went with almost every seigneury represented a baffling obstacle to the operation of the king's lower tribunals.[95] The manorial court, where tenants must bring their complaints not only against each other but also against their lord, placed in the latter's hands a powerful weapon of exploitation.[96] Voltaire had in mind not just the comic aspects of this situation in his *Droit du Seigneur:*

> Car si je suis le magister d'ici,
> Je suis bailli; je suis notaire aussi;

[93] A.N., F^{10}. 215 ff.

[94] See, for example, Roupnel, *La ville et la campagne*, 241.

[95] A.N., AD.II. 3-4, contain a collection of royal enactments concerning inferior jurisdictions which reveals in a striking manner the confusion and maladministration created by the system.

[96] For full discussions of this problem, see André Edmond Giffard, *Les justices seigneuriales en Bretagne aux XVIIe et XVIIIe siècles* (Paris, 1903) and A. Combier, *Les justices seigneuriales du bailliage de Vermandois sous l'ancien régime* (Paris, 1897).

Et je suis prêt dans mes trois caractères
A te servir dans toutes tes affaires.[97]

Such amelioration and regulation of this regime as had occurred had for the most part been imposed during the period between the Edict of Crémieu in 1536 and the Ordinance on Civil Procedure in 1667, that is to say, after the sovereign courts had become powerful, but before their officers had become identified with the feudality. What could be expected of the high robe in the eighteenth century, when most of its members had their own manorial jurisdictions, their own bailiffs, *lieutenants de juge*, and *procureurs fiscaux?*[98]

The agrarian wealth of the magistracy was thus much more than an added prop to its economic position. It had altered the once exclusively urban outlook of the class, had sharpened its opposition to the fiscal and administrative projects of the crown, and last but not least, had given it access to that special prestige which the land and only the land could bestow.

6

Bearing in mind these three major elements, office, urban wealth and land, the reader can more fully appreciate the special characteristics of the typical robe fortune, above all, the peculiar resiliency which it displayed. Consider for a moment the succession of François-Anne Chartraire de Givry, conseiller clerc in the Parlement of Burgundy, as inventoried at his death in 1744:

Notes on the provincial estates	177,531 livres
Notes on private parties	33,683 livres
Town property	20,541 livres
Seigneury of Givry	50,000 livres
Seigneury of Saint-Agnan	70,000 livres
(Parlimentary office already sold for 60,000 livres)	
Total	351,755 livres.[99]

[97] Act I, scene 1, *Oeuvres*, VI, 9.

[98] A.N., K. 1159, no. 13, and KK. 1223^{A} provide lists of "jurisdictions féodales" in which parlementary involvement is clearly revealed, in the former case for Dauphiné, in the latter, for Guienne.

[99] Bib. Dijon, Ms. 1340 (20), Titres généalogiques.

For magistrates with fortunes such as this the declining value of offices and the frequent non-payment of gages constituted a loss; but other sources of income prevented its being a catastrophic loss. The collapse of a business enterprise or a Banque Générale might ruin many investors, but sovereign court officers were not apt to be among them. A drought or blight could desolate a whole area without lasting damage to the prosperity of magistral landowners within it. Only if all these threats to its economic position had occurred simultaneously and for a protracted period would the place of the high robe in eighteenth century society have been seriously endangered. The tripod of wealth was still standing when the Revolution began to shake the ground beneath it.

Even the tradition of testamentary *morcellement*, which had dissipated so many landed fortunes in France by sub-dividing them indefinitely among consecutive generations of heirs, represented less than the usual danger to the high robe. It was possible for the magistrate to distribute his fortune quite equitably among his children without splitting the land which was only one element within it; for he could leave his office to one child, his town house to another, cash and securities to others and his agrarian holdings intact to one alone, often the eldest.

The political and ideological significance of this complex of interests will be clear enough if one reflects on the manner in which it increased the sovereign court officer's sensitivity to a wide range of possible reform efforts. Fiscal reform which involved reduction of gages or liquidation of offices he opposed as the owner of a valuable charge. A royal edict reducing interest rates he opposed as a rentier. An attack on feudal jurisdictions or seigneurial prerogatives he opposed as the lord of a manor. All along the line, in both theory and active politics, he was committed to the defense of privileges. And in defending them he became the shield of the aristocracy in general.

BOOK THREE

LEADERSHIP WITHIN THE NOBILITY

Chapter Nine

The Claims of the Peerage

1

In turning from the individual bases of robe power to the effect of that power on the French aristocracy as a whole, one comes face to face with some exceedingly difficult terminology. For this shift requires the application of concepts of political action, common interests, and group pressures to a situation in which the modern understanding of those phrases is misleading rather than helpful. Walpole, to cite a familiar eighteenth-century case, was a consummate parliamentary tactician; but the British squirearchy which he contrived to manipulate in the 1720's and 1730's had none of the clearly defined organization, internal discipline or recognized allegiance to common aims which the modern mind associates with the ideal party structure. The same was true, to a much greater degree, of the tens of thousands of individuals within the farflung boundaries of the French noblesse.

Yet this same noblesse, dispersed and variegated as it was, nonetheless represented a genuine political force as a mass of individuals whose part in initiating royal policy might be negligible but whose reaction to decisions once taken no government could ignore. It was in this sense, in its resistance to projects which endangered its privileges, that the aristocracy was important in the political history of the late ancien régime. By the same token, the pivotal position within it eventually fell to the high noblesse de robe, because the latter was the group best equipped to fight a defensive action whether against absolutists or democrats, jealous businessmen or discontented peasants. Before the eighteenth century reached its midpoint, this assumption of leadership by the magistracy had become clear enough to Louis XV, to ministers such as d'Aguesseau and d'Argenson, to writers such as Voltaire, and to a large portion of the nobility itself.

The crucial importance of the sovereign courts, however, was by no means as clear to the men of 1715 as to their sons in 1750. This was true partly because the courts had been silenced too long for anyone to be sure just how they could or would employ their restored political privileges under the new government. But even more important in complicating the issue was the fact that the aristocratic group which struck first and with the greatest initial display of success was composed not of magistrates but of the highest ranking nobles de race, the ducs et pairs de France.

The story of the peerage under the Orléans Regency is in one sense only a section of the chronicle of court intrigue, a morass of details, many of them more ludicrous than significant, into which the unwary researcher could vanish without leaving a trace. Beneath this confusion and triviality, however, certain basic issues were at stake, issues sufficiently important to be worth shaking loose from the personal rivalries and inconsequential motives which often threaten to conceal them altogether. In the present chapter I have attempted to deal with several different aspects of the peers' offensive, touching only briefly on portions of the story which have been covered in detail in such works as Leclercq's,[1] devoting more attention to the relations of the peerage with the Parlement of Paris and with the lower nobility. In combination these factors represent an important element in the regrouping of the aristocracy.

2

Like the parlementaires, the ducs et pairs based their political claims on medieval tradition. Specifically, they invoked the memory of the great vassals who under the direct Capetians had been entitled peers of France: the dukes of Normandy, Burgundy, and Aquitaine, the counts of Flanders, Champagne, and Toulouse, the archbishop of Reims, the bishops of Laon, Langres, Noyon, Châlons, and Beauvais. In theory, these twelve peers, six lay and six ecclesiastical, had stood just below the crown, an exclusive feudal group no

[1] *Histoire de la Régence*, ch. 5-28.

member of which could be tried except by the rest. Under the Valois kings and still more under the Bourbons the peerage had undergone great changes since its thirteenth-century apogee. Its numbers had grown as its power had waned, until by 1715 there were no fewer than fifty-five lay peerages, almost all created since 1600.[2] It is worth mentioning, in order to avoid confusion with the five ranks of the British system, that every eighteenth-century French lay peer was a duke, though there were always a few *ducs non pairs* as well.

As already noted,[3] the peers had been absorbed as advisers of the king into the Parlement of Paris, where they had the right to sit as councilors-born.[4] Few of them exercised this right save in unusual situations, but their exact relationship to the greatest of the sovereign courts was nonetheless a problem of considerable institutional importance, for it represented all that was left of their once exalted judicial function. Under Richelieu, Mazarin, and Louis XIV they had been carefully excluded from administrative offices; and yet when the Great Reign ended they were still recognized as just below the royal family in honorific distinction.[5] Furthermore, they had never relinquished a sweeping set of claims, as any reader of Saint-Simon is well aware. In Clairambault's huge *Recueil sur la Pairie*[6] is revealed the endlessly reiterated insistence that the peers were still the king's principal councilors, entitled to first consideration in all matters of influence, as well as etiquette.

The Regent's situation in 1715, as well as his close relations with Saint-Simon, Noailles, and other peers, provided the more active members of the group with a golden opportunity; for the Duc

[2] A.N., K. 616-623, contains papers on the erection of seventeenth- and eighteenth-century peerages. See also Louis de Maslatrie, "Pairies de France," *Annuaire historique* (Paris, 1839), III, 117-140. The oldest peerage existing in 1715 was that of Uzès, erected in favor of the de Crussol family in 1572. Not all of the *pairies* were in fact occupied by adult males at any given time, so that in 1715, there were actually only fifty-three peers, lay and ecclesiastical combined.

[3] See above, 47.

[4] A.N., K. 621, no. 1. Dattes des receptions des Princes du Sang et Pairs de France au Parlement.

[5] A.N., U. 909 contains the edict of 1711 "portant Reglement general pour les Duchez & Pairies."

[6] A.N., KK. 592-604, thirteen volumes.

d'Orléans was momentarily dependent on their support no less than on that of the sovereign courts. The latter he hastened to buy with concessions as soon as he assumed the regency.[7] In the case of the peerage, his initial favors were even more extensive, for it was the peers who dominated the royal administration itself during the ensuing three years.

There is no need here for lengthy discussion of this brief experiment, the *Polysynodie*, which is assigned its own chapter in almost every political history of France. The results, in administrative terms, were about what could be expected from a group of barely literate soldiers and pompous courtiers, who devoted more attention to deciding whether or not a subordinate official might be seated while reporting to a council than they did to the substance of his report. By the end of 1718 power had slipped back into the hands of ministers chosen by the Regent as under the Ludovican system. The Polysynodie perished with scarcely a voice save that of the Abbé de Saint-Pierre raised in its defense.[8] Many of the peers and marshals themselves seemed relieved to be freed of the duties which had proved so much more onerous than had been suspected in advance. Since last their class had played any major role in politics, the national government of France had become a huge and complex piece of machinery, requiring of those who directed it a whole set of skills almost completely lacking in the peerage.

At the very time when they were seeking to control the administration, the peers were also deeply involved in the problem of Louis XIV's illegitimate sons.[9] The old king had heaped honors on the Duc du Maine and the Comte de Toulouse (children of his liaison with Madame de Montespan), conferring upon them an intermediate rank below the royal family but above the peerage, then in 1714 declaring them eligible to succeed to the throne after the collateral houses of Condé and Conti. The new reign had scarcely

[7] See above, 82-84.

[8] In his *Discours sur la polysynodie* (Paris, 1718), Saint-Pierre made a plea for the system of councils the occasion for a general diatribe against the "tyranny" of ministerial government under Louis XIV.

[9] A.N., K. 136-142, K. 621; B.N., LB[38].121, *Recueil des pièces touchant l'affaire des princes légitimes et légitimés* (Rotterdam, 1717), 4 vols.; Saint-Simon, *Mémoires*, XXIV, 348-352; XXVI, 1-59; XXX, 192-195; XXXI, 73-77, 223-224, 247-257; XXXV, 95-150.

opened when both the legitimate princes of the blood and the peers went into action to secure the annulment of these honors. In 1717 the Regent removed the *légitimés* from the line of succession; and for a brief five years after the 1718 lit de justice the Duc du Maine was actually demoted to the ordinary status of peer. It was during this period, before a seldom noted declaration of 1723 restored his intermediate rank,[10] that he became involved in the Spanish plot of Cellamare.

Had the peers done nothing but bungle their excursion into governmental policy-making and involve themselves in a ludicrous prestige controversy, their role might be dismissed as inconsequential from the present point of view. It cannot be thus dismissed, however, because in the network of tensions under the Regency, an alliance against them had taken form between the royal bastards and the high robe, with both relying heavily on the support of the subordinate noblesse. Thus the Polysynodie and the dispute over the légitimés merged with another phase of the ducal offensive: the struggle with the parlementaires.

3

The honorific rights of the peers as conseillers-nés in the Parlement had long been a source of contention. In 1664, for example, Louis XIV had settled one point of difference by ruling that in a lit de justice the peers should give their opinions before the présidents à mortier.[11] The former, however, were far from satisfied with their position; and as soon as the old king died they hastened to raise several other objections to procedural customs of the Parlement. The central one, which has given to the controversy as a whole the name of the "affaire du bonnet," hinged on the momentous question of whether or not the officer presiding in the Grand' Chambre should remove his mortier when asking the opinion of a peer, and whether or not the latter might remain covered in replying. The existing rule at the Palais was that the presiding magistrate removed his hat only when addressing the members of the royal family and

[10] A.N., K. 139, no. 19.

[11] A.N., K. 703 contains documents on this earlier controversy.

that no peer's opinion would be received until its author had uncovered. This situation, the peers insisted, should be exactly reversed. Other grievances included the presence of a councilor as "garde-banque" at the end of each bench otherwise reserved to ducs et pairs and the refusal by regular robe officers to yield special precedence in entrances and exits.[12]

Like other such problems of etiquette under the *ancien régime*, this quarrel called forth floods of literature on both sides, as well as repeated appeals to the crown.[13] As soon as the parlementaires discovered that the peerage intended to raise the question of the "bonnet" at the lit de justice of September 2, 1715, an assembly called to consider the question of Louis XIV's testament, they hurried into an early morning session at which it was resolved that the company would brook no alteration in the existing custom. Thereafter, they published a series of memoranda, some of which had been sent in the original to the Regent, all of which attacked the ducal position. Perhaps the most telling of these was President Potier de Novion's analysis in 1716 of the family backgrounds of existing peers, with emphasis on their obscure origins and the more exalted traditions of the great robe families.[14] At the same time, they lent their support to the royal bastards. Barbier treats as a well-known fact the Paris Parlement's sympathy for the Duc du Maine.[15] It is interesting in this connection to read Saint-Simon's angry assertion that most of the polemics for the légitimés had been prepared by Dadvisard, former avocat-général in the Parlement of Languedoc.[16]

On the peers' side, the strategy of publication and appeals addressed to the Regent was laid out in a long series of meetings

[12] For a full account of all the vagaries in this mock drama, see André Grellet-Dumazeau, *L'Affaire du Bonnet et les Mémoires de Saint-Simon* (Paris, 1913). Saint-Simon's description is scattered throughout his *Mémoires* for the Regency years, but especially in XXVI, 1-65, and XXIX, 3-15, 206-214.

[13] A.N., K. 619 is a carton of handsomely printed pamphlets supporting the peers' demands, while K. 620 and U. 963 emphasize the Parlement's rebuttals.

[14] A.N., K. 619, no. 10, Mémoire pour le Parlement contre les ducs et pairs, présenté à Monseigneur le duc d'Orléans, Régent. Printed in Barbier, VIII, 386-396. The wide circulation of this document is attested by the existence of a manuscript copy in Dijon, A.D. Côte d'Or, B. 12175 *bis*, and printed copies in most other provincial collections.

[15] *Journal*, I, 10.

[16] *Mémoires*, XXX, 191.

which began on the very day of Louis XIV's death. In the Archives Nationales one may still read a thick pack of invitations announcing gatherings at the homes of such leading activists as the Archbishop of Reims, the Duc de La Force, the Duc d'Uzès, and the Duc de Tresmes.[17] At these meetings, of which no fewer than fifty-five took place between September 1, 1715, and February 22, 1717, the peers discussed both the parlementary issue and that of the légitimés. They appointed representatives to carry their case to the Palais Royal and levied contributions in money to pay for the hiring of pamphleteers and for the printing of the latter's products.

The quarrel, however, never reached a point of clear decision; for though the Regent had expressed himself as sympathetic to the claims of the peers before he assumed power,[18] his only official action thereafter was a declaration of 1717 freezing their prerogatives as they had been defined at the end of Louis XIV's reign.[19] Saint-Simon has left an exaggerated impression of the influence wielded by the ducal meetings, which had in any case shrunk to a mere handful of diehards by 1718. This stubborn core remained active for a few years more, but when the Archbishop of Reims died in 1721, Saint-Simon was left almost alone in his desire to continue the fight. Thereafter, he could only vent his spleen on his less determined colleagues (in particular the Duc de Noailles), rail at the bad faith of the Regent and the Parlement,[20] and sadly compose a "Mémoire des Prérogatives que les Ducs ont perdues depuis la Régence de Son Altesse roiale."[21] His fraternity had failed against the parlementaires as it had failed against the ministerial government and the légitimés.

The very fact that numerous peers had so quickly abandoned the position of Saint-Simon and likeminded extremists suggests that more was at stake here than the mere desire to humble the Parlement of Paris. The great memoirist always put that motivation first, to be

[17] A.N., K. 648, nos. 6-11. Four of the meetings were termed "assemblées générales," with thirty or more members present, and for these several of the absent peers sent notarized declarations of proxy.

[18] Saint-Simon, *Mémoires*, XXIX, 3.

[19] A.N., K. 136, no. 17^3.

[20] See his letters and memoranda in the *Écrits inédits*, IV, 61-110; 245-260.

[21] A.N., K. 1712, no. 26. Printed in *Écrits inédits*, IV, 253-260.

sure, and many subsequent writers have accepted his formulation. There was, however, a second and to my mind considerably more important trend in the thinking of the peerage, a feeling that the Parlement of Paris should be dominated by the peers, and that in this form its power should be extended rather than curtailed. The French dukes were by no means unaware of the power still vested in the British peerage, nor were they blind to their own need of some solid institution within which to operate.

At the level of theory their ambivalence is well revealed in the history of the peerage written in the latter part of the seventeenth century by their subsidized research director and publicist, Jean Le Laboureur, Abbé de Juvigné, and printed in several editions during the early eighteenth century.[22] On the one hand, Le Laboureur is arguing that the robe officers are only a technical staff grouped around and subordinate to the peers, and that it is the latter who by their presence lend to the Parlement its true grandeur. On the other hand, he insists that the Parlement of Paris, thus conceived, has taken the place of the medieval court of peers (not the Champ de Mars as in the *Judicium Francorum*)[23] and that as such it is the highest body in the kingdom. It is significant that the final section of his book is an admiring study of the British House of Lords.

The dominant opinion among the peers at any given juncture as to whether they should humble the Parlement or seek to dominate and at the same time elevate it depended, of course, on their political situation. From 1715 to 1718, when the Polysynodie offered them a virtual monopoly of political power, they tended to pursue the former course; but as soon as that abnormal situation came to an end, their feeling for the Parlement as *their* court revived very quickly.

This shift is discernible when one compares two judicial disputes concerning individual peers: the first, the arrest of the Duc de Richelieu for dueling in 1716, that is, during the Polysynodie period, the second, the arraignment of the Duc de La Force for illegal hoarding of commodities in 1721. In the former case the peers'

[22] *Histoire de la Pairie de France et du Parlement de Paris.* The last and fullest edition was that ostensibly printed in "London" in 1740. See Saint-Simon, *Écrits inédits*, III, 508, Annex 3, for the text of the contract by which Le Laboureur entered the paid service of the peerage in 1664.

[23] See above, 93.

insistence that Richelieu could not be tried by the robe officers in Parlement was, if not unanimous, at least not openly opposed by any of the group; and they were able to secure his release without a trial.[24] In 1721, extremists including Saint-Simon and the Archbishop of Reims revived the argument of parlementary non-competence on behalf of La Force. This time, however, there was a strong opposing party of peers, led by the Duc de Luxembourg, who believed that La Force should be tried by the Grand' Chambre, because the alternative would be to create a dangerous precedent in the form of a specially appointed royal board of inquiry.[25] Thus, after the Saint-Simon circle had induced the Regent to evoke the case to the privy council, a number of other peers accompanied First President de Mesmes as part of the delegation which on March 1, 1721, went to the Palais Royal with a protest against the evocation. The return of the case to the Parlement, by a declaration of the following week,[26] and the subsequent escape of La Force with only a reprimand represented the ideal solution from the "Luxembourgiste" point of view.[27]

Now this was not yet that conscious dependence of the peerage on the high robe which I shall have cause to refer to in the next chapter. The ideal of a court dominated, like the House of Lords, by the highest titled nobility was still central to ducal thinking. The application of British institutions to French theory in this respect becomes clearer if one goes beyond the bonnet and préséance to another element which recurred frequently in the demands of French peers under the Regency. This was the claim that the peerage represented an essential part of the Parlement and that no parlementary decision, of a political nature at least, should be considered valid unless taken in the presence of representatives of the peerage—

[24] A.N., K. 619-622 contain published arguments concerning both the Richelieu and the La Force cases.

[25] On this subject see *Les correspondants de la Marquise de Balleroy*, II, 284 ff.

[26] A.N., K. 622, no. 7.

[27] A.N., K. 622, no. 3, Mémoire sur le droit qu'ont les pairs de France de n'être jugés que par leurs pairs, is a tract written by Saint-Simon which contains the clear admission that "C'est en 1721 qu'il a commencé entre [les ducs et pairs] à varier, quelques uns veulent encore aujourd'hui n'être jugés touchant leur personne et leur estat qu'au parlement de Paris toutes les chambres assemblées et les pairs dument convoqués, regardant le parlement comme la cour unique et essentielle des pairs."

unless the Parlement had been "suffisament garni des pairs."[28] Here was a fundamental claim, which the high robe was strong enough to defeat and which the most articulate peers permitted to get lost in ceremonial trivia. Had it been pressed with full vigor and awareness of its implications, it would have confronted the French government with the threat of having a regularly established political institution pass under the control of the great ducal families.

Stated in these terms, the possibilities of the French situation call to mind the British case once more, specifically, the Peerage Bill of 1719. This proposal had envisaged the conversion of the House of Lords into the closed preserve of families whose hold could never again be broken by the crown's creation of new dukes, marquises, earls, viscounts, or barons. Walpole, it will be recalled, was able to defeat the measure in Commons (for his own immediate political purposes, to be sure) by appealing to the lower gentry's hope of someday seeing their own sons enter the House of Lords and by portraying the evils of a distinct and inaccessible corps of titled houses. The parallel between these tactics and those used against the *pairie* in France is inescapable. In the French case, there was no particular problem of inaccessibility (six new peerages were created between 1716 and 1723 alone),[29] but both the Duc du Maine and the Parlement of Paris made use of arguments similar to those of Walpole in their emphasis on the danger of a separate, titled class above the nobility in general. This brings me to one of the most important single aspects of the peerage question: its repercussions within the lower noblesse.

4

The peerage had exposed itself to resentment on the part of other nobles from the very day of Louis XIV's death, when it had demanded of the Regent that the peers be permitted to pay their respects to the new king in a separate body.[30] (Saint-Simon later charged that this inspiration had originated with his enemy, the Duc de Noailles,[31] though he himself had three years earlier agreed that

[28] Saint-Simon, *Écrits inédits*, III, 437; Le Laboureur, *Histoire de la pairie*, 65-75.

[29] Saint-Simon, *Écrits inédits*, IV, 162-163.

[30] Dangeau, *Journal*, XVI, 137.

[31] *Mémoires*, XXVII, 219, 225.

"the equality within the noblesse is insupportable.")[32] The Regent refused and instead personally conducted a mixed group of nobles into the presence of the young Louis XV. But word of the proposal was quickly passed about; and early in 1716, the Regent received a "Requête de la noblesse contre les fausses pretentions de Messieurs les Ducs et Pairs,"[33] which cited the following alleged claims by the peerage: (1) that it was a separate corps "between the king and the people"; (2) that it was sole judge of successions and regencies; (3) that the Parlement of Paris derived its powers solely from the peers' traditional rights; (4) that its members should always be styled "Monseigneur"; (5) that they need not "offer the hand" to lower noblemen; and (6) that they should enjoy a monopoly of the great crown offices.[34]

This petition is of interest from several points of view. For one thing, though it unquestionably gave an exaggerated idea of what most of the peers were asking, it revealed what effective propaganda could be constructed out of the charge that they were seeking to desert the rest of their class. Even more important, the six points set forth in the document embody the grievances not just of lower noblemen but also of the royal bastards (point 2) and the high robe (point 3). The mingling of opposition to the dukes is nowhere more clearly dramatized. In the subsequent barrage of pamphlets against the peerage there were many financed by the Duc du Maine on behalf of the gentry and many others of which the style and format showed the marks of parlementary origin.[35] In this connection it is interesting to observe complaints of robe and sword expressed side by side in such jingles as the following:

> Saint-Simon croit, par son adresse
> Avilir toute la noblesse
> Et subjuguer le Parlement;
> Cette entreprise est téméraire,

[32] *Ibid.*, XXII, 323.

[33] A.N., U. 907; also, in printed form, K. 619, bundle 3, no. 4.

[34] *Op. cit.* "La noblesse une fois reconnue n'admet point en elle de distinction. Un Gentilhomme n'est pas plus Gentilhomme qu'un autre. En France tous Nobles sont égaux quant à la Noblesse."

[35] Saint-Simon, *Mémoires*, XXIV, 199 ff.; XXVII, 214 ff. For an analysis of the légitimés' subsidization of propaganda, see Leclercq, *Histoire de la Régence*, II, 93.

Mais un sot, un impertinent
Croit que tout est facile à faire.[36]

Although only the magistracy and the legitimated du Maine could have paid for large-scale publicity, the nobility's reaction was by no means the product of wholly artificial incitement. The theoretical unity of the noblesse was deeply rooted in the sentiments of the entire class. It might be fanned by burlesques of ducal pretensions, such as the following mock petition:

> It would seem unnecessary for the Dukes to demand the distinctions above the nobility which are so legitimately due them, if this nobility would only do them justice; but since, by virtue of an incredible blindness, the Seigneurs and Gentlemen have sought to compete with persons whom they ought to regard only with respect, Your Royal Highness is requested to put them in their place.[37]

Or it might be given the easy focus which doggerel provided:

Les ducs et pairs du temps passé
Respectables par leurs naissances,
Ne se sont jamais séparés
D'avec la noblesse de France.
Aujourd'hui les nouveaux venus
En appellent comme d'abus.[38]

But it was a genuine swelling of indignation, which had only to be channeled to suit the needs of the princes and the Parlement.

The légitimés issue was the institutional problem which called forth the strongest display of resentment, for here the peerage was publicly accused of usurping the prerogatives of the comatose Estates General by seeking to decide a question of succession "as though it were the College of Cardinals."[39] Anti-ducal feeling spilled over into the historical writings of Boulainvilliers, who cited the original equality of the Franks and charged the peerage with

[36] Émile Raunié, *Chansonnier historique du XVIIIe siècle* (Paris, 1879-1884), II, 229-230.

[37] A.N., K. 619, bundle 3, no. 3.

[38] Raunié, *Chansonnier historique*, II, 221.

[39] A.N., K. 622, no. 18, Contestation entre la Noblesse et les Pairs de France. K. 616, nos. 2, 3 and 5 are other pamphlets containing similar charges.

having broken the whole tradition of aristocratic solidarity.[40] The Parlement's First President de Mesmes obtained the condemnation of ducal claims by the Order of Malta, through his brother, who was Grand Prior; while correspondence with outlying centers produced protest meetings by groups of provincial noblemen.[41]

The uproar reached its peak in the spring of 1717, when the Regent appointed his commission to consider the problem of succession to the crown.[42] On June 17, in defiance of an order in council of the preceding month which forbade joint action by noblemen in the matter, thirty-nine gentlemen sent to the Parlement a petition that the peers be silenced and that no decision be taken in the matter of the légitimés' royal rights except by a full Estates General.[43] Here again is evident the complicity among the sword, the bastards, and the parlementaires (one of the principal signers of the petition was de Mesmes' own son-in-law, Vieux-Pont).[44] The Regent, who had no intention of permitting the Duc du Maine to build a permanent party in support of his claims, immediately ordered six of the petitioners, including Vieux-Pont, arrested and held them in the Bastille until the July edict had settled the succession question. The nobility's intervention had not saved the légitimés from losing their eligibility for the crown; but the government's actions did nothing to restore the popularity of the peerage.

The latter had never had any illusions on one point at least: that whatever ground they lost in aristocratic circles would be so much gained for the parlementaires. A "Lettre des Pairs de France" of this period pleads with the lower noblesse d'épée to support the peerage against the Parlement's effort to destroy honors which constituted "le seul vestige qui reste des anciens droits de la Noblesse."[45] The same appeal for a counter alliance against the légitimés and the magistrates, combined with an indignant denial of the more exaggerated claims imputed to the peerage, is contained in a "Mém-

[40] *Essais sur la noblesse*, 173 and 244. Mme. R. Simon, in her *Henry de Boulainviller* (Gap, 1940), 100-109, seems to have missed an important point in her analysis of Boulainvilliers' support of the royal bastards. The point is that Boulainvilliers was opposed to the peers, and the peers were opposed to the bastards.

[41] Dangeau, *Journal*, XVII, 66; Saint-Simon, *Mémoires*, XXIX, 199-207.

[42] See above, 177.

[43] A.N., U. 907.

[44] Dangeau, *Journal*, XVII, 109-112.

[45] A.N., K. 619, bundle 3, no. 1.

oire d'un homme de condition au corps de la Noblesse sur les veritables interests, dans l'affaire des Pairs contre le Parlement."[46] But the effort was unavailing in the context of events, as Saint-Simon admitted in 1753, when, in the last letter of his which has survived, he ruefully reminded the Duc de Richelieu of "that rising of the nobility against the dukes at the death of the King and during almost the whole Regency."[47]

It should be noted, for the light it throws on the sort of appeal which the high robe made to the rest of the noblesse, that the Parlement chose throughout to fight the peers with the latter's own rhetorical weapons. The magistrates might well have ignored prestige arguments and concentrated on the dukes' governmental incompetence or the ridiculous irrelevance of appeals to a thirteenth-century tradition of twelve real territorial princes. Instead, they met claims of family dignities and institutional age with counter-claims of the same kind: if the peerage was old, the Parlement was older; if robe families dated only from the sixteenth century, those of the peers had for the most part attained their present rank only in the seventeenth. No noble de race ever heaped more scorn upon the lineage of sovereign court officers than did Novion upon the recent rise of the ducs et pairs in his famous memorandum of 1716.[48] The magistrates were fighting not for recognition as a more useful part of French society and government, but for a place of honor and leadership within the aristocracy.

The fact that they were able to take over that place so soon after 1715 must be explained in part by the haughty ineptitude of the peerage and in part by a shift of emphasis in the nobility's political situation. During the first few years after Louis XIV's death, there appeared to be a real chance of aristocratic government. At least until the Polysynodie collapsed, the upper nobility was clearly on the offensive. During this brief interlude the peers, as a small group of highly placed courtiers with easy access to the Regent, might well have claimed to represent the nobility had they not been so intent on raising themselves above it. But even if they had displayed

[46] A.N., K. 619, bundle 3, no. 2.

[47] Supplement to Chéruel-Regnier edition of the *Mémoires* (Paris, 1886), XX, 409.

[48] See above, 178.

the diplomatic skill required to make themselves acknowledged leaders of the entire noblesse, they could, it seems to me, have maintained that status only so long as basically abnormal political conditions continued to exist. As soon as the Regent felt strong enough to re-assert the governmental traditions of his late uncle, the nobility fell back to the defensive position which I have described as its true place in the political history of eighteenth-century France. And for the tactics which such a position demanded, the high robe was eminently well situated. If the peerage had accomplished anything during its short but noisy period on stage, it had been to make robe primacy more apparent and less repugnant to the mass of lower noblemen.

Chapter Ten

The Defense of Privilege

1

FROM THE PRESENT VANTAGE POINT it seems obvious that even in 1715 the high robe, secure in its nobility and with its political rights restored, was the most potent force within the aristocracy. The wealth of its members made possible the publication of remonstrances, the hiring of pamphleteers, the bribing of influential courtiers, and the buying off of unwelcome royal projects. Pensions and gratifications from the king might be welcome enough to individual presidents and councilors, they might even destroy effective opposition in specific instances; but they could never reduce the robe to economic dependence on the monarch's good will nor eliminate resistance when greater sums and more fundamental interests were at stake. The sovereign court officers were the one aristocratic group which avoided both horns of La Bruyère's dilemma—poverty or sycophancy[1]—and their impregnable family positions only added to the sense of independence conferred by economic strength.

One of the special blessings of wealth lay in the accessibility of education. Here again the robe in 1715 already stood out from other noblemen, save perhaps for a scattering of learned prelates. I shall return somewhat later to the question of education; but for the moment it is enough to point out that with a background of childhood tutors, Jesuit or Oratorian college training in rhetoric, literature, the classics, and finally legal studies at the university level, the high robe of Louis XV's time possessed a tremendous advantage over any other noble group of comparable size and distribution. The ability to organize its own arguments, buttress them with the historical data so

[1] See above, vii.

vital in a precedent-minded society, and present them in coherent form was practically a monopoly of the upper magistracy.

Last but not least, the sovereign courts of 1715 represented a set of organized units unparalleled anywhere else in France. Here were thirty-one recognized assemblies, each endowed with its own institutional charter, shaped and strengthened by centuries of corporate continuity, protected by revered traditions and by the government's need of its judicial services. Any collection of confidential minutes, such as Greffier-en-chef Gilbert's for the Parlement of Paris, 1718 to 1720,[2] or Councilor Savignac's for the Parlement of Guienne, 1730 to 1733,[3] will suffice to illustrate the importance which professional solidarity and secrecy could have in the political sphere. Tax issues, theological questions, problems of public relations, dealings with the peerage, with the ministers, with the intendants, all were discussed in perfect freedom at the very same assemblies which deliberated on purely judicial matters. Corporate solidarity might be expressed by the naming of a commission to secure apologies for insults to the company,[4] by resistance to an alleged royal encroachment in a matter of internal discipline,[5] by asking en bloc that some special honor be accorded to a past or present member.[6] A magistrate arrested by agents of the crown could rely on his company's support, including on occasion, as in June 1732, the suspension of all judicial business.[7] And always available was the published remonstrance as an implement for turning public excitement to the service of magistral demands.

[2] A.N., U. 420-421.

[3] Bib. Bordeaux, Ms. 369.

[4] A.N., K. 701, no. 311. On July 20, 1719, Président à mortier Potier de Novion reported to the Parlement of Paris that a full apology had been obtained from one Courcelles whose son had publicly abused several members of the court.

[5] Barbier, *Journal*, II, 317-318. In 1742 Chancellor d'Aguesseau wished to expel six young councilors of the Paris Parlement for having dishonored their offices through questionable fiscal dealings. The Parlement rejected the demand as given, then expelled four sons of older magistrates on its own authority.

[6] In 1716, for example, the Parlement of Burgundy addressed to the papacy an appeal for the canonization of Madame de Chantal, daughter of seventeenth-century President Fremyot. She was beatified by Benedict XIV in 1757 and sainted by Clement XIII.

[7] See Rocquain, *L'esprit révolutionnaire*, 67-68, for a description of this "sympathy strike."

2

It is interesting to speculate as to how different might have been the sovereign counts' political situation if the first Estates General after 1614 had been called in 1715 instead of 1789. The possibility was by no means remote. True, the British demand of 1712 for a national assembly to ratify the permanent separation of the French and Spanish crowns had been rejected by Louis XIV's plenipotentiaries.[8] Even before the old king died, however, several of the Duc d'Orléans' associates, among them Saint-Simon, were urging that the Estates General be summoned to meet at Saint-Germain-en-Laye as soon as the new reign began. They argued that such an assembly would create a surge of popularity in favor of the Regent, would ratify his assumption of power, would remove the Spanish threat by confirming Philip V's exclusion (exactly what the British negotiators had asked three years before), and might even permit the government to obtain a declaration of bankruptcy on other than its own authority.[9] But the Duc de Noailles, chairman-designate of the Council of Finance, opposed this solution; and the Regent himself had by August 1715, decided that the Estates General would be too cumbersome and too dangerous for his purposes.[10] He chose instead to bargain with the Parlement of Paris for suppression of the late king's testament.[11]

The idea remained in active circulation for several years, however. In a memorandum to the Regent in late 1715, Boulainvilliers urged convoking the Estates General at Bourges the following August, in order to consider the financial crisis and incidentally to repeal the anti-aristocratic capitation and dixième.[12] The first of these taxes

[8] Saint-Simon, XXIII, 126: "On leur expliqua la nature et l'impuissance de nos États généraux, et ils comprirent enfin combien leur concours seroit vain, quand même il seroit accordé."

[9] Saint-Simon, XXVII, 63-92.

[10] *Ibid.*, XXVII, 172.

[11] As Ranke has pointed out in his *Französische Geschichte* (Stuttgart, 1879), V, 278: "He was fully aware that in the assembled estates unwelcome speeches also might be delivered, either in favor of the Duc du Maine . . . or in favor of the King of Spain. . . . And what was to happen until they could be summoned, elected, and brought together? For him and for the country an immediate decision was essential."

[12] *Mémoires présentés*, etc., 11-14.

was modified to suit the nobility; the second, suspended without such a convocation; and within two years Boulainvilliers had switched to the opposite point of view concerning its desirability.[13] But early in 1717 the project was simultaneously revived by three different sponsors: first, the Duc de Noailles, now desperate over the financial situation;[14] second, the Duc du Maine, who was publicly insisting that no change be made in the succession without national assent;[15] and third, the thirty-nine nobles who signed the anti-peerage petition and who asserted that not the peers but the three estates of the realm should be consulted on the rights of the royal bastards.[16] In spite of this concerted pressure, the Regent rejected the demands of all three parties.[17] He had no intention of providing the Duc du Maine with a national forum, and John Law had already raised hopes of some fiscal solution other than that of the despondent Noailles. As under Louis XIV, so under Orléans and Louis XV the policy of the crown remained one of minimizing the possibilities for public expressions of resentment.

It is worth adding that the two most potent elements within the nobility were as opposed to the Estates General project as was the Regent. The peers had long been hostile to this institution which, when it had been active, had made of them only a segment of the general order of noblesse.[18] As for the high robe, its whole position of unique institutional importance rested on the absence of any body more representative than the sovereign courts. As far back as the Fronde, Henri de Mesmes, great-uncle of the first president under the Regency, had admitted that "the Parlement used to take rank below the Estates General by virtue of their verification of what it decided."[19] Had the Estates General actually been summoned, both

[13] *Ibid.*, 157-159. [14] Saint-Simon, *Mémoires*, XXXI, 268-327.

[15] A.N., K. 136, no. 21. Letter from the légitimés to the king: "Plaise a Vostre Majesté . . . ne rien prononcer sur la question de la succession a la Couronne que les Estats generaux du Royaume juridiquement assemblés ayent deliberé sur l'interest que la nation peut avoir aux dispositions de l'Edit du feu Roy." The same argument appears in a pro-légitimés pamphlet of 1717 called "Lettre d'un avocat de province," A.N., K. 621, no. 48.

[16] A.N., K. 616, nos. 2, 3, 5.

[17] Dangeau, *Journal*, XVII, 97 (May 27, 1717).

[18] A.N., K. 616, no. 3, *Faits sur la séance des Pairs aux États du Royaume;* Le Laboureur, *Histoire de la pairie*, 147.

[19] *Journal d'Olivier Le Fèvre d'Ormesson* (ed. A. Chéruel, Paris, 1860-1861), I, 698.

peers and parlementaires would doubtless have fought hard for control of the chamber of nobility. But neither group was sorry to be spared the test in 1717.

3

If the high robe was unenthusiastic about any legislative body of national scope, this was partly because both the structure and the traditions of the sovereign courts inclined them to put their trust in the province as the safest political unit. There were, it is true, numerous symptoms of integrated effort by widely separated companies acting in concert.[20] Nevertheless, a frontal attack by the government on the special rights of any province was still primarily the affair of the local sovereign court or courts.

Thus the Breton nobles in their insurrection of 1717-1720 were strongly defended by the remonstrances and memoranda of the Parlement at Rennes.[21] This revolt, in which several of the magistrates were arrested for treason, is one of the main reasons why no provincial parlement has been so fully treated in past studies as has that of Brittany.[22] The rebellion was in itself a fascinating and highly complex affair, but I must here limit myself to pointing out two of its aspects which were specifically related to the parlement's attitude. One of these was the insistence on royal respect for the 1532 *Contrat* of union, which had guaranteed that "no edicts, declarations, commissions, orders in council or letters patent in general . . . are to have any effect if they have not been accepted by the Estates and verified by the sovereign courts of the province."[23] The other was the part which the parlement played in actually reinforcing the intransigence of the Breton nobility, while at the same time assuring the crown that it was the latter's feelings which necessitated magistral protests. In

[20] See above, 89-90.

[21] A.N., K, 712, nos. 65 *bis* and 66; B.N., Ms. fr. nouv. acq. 9640, fol. 211-221; and A. Le Moy, *Remontrances du Parlement de Bretagne au XVIIIe siècle* (Anger, 1909), 1-24. Le Moy provides several valuable documents from the Archives Départementales d'Ille-et-Vilaine which would not otherwise be available to the non-Breton researcher.

[22] Carré in Lavisse, VIII (2), 55-57; Leclercq, *Histoire de la Régence*, II, 331-364; Armand Rebillon, *Les États de Bretagne de 1661 à 1789* (Paris, 1932), 249-268, are all instructive on the subject of the rebellion.

[23] Le Moy, *Remontrances*, lii.

May 1718, the Bishop of Vannes wrote to the Marquise de Balleroy apropos of some peace overtures from the Regent: "the Parlement, it if had lent itself to them, could have easily secured from the court the re-establishment of the Estates [dissolved the preceding year]; it has preferred to make remonstrances."[24]

Less violent but equally significant was the reaction to d'Aguesseau's codification project of the 1730's; for resistance came independently from several provinces at once, especially from those still governed by legal customs which antedated direct French rule. The Parlement of Dauphiné, for example, invoked the whole tradition of pre-fourteenth-century peculiarities to combat the Chancellor's standardizing ordinance on testaments.[25] The reaction from Franche-Comté was similar.[26] Rouen's defense of its revered *coutume* was the fiercest of all, if one may judge by d'Aguesseau's exasperated remarks in a letter to his son: "A change of religion would perhaps be easier to introduce in Normandy than a change in jurisprudence."[27] It was only at the cost of numerous compromises and several lettres de jussion that the new ordinances were pushed through, some of them in barely recognizable form.

How should this continuing particularism be assessed, as against the awakening sense of robe solidarity? It must, I think, be concluded that as governmental centralization increased in the latter half of the seventeenth and first half of the eighteenth centuries, local patriotism, as expressed by the high robe at least, underwent a dual reformulation. On the one hand, it was modified and brought under restraint insofar as was necessary to permit greater cooperation in opposing the crown. On the other hand, it was harnessed to the service of privileged groups whose special rights and exemptions were hardest to sustain in tests of nation-wide dimensions, but could be defended quite effectively when confounded with the "liberties" of Brittany, for example, or the "constitution" of Franche-Comté.

It is only in juxtaposition with the activities of the provincial courts that the performance of the nobility in the provincial estates becomes comprehensible. Numerous provinces had at least occasional assem-

[24] *Les correspondants de la Marquise de Balleroy*, I, 319.

[25] Egret, *Le Parlement de Dauphiné*, I, 12-13.

[26] D'Aguesseau, *Lettres inédites*, 459. [27] *Ibid.*

blies; but the only four which exercised functions of any importance (beyond solemnly voting the *don gratuit* to the crown, as in Artois)[28] were those of Brittany, Languedoc, Burgundy, and Provence. The dominant role of the high robe among noblemen at these provincial estates becomes clear enough when one considers by contrast the results in instances which involved no sovereign court officers. The estates of Vitry-le-François, for example, in 1744 brought together numerous military noblemen of Champagne-Brie; but the record left by their president is one of ineffectual uproar, with the royal commissioners ultimately dictating all decisions with perfect ease.[29]

In the estates which included high robe officers there was still no possibility of flatly refusing fiscal demands of the crown, but here the privileged groups were better able to exact respect and in some cases appreciable concessions from the royal agents. This was in no small part due to the interaction of deliberations in the estates and the sovereign courts' remonstrances. The demands of the Estates of Languedoc, for example, were on the one hand partly shaped by parlementary representatives. On the other hand, these same demands were apt to re-appear in formal pronouncements of the Parlement at Toulouse, the Chambre des Comptes at Montpellier, and the Cour des Aides at Montauban, as occurred in the successful fight against the cinquantième in 1725.[30] What might have been a negligible protest, if it had come from only a group of illiterate and inept gentry, called together briefly and quickly dispersed, took on real weight by virtue of the high robe's place in the Second Estate and its close contacts with privileged elements in the First. Colbert's dislike of the provincial assemblies had resulted in part from this circumstance,[31] and in the eighteenth century the robe preponderance was much greater.

The Estates of Burgundy in 1736 contained one magistrate who marched with the commoners, but this was only because Councilor Burteur, as mayor of Dijon, was ex officio president of the *Chambre*

[28] A.N., H. 11-23.

[29] Claude-Lamoral, Prince de Ligne, *Journal sur les États tenus à Vitry-le-François en 1744* (Vitry-le-François, 1887).

[30] K. 138, no. 13[4]; see above, 85 and 90.

[31] *Correspondance administrative sous le règne de Louis XIV* (ed. Depping, Paris, 1860-1865), 4 vols. Also Hedwig Hintze, *Staatseinheit und Föderalismus im alten Frankreich* (Stuttgart, 1928), 87, 526.

du Tiers État. Berbisey, first president of the Parlement, sat at the right hand of the Duc de Bourbon. During the Regency and for some years after, the nobles' president was the Comte de Montal, the heir of an old feudal family; but it was a Rigoley whose signature, inscribed with the flourishes of a palais-trained hand, appears on the records as *Secrétaire des États*.[32] In the eleven triennial sessions between 1718 and 1748, there were a total of 195 individuals received as new deputies of the Second Estate; of these 42 were nobles de robe, as compared with 37 out of 302 between 1658 and 1715—more than one out of five as contrasted with less than one out of eight.[33]

In Provence, the robe enjoyed parity with the sword, in that it was guaranteed six of the twelve syndics elected every three years by the Second Estate. From 1714 to 1717, for example, the robe syndics were Councilors Charles de Grimaldy, Jean Baptiste de Coriolis, Jean de Félix, Pierre de Laurent, Jacques-Joseph de Gaufridy, and Elzéas d'Arbaud—five from the Parlement of Provence and one, Coriolis, from the Chambre des Comptes at Aix. In 1736, the twelve-man committee comprised:[34]

As syndics d'épée:	*As syndics de robe:*
Marquis de Saint-Martin*	Comte de Grimaldy
Marquis de Pierrefeu	Comte d'Espinasse
Marquis de Simiane	Monsieur Le Blanc Ventabren
Monsieur de Rognes	Monsieur Thomassin
Monsieur de Roux de Bonneval	Monsieur de Sagui
Monsieur Laurent de Peirolles*	Monsieur Piton de Tournefort

*Saint-Martin and Laurent de Peirolles both came of magistral families.

The Estates of Burgundy and those of Provence, though more important than any left in most of the other provinces, were nevertheless weak assemblies, whose cahiers of grievances seldom carried any weight unless seconded by the sovereign courts.[35] It was only in two provinces —Languedoc and Brittany—that the estates in their own right still

[32] Bib. Dijon, Ms. 1322 (Juigné 11), Tenues des États de Bourgogne, 1653-1760.

[33] A.D. Côte d'Or, C. 3037.

[34] Bib. Méjanes, Ms. 1144 (1074).

[35] Burgundy's cahiers for this period are in A.N., H. 100–115; those of Provence, A.N., H. 1191-1217.

wielded substantial authority over local taxation and public works.[36] The Estates of Languedoc, buttressed by close cooperation with three sovereign courts, not only regulated assessment of the taille and directed the building of roads but also voiced regional opposition to crown policies in no uncertain terms.[37] Their commissioners, one of whom was regularly a magistrate, carried the cahiers of each session up to Versailles; and though the Third Estate was unusually strong in this province, the grievances of the noblesse always received adequate expression.

In turning to the Breton case again, it becomes necessary to make one general observation about the cahiers of all the other estates so far discussed. This is that although robe noblemen had a large part in framing them, and though they almost invariably contained references to special desires of the sovereign courts in matters such as taxation of offices, judicial appeals, interest rates and gages, they never became the primary vehicle of political expression for high robe interests. Down to 1789 the favorite weapon of the magistracy of Burgundy, Provence, and Languedoc remained its own remonstrances, often synchronized with the *cahiers* but never replaced by them.

It is in the light of this distinction that the uniquely close relationship between courts and estates in Brittany becomes most apparent. The Breton robe, which steered not only the nobility of the province but in many instances the clergy and the commoners as well, seems to have looked upon the estates and the courts as practically interchangeable mechanisms of political action. Remonstrances defended special immunities of the province as a whole against intendants and governors general. The estates sent petitions to the crown in favor of the magistracy. The parlement at Rennes paid for the publication of memoranda issued on behalf of the whole nobility and pleading the cause, to cite a famous instance, of the gentlemen sentenced to death after the abortive revolt of 1718.[38] An observer well acquainted

[36] Émile Appolis, "Les états de Languedoc au XVIIIe siècle: Comparaison avec les états de Bretagne," in *Études présentées à la Commission Internationale pour l'Histoire des Assemblées d'États*, Fasc. 2, *L'organisation corporative du moyen âge à la fin de l'ancien régime*, 129-148. Émile Lousse, ed., Louvain, 1937.

[37] A.N., H. 748[25,28,245], 751, 842.

[38] B.N., Ms. fr. nouv. acq. 9640, Apologie de la noblesse et du Parlement de Bretagne. For detailed accounts of this recurrent phenomenon see Le Moy, *Le Parlement de Bretagne*, and Rebillon, *Les États de Bretagne*.

with the Breton precedent might have foreseen the part which the high robe was to play in the affairs of a nation in 1788 and 1789.

In assessing the general significance of provincial assemblies, one should not, I repeat, permit them to overshadow the crucial importance of the courts themselves as political institutions. It was in the power of the sovereign companies that the nobility's best hope resided. If the provinces which possessed vestigial estates displayed a more articulate and more clearly recognized alliance of privileged groups, it was because in those provinces robe power and the possibilities it offered were constantly being demonstrated to a nobility which could still come together from time to time in large numbers.

4

I have delayed raising the issue of the aristocracy's *conscious* reliance on protection by the courts because such reliance presupposed an awareness of what the high robe could do for the noblesse as a whole; and that awareness could only take shape out of the public furor under the Regency, publicity of magistral campaigns in the form of printed remonstrances, and the demonstration of the robe's leadership among nobles in the provincial estates.

The immediate political demands put forward by noblemen at the death of Louis XIV are well illustrated in a thick sheaf of anonymous letters, sent to the Regent late in 1715 and early in 1716, often with signatures such as "A loyal gentleman" or "A nobleman devoted to Your Highness."[39] The demands repeated most often in this correspondence are for suppression of the capitation and dixième, the righting of wrongs done by intendants to privileged subjects, and punishment of profiteers who had plundered the country during the recent wars. Now compare with this the role of the sovereign courts. Their pressure was largely responsible for suspension of the dixième in 1717 and for the progressive easing of the capitation as applied to privilégiés. Later, when new taxes were devised, their remonstrances continued the defense of exemptions—against the cinquantième in 1725, for example, or the *centième* in 1748—"After having spoken, Sire, in favor of the people, could your Parlement forget that generous

[39] A.N., K. 138, nos. 1-1[87].

nobility which merits so much respect and consideration?"[40] Their influence and the worry it caused to ministers and intendants are apparent in this letter of 1716 from the Duc de Noailles, President of the Council of Finance, to Lamoignon de Courson, intendant at Bordeaux:

> The receivers general of finance in the généralité of Bordeaux continue to complain, Monsieur, of the extreme difficulty which they are encountering in the collection of the dixième and capitation; they believe the principal cause to be the bad example of some individuals, even among the nobility, and Messieurs the officers of the Parlement of Guienne, who not only refuse to pay what they owe of these taxes, but incite others to do likewise.[41]

Their part in the Chambre de Justice of 1715-1716, established to punish war profiteers, was at least a step toward satisfying noble resentment of the nouveaux riches, while the Parlement's remonstrances of April 1720, like the letters from aristocrats to the Regent five years before, specifically blamed the whole class of bankers and tax farmers for the country's financial predicament.[42] If any doubt remained as to the robe's position between the old noblesse and the financiers, it should have been dispelled by the following from a remonstrance published by the Paris Parlement in 1748:

> What spectacle more afflicting to behold for gentlemen of old extraction, often returned to their lands with honorable marks of their services and their courage, than to see at every turn their escutcheons mingled with those of persons who have barely had time to buy the right to possess them, and to find themselves compelled at church to share with these newcomers the honors which for several centuries have been rendered only to them [the real gentlemen] and their ancestors.[43]

In countless other ways the high robe under Louis XV was rendering services to the aristocracy. Against the peers, it was to the Parlement of Paris that the lower nobility addressed itself: "A nosseigneurs du parlement, supplient, etc."[44] In 1716 it was the Parlement of Dauphiné which assembled the precedents and framed the petition to the crown

[40] Flammermont, *Remontrances*, I, 386.
[41] A.D. Gironde, C. 3145. [42] Flammermont, *Remontrances*, I, 138.
[43] *Ibid.*, I, 387. [44] Duclos, *Mémoires*, 517.

against the billeting of troops in the homes of noblemen in that province.[45] In 1735 it was the Parlement of Franche-Comté which forbade the Confrérie de Saint-Georges, an exclusive circle of chevaliers, to interfere with the admission of noble persons to religious orders.[46] When the bishops and *abbés commendataires* submitted their protest against the cinquantième in 1725, they not only took sections from various sovereign courts' prior remonstrances but explicitly referred to them.[47] In 1748 and 1749, the centième again set the church nobles to framing a petition which cited robe remonstrances and concluded with a lament on behalf of prelates "for the first time degraded and reduced to the condition of your other subjects . . . confused with the very people they govern."[48] Few bishops had any love for parlementary pretensions, but against the crown one took help where one could find it.

Appreciation of what the sovereign courts represented becomes common in aristocratic memoirs and letters by the 1730's at the latest. Looking back on the Regency from a point ten years after its close, the Duc de Villars comments warmly: "There were sent to the Parlement a variety of edicts which with respectable firmness it always refused to register."[49] A letter written in 1733 by Sévigné's daughter, Madame de Simiane, begins: "What will come of the Parlement's affairs? I am very anxious!"[50]—an expression of infinitely more intense political interest in the high robe than had ever come from the pen of her gifted mother. And here are the words of a crusty old soldier, the Marquis de Franclieu, writing from his seigneury near Auch in the 1740's: "How fortunate we should be if all our affairs were judged by the parlements. They may be expensive, but at least they are reliable."[51] The Grands Jours seem far away in

[45] A.D. Isère, B. 2322.

[46] "La noblesse et les chapitres deviendraient la victime des caprices, des inimitiés, des préventions ou de la faveur des confrères de Saint-Georges." A.D. Doubs, C. 633, quoted by Estignard, *Le Parlement de Franche-Comté*, II, 161.

[47] A.N., K. 138, no. 13[4].

[48] Bib. Méjanes, Ms. 730 (826).

[49] *Mémoires*, IV, 139.

[50] *Lettres de Madame de Sévigné, de sa famille et de ses amis* (ed. Monmerqué, Paris, 1862-1866), XI, 145.

[51] *Mémoires* (ed. Germon, Paris-Auch, 1896), 221.

the past: the parlements are now the nobleman's courts of choice.[52]

Perhaps most significant of all, however, was the shift of the peerage itself, away from scornful opposition to support of magistral independence. It will be recalled that even Saint-Simon came to the defense of venality because of its part in keeping the sovereign courts beyond the reach of absolutist interference. If the less determined peers began to drop away from the group of titled diehards after 1718, it was partly because they dreaded the advantages which might accrue to the royal administration if their order remained at war with the high robe. And in 1721, as noted above, a strong party within the peerage supported the Parlement's claim to jurisdiction over their colleague, the Duc de La Force.[53]

As the hard feelings of the Regency period waned in intensity, the peers came to associate themselves more and more willingly with high robe institutions. In 1746, the delegation which went to congratulate Lamoignon de Blancmesnil on his reception as First President of the Paris Cour des Aides included several peers with four présidents à mortier from the Parlement and First President Nicolay of the Chambre des Comptes.[54] It is significant that the next time a public issue concerning both the peerage and the Parlement of Paris was raised, it took the form of solidarity against the crown, again, as in the La Force case, over an issue of royal evocation. This was after my defined period, in 1756; but it is worth looking ahead to take note of the joint memorandum prepared on that occasion by the two groups to raise the question "si le Parlement peut sans la permission du Roy inviter les Princes et les Pairs à venir prendre séance à la Cour."[55] It was also in the 1750's that Horace Walpole, after years of association with the French aristocrats, wrote in a letter to Henry Seymour

[52] The great collection of letters to the Marquise de Balleroy, Bib. Mazarine, Mss. 2334-2338, is extremely valuable for the evolution it reflects. Under Louis XIV (vol. I) the high-born correspondents of the Marquise express little save indifference toward the parlements; by 1718 (vol. III) their attitude is changing, subtly but unmistakably, to one of curiosity concerning robe affairs, and in the 1720's (vols. IV-V) to one of serious interest (friendly in the letters of nobles de race, hostile in those of most *nobles des fonctions gouvernementales*). Barthélemy's printed selection of these letters, already referred to, is worth consulting on this change.

[53] See above, 180-181.

[54] Barbier, *Journal*, II, 489.

[55] B.N., Ms. fr. nouv. acq. 7982, fol. 189-227.

Conway: "I say nothing of the exile of the Parliament of Paris, only, as we are going to choose a new Parliament, we could not do better than choose the exiles: we could scarce choose braver or honester men."[56] In the voice from Strawberry Hill was the echo of others from countless châteaux across the Channel.

I return to the fact that under eighteenth-century conditions leadership of the nobility could never denote fully recognized direction of a compact class. But leadership, as Louis XV's era knew it, had passed unmistakably to the high robe within only a few years after 1715. The proudest peers might still deny it for awhile; perhaps some sensitive gentlemen in provincial estates still writhed at the sight of confident magistrates dominating their order. Condescension and hostility, however, were fast yielding to recognition of services rendered. There was in the 1730's and '40's no longer any doubt that without the sovereign courts the noblesse was an impotent horde of individuals and that with them it could function as an increasingly effective alliance in defense of privilege.

[56] *Letters* (ed. Mrs. Paget Toynbee, Oxford, 1903-1905), III, 162.

Chapter Eleven

Social Aspects of Fusion

1

The fact that non-robe nobles were coming more and more to rely on the political power of the sovereign courts is in itself, of course, no infallible proof of changes in social attitudes and relationships. The defensive alliance of privilégiés might conceivably have been an expedient rationally arrived at, but accepted by the noblesse d'épée as nothing better than a distasteful necessity. For some old-line aristocrats it remained just that. The purpose of the present chapter, however, is to demonstrate that the political closing of ranks did have its social concomitants. What these were and what sort of robe-épée distinction still existed by the mid-eighteenth century are the two sides of a single question, namely: to what extent had the high robe of the 1740's become part of a fused aristocracy?

When one enters upon a discussion of any phenomenon as subtle as class assimilation, he inevitably feels the loss of that framework of institutions, statistics, and narrative facts to which he has been able to cling in considering the less elusive aspects of a general problem. For when the focus shifts to attitudes and social behavior, the subject matter becomes a fragile network of half-explained references, suggestive omissions, increased representation of certain elements in the sort of informal gatherings which leave no minutes nor membership lists but which influence men's actions as powerfully as do laws or ledgers. There are exceptional points of view to be noted, eloquent outbursts which may threaten to obscure less articulate but nonetheless basic trends in thought and habits. Gone is any satisfying sense of cleavage or dramatic change from the old to the new in neatly defined stages. But for all the difficulties inherent in measurement by relative as opposed to absolute dimensions, it must be conceded that a significant shift of emphasis is itself an important historical datum.

This is exactly what one encounters in comparing the attitude of the noblesse d'épée toward the robe most commonly encountered in the 1720's, '30's, and '40's with that of the century's early years. It was a matter of the fading, not the total disappearance of hostility. Magistral wealth was a cause for some continued bad feeling. A "Lettre de M. ——" in 1716, for example, complains that among the noblesse de race:

> there is hardly to be seen at present anything but a certain base luxury . . . no-one has the slightest conception of the magnificence which used to distinguish great houses and which would still make them respected today. The robe, inflated with the wealth of commerce, would not dare to imitate or insult them.[1]

In districts such as Auvergne, where urban influences were weak, the seventeenth-century atmosphere seems to have persisted well into the eighteenth;[2] and in the youthful writings of Mirabeau *père*, the future "ami des hommes," one finds the old scorn for the parlementaires (in this case, those of Provence) still active in the 1730's.[3]

Against these increasingly rare instances, however, must be set that whole trend which excited Boulainvilliers to rail in the 1720's against what he considered the old nobility's loss of class pride.[4] This, after all, was the century in which even such a purist as Guyot was content to insist that it took four generations of nobility to make a "gentleman."[5] His aim was to exclude recent anoblis who did not have four degrees, but by implication he accepted all the many nobles de robe who did.

In the great mid-century collections of letters there are to be found dozens of correspondents, nobles d'épée and nobles de robe alike, writing about persons and events with none of that conscious

[1] Dangeau, *Journal*, XVIII, 398.

[2] Jalenques, "La noblesse de la province d'Auvergne," 384-385.

[3] "Journal de la jeunesse de Victor de Riqueti, marquis de Mirabeau," *Revue rétrospective* (Paris, 1834), V, 21-24.

[4] *Essais sur la noblesse*, xiv, 251, and *passim*.

[5] *Répertoire*, XII, 71.

distinction between robe and sword which is present in Madame de Sévigné's letters. Another arresting indication of mounting respect for robe status is to be found in the references made by military noblemen in discussing their ancestry. In 1729, for example, the Comte de Forbin, naval commander and chevalier de Saint-Louis, wrote proudly:

> Je ne m'arrêterai point ici à parler de ma Famille, le nom de Forbin est assez connu par le mérite de ceux qui l'ont porté, & qui depuis longtems se sont distinguez dans l'Église, dans l'Épée & dans la Robe.[6]

Similarly, the Marquis de Franclieu, composing his memoirs in the late 1740's began by citing the fourteenth-century military origins of his house but was quick to add that "my grandfather . . . married a Chauveau, which makes me related to the Chauvelins, to President Robert . . . [and to] the Le Pelletiers, the Le Telliers, the Chamillards."[7]

Even more significant than the change in written references was the great increase in robe-épée social contact, a phenomenon which appeared in different areas at different times. From what has previously been said of Brittany it should be no surprise to find Madame de Sévigné reporting as early as the late seventeenth century that there an aristocrat could enjoy himself in parlementary society and that "on ne peut recevoir plus de politesses."[8] At Paris, on the other hand, it seems to have been a major surprise for the same lady to discover the charm of Procureur-Général de Harlay—"il cache sous sa gravité un esprit agréable et très poli."[9] This incredulous reaction would have been typical for most of France in Madame de Sévigné's day. Outside of Brittany, it was left to the early eighteenth century to bring that social intermingling of nobles de robe and nobles de race in academies and private homes which had such important effects on the intellectual and political development of the aristocracy. The personification of magistral success in the *beau monde* has long been President Hénault, wit, playwright, lover of the Duchesse du Maine and Madame du Deffand; but he was only the most famous among many others.

[6] *Mémoires du comte de Forbin* (Amsterdam, 1729), I, 3. The author's ancestors had served in the Parlement of Provence in the seventeenth century.

[7] *Mémoires*, 2. [8] *Lettres*, IX, 143. [9] *Ibid.* 2; IX, 246-247.

In the capital the social acceptance of the high robe was made easier by the importance of governmental positions, by the prestige of academic honors, and by the relative security of great nobles de race who still had a monopoly of distinctions at Versailles. In the provinces a large portion of the old nobility unquestionably clung the more desperately to its narrow pride of caste because it had so little else. But the main provincial centers were rapidly developing replicas of Parisian society, and in the process offering the eighteenth century magistrates ever greater opportunities to move amid the representatives of the richest and most revered territorial families. When the Marquise de Roussille, daughter of a president in the Clermont-Ferrand Cour des Aides, arrived at Riom in 1723 for a visit with the Duc and Duchesse de Noailles, she reported to her husband that "I was received with infinite cordiality. . . . As soon as I was announced, Madame de Noailles broke through the crowd in her reception room to come to me and embraced me tenderly."[10] In about 1720 a secret agent in Lyon sent to the future Cardinal Dubois a list of some eighty leading residents whose social and political contacts might be of moment to the crown; included in this circle were not only the Marshal de Villeroy, the archbishop (Villeroy's son), numerous clergymen and thirty-six nobles de race, but also the eleven highest officers of the local Cour des Monnaies.[11]

In all the sovereign court towns the robe hotels were under Louis XV, as they had much earlier become in Rennes and Nantes, among the principal sites of aristocratic mingling. When the Turkish ambassador, Mehemet Effendi, visited Toulouse in 1721, he was lodged at the home of Président aux Enquêtes d'Aguin. There, in the midst of paintings specially executed by Rivals and with a military guard of honor surrounding the establishment, the noblesse of Languedoc came to pay its respects to the visitor and his host.[12] Even in remote Navarre, the Marquis de Franclieu discovered that by the 1740's

> one could be quite satisfied in Pau. Madame la Présidente de Gassion, for example, is the most accomplished lady I have ever seen. I used to go

[10] Scoraille, "Un lieutenant du Roi en Haute Auvergne," 378.

[11] Bib. Méjanes, Ms. 565 (39).

[12] J.-B. Dubédat, *Histoire du Parlement de Toulouse* (Toulouse, 1885), II, 342-343.

often to her house. There the conversation turned on history, on general news, and on all that concerned the people who had earned her esteem.[13]

No group did more than the high robe to bring Parisian standards of salon society to the provinces.

2

The mounting respect for and acceptance of the magistracy appears puzzling only in terms of the traditional formulation which concentrates on the robe's position vis-à-vis none but the highest circles of Parisian and provincial nobles de race. The weakness of that approach is that it limits its view to a thin band of the most affluent and prestigious aristocrats. The genuine noblesse de race of the eighteenth century has been reliably estimated at only about 5 percent of the nobility;[14] and even within this 5 percent, not all individuals possessed wealth and position to match their proud origins. The rising consideration of the robe bestowed by the social group just above it was all-important for its position; but that position cannot be understood simply in terms of two very limited groups, one portrayed as aspiring, the other, condescending. In order to assign the magistracy its correct place on the scale of prestige, one must visualize as well the horde of infinitely *less* distinguished nobles: poor gentry (some nobles de race, others of recent, usually military, origin), ennobled businessmen, and last but not least, outright usurpers.

A difficult problem in this connection is that of calculating the reciprocal effects of aristocratic standards on public opinion and conversely of popular standards on the thinking of the aristocracy. The literate portion of the early eighteenth century populace devoured fiction concerning the noblesse with an insatiable passion which led one critic to remark in 1749:

> In France roturier novels are scarcely to be seen; they are almost all of high degree; few but are decorated with the name of some land erected into a duchy, marquisate, or county . . . *Les Mémoires du duc de . . . Les aventures de la comtesse de* . . . .[15]

[13] *Mémoires*, 216-217. [14] Kolabinska, *La circulation des élites*, 84.

[15] *Observations sur la littérature moderne* (s. 1, 1749), I, article 8, quoted by F. C. Green, *La peinture des moeurs de la bonne société dans le roman français de 1715 à 1761* (Paris, 1924), 5.

Furthermore, popular attitudes toward various types of aristocrats received expression in the numberless burlesques and ballads preserved in the pages of collectors such as Raunié.[16] The noblesse might pretend to deny the right of the public to shape its internal standards of prestige; but it could not actually escape the effects which general recognition had in establishing a position of honor, nor the seepage of popular esteem or contempt into its own attitudes. In the pages of Saint-Simon, Villars, Luynes, and Richelieu (all dukes) are revealed constantly recurring traces of the people's praise or blame.

Literature and doggerel, if they were to sell, might have to keep close to noble subject matter; but the treatment was by no means necessarily respectful. Ridicule of the hobereau, for example, had constituted a genre in itself ever since the 1660's, when Molière had written his *Monsieur de Pourceaugnac* and Poisson, his *Baron de la Crasse*. In the early eighteenth century the tradition lived on in such popular works as Marivaux' *Vie de Marianne*, La Bataille's *Nouvelle paysanne parvenue*, and Bonneval's *Voyage de Mantes*.[17] The small country squire as an uncouth and poverty-stricken ignoramus appeared as well in tavern songs such as that which concerned itself with a certain

> . . . . gentilhomme de Bauce,
> Qui reste au lit pendant qu'on raccommode ses chausses.[18]

Vaissière has demonstrated the injustice of the popular picture when applied to many individual cases;[19] but to the more affluent sections of the noblesse the hobereau remained what the people had made him: an object of contempt.

The anobli was a more controversial figure. A rich purchaser of lettres de noblesse, whose bourgeois youth was still a matter of first-hand recollection by his contemporaries, might be treated as a ridiculous *Bourgeois gentilhomme;* but in the eighteenth century he was not to be dismissed as simply a clown. His wealth was a fact to be

[16] *Chansonnier historique du XVIIIe siècle.*

[17] For a detailed discussion of the hobereau in literature see Vaissière, *Gentilshommes campagnards*, 261 ff.

[18] René Vallette, "Le mobilier d'un gentilhomme rural au siècle dernier," *Revue de la Société littéraire, artistique et archéologique de la Vendée* (Fontenay-le-Comte, 1884), III, 114.

[19] *Loc. cit.*

taken seriously, both by jealous aristocrats and by resentful commoners who saw him now exempt from taxes which still bore down on them.[20]

It is all too easy to pass from the eighteenth century's increased consciousness of the distinction between noble and roturier to the assumption that nobility as such was becoming inaccessible. Nothing could be further from the truth. The fiscal requirements for entrance were unquestionably excluding many whose ability and ambition made them enemies of existing inequality. The exclusivism of the high noblesse de robe and the old noblesse de race made mere ennoblement only the first step in the long, slow ascent to aristocracy, more narrowly defined. But the rich bourgeois who was willing to invest in prestige for his posterity three or four generations hence and who wished to buy for himself the immediate privileges and exemptions of legal noblesse could do so without difficulty. Between 1732 and 1748, in the Paris area alone, there were 1,207 payments of finances for ennoblement or confirmation (often the same thing applied retroactively to prior usurpation).[21] For other evidences of activity, one can peruse Campardon's two-volume catalogue of such letters patent registered in the Paris Cour des Aides.[22] And in provincial archives there are ennoblements recorded for almost every month of every year. At Bordeaux in August 1733, for example, royal letters were registered in favor of Joseph Dupin (shipper), Pierre-Noël Saincric (wholesaler), Jean-Baptiste de Maignol (lawyer), and Pierre de Kater (merchant, naturalized Hollander).[23]

Even after giving up their direct commercial activities such men as these stood infinitely lower on the social ladder than did magistrates whose families had been noble under Mazarin or before. But at least the bona fide anobli possessed an unimpeachable claim to legal recognition. How many other "nobles" had no basis for their assumed rank except forged genealogies and fraudulent coats of arms! Here, in the

[20] Lower class resentment of anoblis was still extremely active in 1789. In a cahier of Vic-le-Comte for that year, we read: "C'est une bien mauvaise dénomination d'appeler noble cette noblesse factice qui n'est que le prix de l'or et le fruit de la fortune." Quoted by Jalenques, "La noblesse d'Auvergne," 74-75.

[21] A.N., Q^3. 90-92.

[22] This meticulous compilation exists only in manuscript at the Archives Nationales. The Cour des Aides' extracts are in A.N., Z^{1A}. 134-144 and 524-633.

[23] A.D. Gironde, IB. 45.

usurper, is reached the bottom of the scale of apparent nobility. The eighteenth-century Frenchman, whether roturier or aristocrat, was acutely conscious of the ease with which a clever man could become ennobled in the course of a move from let us say Provence to Champagne, with the aid of a little documentary improvisation by a hired scribe.[24] Contemporary publications were full of such stories: Mauvillon's *Soldat parvenu*, Mouhy's *Paysanne parvenue*, Magny's *Spectacles nocturnes*, Marivaux' *Prince travesti*, to mention only a few of the countless examples, all featured real or suspected usurpers. That tireless publicist, the Abbé de Saint-Pierre, proposed the establishment of special bureaus attached to the various intendancies, simply to investigate frauds and to supervise the official registration of genuinely noble births.[25] Royal prosecution, inspired by the need to prevent tax evasion and to protect the sale value of lettres de noblesse, was less publicized than it had been under Louis XIV;[26] and the machinery of the Grande Recherche was abandoned in 1729. Nevertheless, it still required two thick folio volumes to record the routine *Relevés d'amendes pour usurpation de noblesse* in the eighteenth century.[27]

In order to place the position of sovereign court officers in better perspective it has been necessary to visualize, as contemporaries did, the poorer gentry, the anoblis, and the usurpers trailing away beneath them. Once it is apparent that the high robe and the aristocratic circles it was invading constituted *in combination* an especially honorific level of the nobility, the invasion itself becomes much less surprising.

3

The heightened social standing of the magistrates could scarcely fail to be reflected in their own attitudes and manner of living. First of all, by the 1740's they no longer poured forth those elaborate polemics against the noblesse d'épée which had appeared in abundance

[24] A.-L. Fontaine, "Une usurpation de noblesse," *Journal de la Société d'archéologie lorraine* (Nancy, 1897 and 1900), XLVI, 176-182 and XLIV, 80-92, is an interesting bit of documentary detective work on a fraud of just this type.

[25] Chérin, *La noblesse considérée sous ses différents rapports*, I, 45. Chérin was himself a councilor in the Paris Cour des Aides.

[26] See above, 13-14.

[27] B.N., Mss. fr. nouv. acq. 22357-22358.

under Louis XIV and until the prestige conflicts of the Regency had subsided. Gone from public debate were the bombastic claims of robe superiority and the heavy scorn which once had sought to conceal the defensive insecurity beneath an aggressive surface.

Not that the hauteur of the robe had become any less pronounced. Professional pretensions had in some instances reached ridiculous heights, as revealed in the Portail correspondence of 1731 to 1740 concerning the claims of the first presidents to be styled "Monseigneur," even by princes of the blood.[28] And the parlementaires of Brittany modestly described themselves as the "chevaliers de Malte de la robe."[29] This pride, however, was no longer the by-product of resistance to pretensions of the sword. The high robe was more and more inclined to take for granted its own nobility and to direct its aspersions at groups below itself.

In this respect, the general attitude of the magistrates had come to coincide with First President Brulart's reference to the town officers of Dijon, "ces bourgeois . . . sans autorité et sans considération."[30] I have already noted that sovereign court remonstrances embodied aristocratic attacks on newly risen financiers. When the Parlement of Languedoc lashed out in 1720 at "cette abondance chez des hommes que nous avons vu s'elever parmi nous et qui nous etoient jusqu'a lors inconnus,"[31] it was speaking for an established nobility against a pressure which was as menacing in the social sphere as was royal policy in the political. Common enmities were doing their work of strengthening common interests.

Hand in hand with this shift in class outlook went changes in the magistracy's way of life which stemmed partly from the desire to conform to older aristocratic standards, especially in seigneurial living,

[28] A.N., K. 703, nos. 4-12. Voltaire has an amusing section on robe pride in his *Dictionnaire philosophique* (vol. XVIII of his *Oeuvres complètes*, Paris, 1878), 116. He points out that by the 1760's even the présidents à mortier and councilors were imitating the peers in their demand to be addressed as "Messeigneurs." One councilor of the Paris Grand' Chambre showed himself more sensible, however; for on one occasion when an avocat had begun his pleading with "Monseigneur, monsieur votre secrétaire . . . ," the jurist cut him short by snorting: "You have committed three blunders in three words—I am not 'monseigneur,' my secretary is not 'monsieur,' and he is not a secretary, he is my clerk!"

[29] Saulnier, *Parlement de Bretagne*, lix.

[30] E.F. de La Cuisine, *Esquisses dijonnaises* (Dijon, 1850), 29-30.

[31] A.N., K. 713, no. 4 *bis*.

but which also reflected the robe's assimilation of and reciprocal influence upon the rules of a more elegant urban society. Bastard d'Estang has left an admiring account of a typical souvereign court officer's daily routine: early audiences at the palais, mass by the company's chaplain, commission meetings, study of evidence and precedents relating to cases on the docket, editing of arrêts, visits to prisons, distribution of alms, and perhaps a quiet supper at home, followed by an evening spent in sober contemplation of the Roman law or some classic author.[32] This Spartan regime, however, though it may still have applied to a few of the most conscientious among early eighteenth-century presidents and councilors, is hardly the norm revealed in contemporary documents.

Considering the rise in the standards of pleasant living since the crude days of a century earlier, one would scarcely expect the parlementaires to have denied themselves the creature comforts which their economic position made possible. The households described above, in connection with the robe fortune, were designed for something more than the routine Bastard d'Estang portrays. It did not require a cook and two helpers to give the master breakfast before a pre-dawn departure to his chores, nor a maître d'hôtel and several lackeys to set out a volume of Livy for fireside reading when he returned home.

The officers of the Parlement of Paris spent their five months' exile at Pontoise in 1720 amid banquets, gaming, and entertainments, both musical and dramatic. The magistrates' chamber music group consisted of the two La Landes (violins), President de Lubert (clavecin), and Councilor Roujault (bass viol), abetted by several hired performers. In the house loaned to him by the Duc d'Albret, First President de Mesmes gave daily feasts for forty or more of his colleagues, with the aid of seafood and creamery products supplied by wagons which were diverted from their normal route to Paris.[33] In this society the premier's hospitality set a standard for emulation; it was unique only in degree.

The bottle and the baize-covered table had a share in more than one eighteenth-century robe nobleman's existence which must have tortured the shades of his Jansenist forebears. In a satirical account

[32] *Les parlements de France*, I, 198 ff.

[33] A.N., U. 747, Journal du Parlement séant à Pontoise; Barbier, *Journal*, I, 188-189.

of the Dijon parlementaires' adoration of the Christ Child one reads numerous verses such as the following:

> Courtivron comme un arlequin
> Y vint en habit tout de pièces
> Mais n'ayant point trouvé de vin
> Soudain il tomba en faiblesse.[34]

Some of the old frugality lingered in the habits of many cooler magistrates, who now would spend for luxuries but would not join in that wild bravado of risk which sought to bring battlefield virtues to the baccarat game. "It is said," noted Pöllnitz in the 1730's, "that the jurists are less subject to this contagion."[35] Yet the robe noblemen who had gained admission to salon society could not wholly escape its fads, including that of gambling; and some, including President Hénault, did not even attempt to do so.[36]

Standards of sexual conduct, of course, played a large part in the era's definition of elegant living; and in this department of polite existence the eighteenth-century magistrate showed himself the equal, mistress for mistress, of any other nobleman. The Dijon satire quoted at the top of this page specifies, in execrable rhyme, some professional implications of non-professional appetites:

> Lantenay dit pour mes amis
> Je renverse Loix et Coutumes,
> Mais c'est bien pis, quand il s'agit
> De servir la Blonde ou la Brune.[37]

The judge might, of course, be victim rather than exploiter, as a Bordeaux versifier suggests in warning Président de Pommiers that he is playing the cuckold in favor of his own brother;[38] and in 1726 Président aux Requêtes Lambert de Torigny at Paris, avowed lover of Madame la Première Présidente Portail, had the misfortune to

[34] A.D. Côte d'Or, B. 12175 *bis*, Relation de tous les Compliments et Discours faits par MM. du Parlement de Dijon à l'Enfant Jésus, le Jour de Sa Naissance en 1720.

[35] *Mémoires*, III, 174.

[36] In 1720 the Marquis de Balleroy wrote to his wife: "They say that Madame La Riche, now that she has a son councilor at the Parlement of Paris . . . no longer knows who she is and cannot find a game big enough to suit her." *Correspondants de la Marquise de Balleroy*, II, 212.

[37] A.D. Côte d'Or, B. 12175 *bis*.

[38] Bib. Bordeaux, Ms. 713, Bernadau papers, XLIII, 37-40.

catch from her a fatal case of smallpox. (His ignominious death in the house of her husband made him the object of considerable posthumous sympathy.)[39] In general, however, the robe nobleman seems to have abided by the canons of aristocratic love without suffering any more than its other devotees: Councilor de Brégis could feel honored to see his daughter, Madame d'Averne, become one of the Regent's long series of mistresses;[40] and Councilor Antoine-Nicolas Nicolay de Goussainville, who had "wit, good sense, and a probity which seems ferocious in this century," lived contentedly with Madame Pinon for ten years before his death in 1731.[41]

The evolution of physical appearance is not easy to document; but the various collections of magistral portraits are nonetheless interesting for what they show of the high robe's conception of itself. I have already mentioned the series of Secondats who line the walls of Montesquieu's salon at La Brède.[42] The same gradual change in expression, in pose, and above all in what the subjects wanted shown of their characters impresses the beholder of the long row of paintings in the gallery of first presidents in the Palais de Justice at Toulouse.

Among the manuscripts in the Bibliothèque Méjanes at Aix, one may study a volume showing Jacques Cundier's engravings of first presidents of the Provençal Parlement: Riccio, Beaumont, Chassannée of the early sixteenth century, with their broad, clean-shaven faces and close-cropped hair; Maynier and Foresta, with the pointed, Italianate beards of the 1550's to 1580's; du Vair, glowering from behind his square "Navarre whiskers" in 1600; the two Forbins, L'Aisné, and Bernet, stubborn countenances adorned with mustachios and goatees of the Richelieu era; Marin, with the small Ludovican mustache and hair in long, soft curls; and finally the Le Brets, father and son, with calm yet haughty faces, clean-shaven, wigged with heavy perukes of the early eighteenth century.[43] Had Cundier gone beyond the Regency period, he would have shown a final stage which is to be seen elsewhere: the less formidable, more refined features of Louis XV portraiture, with smooth powdered hair and perhaps an artificial mole at one corner of the mouth. The older

[39] Barbier, *Journal*, I, 241. [40] *Ibid.*, I, 90.

[41] Barbier, *Journal*, I, 349. See Marais, *Journal*, I, 277 and *passim.*, for other examples.

[42] See above, 138. [43] Bib. Méjanes, Ms. 951 (963).

professional virtues of equity, sternness, and somewhat ponderous honesty had yielded to other qualities which the eighteenth-century magistrate preferred to see looking down from his own likeness: haughty poise, refinement of taste, and sensitivity to forms of expression beyond the reach of roturier comprehension. Cato could scarcely remain as idol where Ovid was enthroned.

4

After all this discussion of mutations, there still remains the question: what was left of the robe-épée line by mid-century? I have suggested that in the urban society of Paris and the provincial centers having sovereign courts it had become socially blurred and politically all but meaningless. In published writings of nobles de race—admittedly, these literate ones were the most likely to be on cordial terms with magistrates—it survived in only a handful of atypical passages reminiscent of Saint-Simon's diatribes. In rural areas, where jealousy and a desperate clinging to remembered honors combined to keep the hobereaux hostile, it still produced bad feeling, but bad feeling directed primarily against the officers of the scattered lower courts. So far as the high robe was concerned, in other words, within what I have called the politically significant aristocracy, its external marks were scarcely visible save at Versailles.

There, in the king's immediate surroundings, were still to be found special honors reserved to the oldest noblesse de race or the greatest among nobles d'épée, regardless of lineage. Sovereign court officers, it is true, now appeared in those surroundings with growing frequency. The first president of the Parlement of Paris had New Year's dinner with Louis XV and the princes of the blood in 1725, for example; and he was one of the 120 noblemen who had places on the official roster of "Logement du Château de Marly" that year and again in 1731.[44] Such magistrate-diplomats as Claude-Antoine Boquet de Courbouzon (councilor at Besançon)[45] or Councilor de Chateauneuf of the Paris Parlement (ambassador successively to Portugal, the Sublime

[44] B.N., Ms. fr. nouv. acq. 9641.

[45] Estignard, *Le Parlement de Franche-Comté*, II, 123-125.

Porte, and Holland)[46] came and went in the royal establishments with perfect ease.

Nevertheless, they suffered from certain disabilities which survived as long as the old monarchy itself. For example, they might hold administrative offices attached to the royal Ordre du Saint-Esprit and in such cases were authorized to wear a distinctive variant of the *cordon bleu;*[47] but in the rolls of regular Chevaliers du Saint-Esprit there was not one high robe officer inscribed in the eighteenth century.[48] Similarly, the 323 persons listed by the *Petite Écurie* at one time or another between 1715 and 1748 as eligible to ride with the king in his own carriage included the princes and princesses of the blood, most of the peers, marshals, the highest ministers, and numerous army officers, but no regular member of a sovereign court.[49] D'Aguesseau and Chauvelin had their "entrées de carrosse" as ministers, not as former magistrates. Carré points out that in the 1780's the wives of robe officials were still staying away from the court because they could not be honored with the king's (ceremonial) kiss—only with a "simple greeting."[50]

These, however, were gauzy barriers indeed. The condescension of courtiers, like the resentment of hobereaux, counted for little in the position of the high robe as dramatized in the various settings which had real importance for the class: in public ceremonies, in the salons and academies, in the provincial estates, and in the sovereign courts themselves. The line which still existed between the robe and the sword in the mid-eighteenth century can never be understood purely in terms of ceremonial rules and verbal niceties. It lay much more in the residual margin of difference in ways of life. For as marked as had been the magistracy's assimilation of seigneurial interests and salon manners, there remained certain characteristics peculiar to the the parlementaires.

[46] Barbier, *Journal*, I, 33, note 1.

[47] A.N., K. 619, no. 6. In 1717 First President de Mesmes of the Parlement and First President Camus of the Cour des Aides were provosts of the order, while parlementary Président à mortier de Lamoignon and First President de Verthamon of the Grand Conseil were among its five greffiers.

[48] A. Teulet, *Liste chronologique et alphabétique des chevaliers de l'ordre du Saint-Esprit, 1578-1830* (Paris, 1864).

[49] A.N., MM. 817. [50] *La fin des parlements*, 17.

Most obvious of the surviving distinctions were those growing out of the high robe's professional status and organization. No matter how lax a president, councilor or maître des comptes might be about his judicial functions, no matter how inclined to recognize only their prestige value, he was still a titular judge in one of the high courts of French justice. He might never appear except at great ceremonies and might never be seen outside the palais in a robe; but he still wore the rabat above his brocaded waistcoat, still took pride in his official title as well as in his landed one, still jealously guarded his right to sit in a secret assembly which was forbidden ground to the haughtiest non-robe marquis or count. Finally, he had one further attribute which set him apart from most other noblemen: his education.

It would be all too easy to let one's view of magistral education remain fixed on some of its most imposing products: Montesquieu, for example, or Jean Bouhier, président à mortier in the Parlement of Burgundy, student of Greek literature, author of the authoritative *Coutume de Bourgogne*,[51] and predecessor of Voltaire in the Académie Française.[52] One is tempted perhaps to overweight the cases of President de Brosses, Bouhier's younger colleague in Dijon (he entered the Parlement in 1730), historian, geographer, friend of Buffon;[53] President de Valbonnais of the Grenoble Chambre des Comptes, author of the *Histoire du Dauphiné*,[54] member of the Académie Royale des Inscriptions et Belles-Lettres;[55] and Jean II de Castellan, conseiller clerc in the Parlement of Languedoc, son of an old Toulouse robe family, author of *Les antiquités de l'Église de Valence* in 1724, as well as works on jurisprudence.

Even if the above examples must be treated as atypical, however, it is impossible not to be struck by a literary circle such as that which met at Dijon in the 1730's and 1740's: Bouhier and de Brosses, President Legouz de Saint-Seine, Councilors Loppin, Bernard de Blancey, de Migieu, Fevret de Fontette, and Procureur-général Quarré de Quintin (all of the Parlement), Presidents Rigoley de

[51] (Dijon, 1717).

[52] Charles des Guerrois, *Le président Bouhier* (Paris, 1855).

[53] Henri Mamet, *Le président de Brosses* (Lille, 1874).

[54] (Geneva, 1722).

[55] Bib. Grenoble, O. 10045 (printed), *Éloge de M. le Président de Valbonnays;* O. 10044 (printed), *Vie de Messire Jean-Pierre de Valbonnais* (s. 1, 1732).

Migeon and Richard de Ruffey of the Chambre des Comptes.[56] In the public library of Dijon, itself founded by the bequest of a Fevret in 1701, one may read Councilor Devoyo's translations from Erasmus[57] and Councilor Jehannin's from Shaftesbury,[58] Councilor Fleutelot's *Voyage en Provence*,[59] and Councilor Bazin's *Remarques sur les auteurs latins*.[60]

These and similar examples elsewhere illustrate the dual nature of robe writing under Louis XV: on the one hand, a faithful continuation of seventeenth-century emphasis on classical commentaries or scholarly histories; on the other hand, a growing admixture of favorite eighteenth-century subjects, such as travel, science, new political ideas, belles-lettres. The same combination is to be seen in the catalogues of robe libraries, some of them huge collections: Valbonnais' at Grenoble,[61] Councilor de La Mare's, Councilor de Chevigny's or President Bouhier's at Dijon,[62] and Montesquieu's, much of it still on its original shelves at La Brède. The transmission of such libraries forms an important chapter in the history of modern French collections, as one realizes when reading the names of principal donors inscribed in the foyer of the Bibliothèque Municipale of Bordeaux: eleven in all, including for this period Jean Jacques Bel (the founder in 1720), Godefroye de Baritault, François de La Montaigne—all councilors in the Parlement of Guienne—President Jean Barbot of the Cour des Aides, and Montesquieu himself. Burgundian Councilor Fevret de Fontette's huge accumulation of prints is one of the richest *fonds* in the Bibliothèque Nationale's Cabinet des Estampes, and Jourdain's *Journal* of eighteenth-century additions to the Bibliothèque Royale is filled with references to acquisitions from such libraries as President Lambert's.[63]

56 André Bourrée, "La société dijonnaise vers le milieu du XVIIIe siècle," *Mémoires de l'Académie des Sciences, Arts et Belles-Lettres de Dijon* (Dijon), vol. 1927-1931, 197-217.

57 Bib. Dijon, Ms. 256 (Ancien 202[3]).

58 Bib. Dijon, Ms. 531 (Ancien 303).

59 Bib. Dijon, Ms. 982 (Baudot 65).

60 Bib. Dijon, Ms. 1114 (Baudot 164).

61 Bib. Grenoble, Ms. 1263 (R. 6254).

62 Bib. Dijon, Ms. 987 (Baudot 70), fol. 16 ff. for La Mare; fol. 29 ff. for Chevigny; fol. 43 ff. for Bouhier. Also Ms. 1112 (Baudot 162) for the Catalogus Librorum of Councilor Bazin.

63 B.N., Ms. fr. nouv. acq. 6516.

The characteristic subject matter of the new era emerges most clearly, however, from the robe scholars' correspondence. There, in the thick, yellowed bundles, are displayed the omnivorous interest and amazing epistolary productivity which we associate with the Enlightenment. Science and religion, politics and painting, society gossip and literary criticism, all were grist for the letter-writer's mill. Here is Justus Fontanini writing to Valbonnais from Rome,[64] there, Bouhier to the Abbé d'Olivet or to Mathieu Marais (to the latter at least once every fortnight for five years),[65] and there, La Mare to Du Cange, Heinsius or Pierre Gassendi.[66]

The mere citation of *érudits*, though it could be spun out to great length, would still not make clear the whole contrast between robe and sword in terms of literacy. Some members of the noblesse d'épée also wrote, with the learning of Boulainvilliers or the subtlety of Vauvenargues. Boulainvilliers' library too contained thousands of volumes, chiefly history and astrology,[67] while that left by the Marquise de Vielbourg had to be catalogued under 306 subject headings, including theology, Italian history, diplomatic history, geometry, astronomy, and parlementary remonstrances.[68] It is rather in the education of an average noble d'épée in the 1740's, as opposed to that of a typical noble de robe, that evidence emerges of the latter's superiority in this important aspect of both social and political life.

In the Archives Nationales there is a memorandum addressed to the king in 1750 and largely devoted to an appeal to rescue the old aristocracy from a system of education "so neglected, so defective, one can even say so evil, that to it alone must be attributed the paucity of outstanding servants which the state has a right to expect from [the nobility]." In the anonymous writer's view, "the education of youth among us still shows the effects of the grossness of barbarous ages."[69] For a large part of the gentry this gloomy diagnosis was all too accurate. Tutors who would come to remote and perhaps dilapidated manors, there to labor for little beyond board and room, were apt to be at best incompetent and at worst corrupting. The Marquis

[64] B.N., Ms. fr. nouv. acq. 3543.

[65] B.N., Mss. fr. 24409-24421; Marais, *Journal*, I, 62–63. (Volume IV of this *Journal* contains dozens of these letters.)

[66] B.N., Ms. fr. 24423. [67] Buvat, *Journal*, II, 171, note 1.

[68] A.N., U. 1013. [69] A.N., H. 1459.

de Franclieu, having just expelled a tutor for having seduced a chambermaid while completely neglecting his pupils, wrote sadly:

I think things would be different if we could keep our children in the good colleges at Paris, but how can a father of such a family as mine [ten children] arrange to have his children educated far from home?[70]

Even in the wealthier noble families education was apt to be viewed as little more than training in social accomplishments; and a young aristocrat could pass through one of the many Jesuit colleges with nothing to show for it but improved manners, the ability to dance, perhaps the knack of writing bad poetry, and in any case a set of success values considered appropriate to a career at court and in the army.[71] The Marquis de Valfons has left an account of how his father had sent him up from Languedoc to the Collège des Jésuites at Paris in 1719. Less than a year-and-a-half later "one of my uncles, major in the cavalry and a friend of the Comte d'Evreux, secured me a lieutenancy in the Regency Horse"—his formal education was at an end.[72]

Boulainvilliers was one of those nobles d'épée who had made the most of his schooling, in his case at the Oratorian College of Juilly. The note inserted by the publisher in his *Essais sur la noblesse de France* (1732), however, speaks volumes concerning the class as a whole:

M. de Boulainvilliers takes for granted in his readers a more profound knowledge of our History than is generally to be found among the rank and file [*commun*] of the Nobility, especially in the Provinces & the Country. Their responsibilities, the care of their property, often just the earning of a livelihood, and finally, their differing talents do not permit us to picture them as normally devoted to study & reading.[73]

To find any large group of noblemen who could read Boulainvilliers with interest and appreciation, it would be necessary to go not to his beloved gentry but to the magistracy.

[70] *Mémoires*, 219 ff. concern this incident.

[71] Sagnac, *Formation de la société française*, II, 41 applies this description even to Jesuit schools like Louis-le-Grand. It is only fair to point out that the rare aristocrat who went to one of these colleges with the serious intention of learning seems to have been able to obtain a solid education.

[72] *Souvenirs* (ed. Marquis de Valfons and G. Maruin, Paris, 1860), 1-2.

[73] *Op. cit.*, ix-x.

No doubt the decline of sovereign court standards in the eighteenth century had its effect on the seriousness of robe education. The new generation of magistrates no longer had the careful grounding which Oratorian, Jesuit, but most of all, Jansenist teachers had given so many of their fathers. Against the cases of scholars such as de Brosses and Valbonnais must be set those of indolent sons of secure robe houses, young men who went through the motions of a legal education with no intention of putting its substance to any real use. The schooling which had once been a priceless means of social and political advancement had become for many a professional adornment.

Nevertheless, the robe as a class never lost its tradition of interest in and close connection with the universities, each of which was a corporation responsible solely to the king *and* to the parlement of its province.[74] On occasion a court might assert its authority over a university, as when the Parlement of Franche-Comté denounced the rector at Besançon for having claimed criminal jurisdiction over his students.[75] But just as frequently it was as the protector of higher learning that a sovereign company took the field. Had the Parlement of Burgundy not successfully fought those of Paris and Franche-Comté (defending their own schools) all the way to the royal council,

[74] The following list indicates the system of parlementary supervision of universities:

Parlements	*Universities*
Paris	Paris, Orléans, Bourges, Angers, Poitiers, Reims
Languedoc	Toulouse-Cahors, Montpellier
Dauphiné	Grenoble-Valence
Guienne	Bordeaux
Burgundy	Dijon
Normandy	Caen
Provence	Aix
Navarre	Pau
Brittany	Nantes
Metz	Pont-à-Mousson
Franche-Comté	Besançon
Flanders	Douai
Roussillon	Perpignan

Cf. Bastard d'Estang, *Les parlements de France*, I, 504 ff. The University of Strasbourg, the only Protestant center of higher learning in France, remained under the direct control of the municipal government.

[75] B.N., Ms. fr. nouv. acq. 8795, fol. 434 ff.

the University of Dijon could not have made its modest beginning with a faculty of law in 1722.[76]

In the 1740's a future robe officer was still expected to complete at least two years' work in law at a university after finishing college-level preparation in philosophy and the classics. Even the dullest or laziest could scarcely emerge without having picked up some advantages over the needy sons of the gentry. The young magistrates' performances might differ widely, but it is impossible to deny the opportunities provided them by the wealth of their fathers and the traditions of their caste.[77]

I have permitted myself this digression on learning, at the end of a chapter on social assimilation, because it is essential to bear in mind this fundamental factor in the robe-épée distinction as it survived in the late 1740's. The noble de robe had gained admission to salon circles; he suffered far less than had his forefathers from the slurs of other aristocrats, who now joined him in ridiculing the hobereaux and despising the anoblis. But he was still officially a guardian of the law, a member of a tightly-knit professional corporation; and he was better educated than any but a handful of non-magistral noblemen. in that combination of remaining peculiarities lay the key both to the political importance of the robe and its special role in the intellectual development of the aristocratic position.

[76] A.D. Côte d'Or, B. 12208.

[77] For a discussion of robe education at Dijon, see Marcel Bouchard, *De l'humanisme à l'Encyclopédie. L'esprit public en Bourgogne sous l'Ancien régime* (Paris, 1930). Enlightening comments with regard to Paris are to be found running through the *Lettres inédites* of Chancellor d'Aguesseau (ed. D. B. Rives, Paris, 1823), in his letters to his two sons working for their *licences* there.

Chapter Twelve

The Restatement of the Thèse Nobiliaire

1

OUT OF THE GROWING social fusion within the French aristocracy came a corresponding amalgamation of doctrines. The newly won political leadership of the high robe within the noblesse found its parallel in the realm of ideas. For it was a parlementaire, writing in the 1740's under conditions very different from those of only a quarter-century earlier, who gave a powerful restatement to the theory of monarchy limited by group privileges. Into this restatement went traditional arguments previously as much at variance with one another as with the claims of absolute kingship. Into it too went observations on the English constitution as it had emerged from the crises of the seventeenth century. With no more than her customary obliqueness, history has decreed that Montesquieu should be remembered best as the interpreter of England to France and scarcely at all as the reconciler of feudal and magistral traditions.

Yet this was to be in fact his most important achievement from the point of view of his own class.[1] The developments traced in the preceding chapters had reduced the gap between robe and sword in most respects quite rapidly after 1715, but at the level of political theory two bodies of thought which had co-existed since the sixteenth century at the latest still split the opposition to absolutism in the years just before 1748. Neither had changed its essential form since the Valois epoch; both had been restated in uncomprising terms during the 1720's and 1730's.

[1] No one has more clearly demonstrated Montesquieu's role in this regard than Friedrich Meinecke, *Die Entstehung des Historismus* (Munich-Berlin, 1936), I, 125-193.

On one side stood the parlementary tradition which has been noted in connection with the *Judicium Francorum* and the great remonstrances of the early eighteenth century.[2] Many of the principal arguments there employed had been used by Claude de Seyssel, writing in 1519 that no reliance could be placed on the feudal nobility or its organ, the Estates General, that to the parlements alone was entrusted the maintenance of traditional order and the fundamental rules of justice.[3] By the eighteenth century the Frankish Champ de Mars, central to the historical constructions of Pasquier and Girard Du Haillan in the 1560's,[4] had become a jealously guarded heirloom of the sovereign courts.

Most important of all in the parlementary past were the *Treize livres des parlements de France*, of Toulousain President La Roche Flavin, published at Bordeaux in 1617. In the eyes of its author the parlements were to the state as the soul to a body. They were the heirs of both the Frankish *Märzfelder* and of the Roman Senate. They were also the legal successors to the recently suspended Estates General. Only God, wrote La Roche Flavin, is above the king; but between the king and the people are the parlements, whose members are irremovable and whose verification of legislative enactments is necessary to bind the populace to the law. France, with its mixed government, was not to be confused with a despotism.[5]

Once enunciated, the phrases of the jurist from Toulouse had never relaxed their hold on the magistral mind. They are to be found in the pamphlets of the parlementary Fronde,[6] in countless remonstrances, and in the *Judicium Francorum*. They remained under Louis XV an element which contributed to the ambivalence of the courts' pronouncements. To a magistracy which owed its rise to that of the monarchy, the king had long stood as the supreme legislator, lending

[2] See above, 90 ff.

[3] *La grande monarchie de France* (Paris, 1519). For an excellent analysis of Seyssel's thought, see W. F. Church, *Constitutional Thought in Sixteenth-Century France* (Cambridge, 1941), 22-42. Also, Martin Göhring, *Weg und Sieg der modernen Staatsidee in Frankreich* 66-68.

[4] Étienne Pasquier, *Des recherches de la France*, book 2 (Paris, 1565); Girard du Haillan, *De l'estat et succez des affaires de France* (Paris, 1570).

[5] Church, *Constitutional Thought*, 133, 147.

[6] Such as the *Véritables maximes* of 1652; and Claude Joly's separate though similarly entitled *Recueil de maximes véritables et importantes* of the same year.

grandeur to the functions of the sovereign courts. As late as 1732 the Parlement of Paris still conceded that "We recognize the full extent of Your absolute and sovereign power,"[7] even though it echoed La Roche Flavin in insisting that this power must be exercised through legal channels, through the *corps intermédiaires*. The conflicting tendency took the form of increasingly frequent references to a contractual theory of state, in which feudal concepts and biblical allusions took renewed vigor from the example of England's Glorious Revolution. Here are the words of the Parlement of Brittany, remonstrating in 1718:

> One cannot, Sire, too often place before the eyes of a young sovereign the example of Him whom he represents on earth. The Lord never breached the alliance and treaty which He had made with His people, so long as they remained faithful to His laws and did not seek aid from foreign gods. Your people, Sire, ask of you today the same favor, for their repose, for your glory.[8]

The threat is veiled but unmistakable. Locke has taken his place beside La Roche Flavin.[9]

Quite different from the doctrines of a corps of royal functionaries who had cut themselves adrift from their once total dependence on the crown were the arguments of a class which had felt itself to be the victim of royal usurpation since the medieval Capetians had first begun to tighten, then extend, their grip on the Île de France. The protests of the feudal nobility had been numerous and loud by the time of Saint Louis' minority. In the crisis of 1314-1315, in that of the 1350's, and throughout the anarchy of the Hundred Years' War they had continued. It was their adoption by Huguenot scholars and pamphleteers in the sixteenth century, however, which had first

[7] Flammermont, *Remontrances*, I, 300. Roger Bickart points out that not until the latter half of the eighteenth century did the courts begin openly and consistently to assert that royal authority was not above the law. *Les parlements et la notion de souveraineté nationale au XVIIIe siècle* (Paris, 1932), 13 ff.

[8] A.N., K. 712, no. 65 *bis*.

[9] Concerning parlementary theory in eighteenth-century France, see André Lemaire, *Les lois fondamentales de la monarchie française d'après les théoriciens de l'ancien régime* (Paris, 1907); Henri Sée, "La doctrine politique des parlements au XVIIIe siècle," *Revue historique de droit français et étranger*, 4th series (Paris, 1924), III, 287-306.

placed them on a standing of intellectual parity with the claims of the magistracy.

The greatest single effort to combine Protestant theories of resistance with those of the non-robe nobility appeared when François Hotman published his *Francogallia* two years after Saint Bartholomew.[10] For Hotman the history of the French monarchy had been one of degeneration from the free society established by the Franks after their expulsion of the oppressive Romans. Here was the Germanist theory in all its rigor, crediting the Franks with the institution of an elective kingship, guided by public-spirited councilors and responsible to annual assemblies of warriors. Conversely, of course, it blamed the re-Romanization of the state under the Capetians for the loss of these salutary features.[11] It was not the sovereign courts, too Catholic for the Calvinist author and too deeply involved in royal aggrandizement, which could claim descent from the Champ de Mars.[12] Instead it was the Estates General and, above all, the nobility. To Hotman, as to the author of the *Vindiciae contra tyrannos* of 1579, *optimates* meant feudal rather than parlementary magistrates, though both Du Haillan, in his later writings, and Loyseau reflected early influences of *Francogallia* on the magistral viewpoint.[13]

Not all eighteenth-century thought in this succession had descended from Protestant polemics, of course. Henri Estienne and Olivier de Serres, contemporaries of Hotman, had hated Catherine de Medici for what she had done to the gentry rather than for what she had permitted to be done to the Huguenots.[14] The Duc de Montpensier's proposal of 1595 had been a prescription for unadulterated feudal decentralization, with the governors general to rule their provinces and to serve the king as had the great vassals of the middle ages.[15] The cahier of the noblesse at the 1614 Estates General (where, it will be remembered, the parlementaires still sat as part of the Third Estate) survived as a list of grievances against the pride of office-

[10] (Cologne, 1574), in both Latin and French. (English edition, tr. Robert Molesworth, London, 1711, 1721, and later dates.)

[11] *Francogallia*, ch. 10.

[12] *Ibid.*, ch. 21.

[13] Church, *Constitutional Thought*, 88, 203.

[14] Vaissière, *Gentilshommes campagnards*, 192 ff.

[15] Hintze, *Staatseinheit und Föderalismus*, 39, 511.

holders, the insolence of peasants, and the inconvenience of royal restrictions on seigneurial rights.[16] Finally, the memoirs of Cardinal de Retz offered readers of the Regency period a record of the nobles' Fronde in the time of Mazarin.

Yet the Protestant influence remained important, especially after the transfusion administered by post-1685 exiles such as Pierre Jurieu and the author of the *Soupirs de la France esclave*.[17] In that famous series of tracts the souvereign courts occasionally receive a word of sympathy as fellow-sufferers under Ludovican tyranny, but more often they are abused as victims of a monster they had themselves helped to create. In general, the arguments are those of Hotman, brought up to date by the addition of a lament for the failure of the Fronde, which "might have made France the happiest kingdom in the world," and by timely references to the English revolution which had just restored the government of that fortunate island to a sound, aristocratic basis.

To complete the set of feudal theorists at the disposal of the early eighteenth century aristocrat, one must include Fénelon, Saint-Simon, and Boulainvilliers, all of whom derived at least part of their importance from the good will of Louis XIV's grandson, the Duc de Bourgogne.[18] If the *Télémaque* was primarily the work of a churchman and moralist lecturing his royal pupil, the so-called *Tables de Chaulnes* of 1711 were much more, for they embody the principal contributions of Fénelon to the tradition here under discussion.[19] In the *Tables* he steps forth as the proponent of contractual kingship, the champion of the Estates General, and the enlightened critic of both venality of offices and seigneurial excesses. But he is also the feudal enthusiast,

[16] Chérin, *La noblesse considérée*, part 2, 193-230.

[17] (S. 1., 1689-1690). Gotthold Riemann, *Der Verfasser der "Soupirs de la France esclave qui aspire après la liberté"* (Kiel, 1937); Henri Sée, *L'évolution de la pensée politique en France au XVIIIe siècle* (Paris, 1925), 22; and Göhring, *Weg und Sieg*, 119, all agree that the *Soupirs* was probably written by Michel Le Vassor, a former Oratorian priest. See also Guy Howard Dodge, *The Political Theory of the Huguenots of the Dispersion, with Special Reference to the Thought and Influence of Pierre Jurieu* (New York, 1947).

[18] G. Tréca, *Les doctrines et les réformes de droit public en réaction contre l'absolutisme de Louis XIV dans l'entourage du duc de Bourgogne* (Paris, 1909).

[19] The actual title of this memorandum is *Plans de gouvernement concertés avec le duc de Chevreuse pour être proposés au duc de Bourgogne*, in Fénelon's *Oeuvres complètes* (ed. Gosselin, Paris, 1850), VII, 182-186.

proud of his own rank and family, anxious to provide for the education, honorific recognition, and political utilization of noblemen. He is no more a friend of the parlements than of absolute monarchy.[20]

These latter characteristics of Fénelon's complex attitude stand almost alone in Saint-Simon's far narrower one. They dominate his reactions to political events as seen in his *Mémoires* and receive explicit formulation in many of his *Écrits inédits*.[21] From thousands of pages of deft but often inconsequential prose emerge Saint-Simon's opposition to religious persecution (easily his most attractive intellectual trait), his demand for an ordered hierarchy of titled ranks, his loathing for bourgeois ministers and robe magistrates, his almost pathological pride in the dignity of the peerage.

The real standard-bearer of feudal doctrine at the third and fourth decades of the eighteenth century, however, was neither an archbishop nor a duke, but an impecunious, unusually erudite Norman gentleman, Henri de Boulainvilliers, Comte de Saint-Saire. Even before his death in 1722 he was widely known as an amateur scientist and as the author of a highly praised life of Mohammed; but it was his posthumously published works, appearing in the 1720's and '30's, which made his name the symbol for the *thèse nobiliaire* prior to 1748.[22] Boulainvilliers' historical vision was essentially that of Hotman; but he placed more emphasis than had any of his predecessors on individual rights, such as seigneurial justice, hereditary fief tenure, and exemption from taxes, which he insisted had been won by the free Frankish warriors in their conquest of Gaul. The eighteenth-century

[20] For an analysis of Fénelon's influence on widely separated thinkers who followed him, see Albert Chérel, *Fénelon au XVIIIe siècle en France (1715-1820): Son prestige, son influence* (Paris, 1917). Discussions of his own thought include Georges Flamand, *Les idées politiques et sociales de Fénelon* (Grenoble, 1932); Élie Carcassonne, *Fénelon, l'homme et l'oeuvre* (Paris, 1946); and Henri Sée, "Les idées politiques de Fénelon," *Revue d'histoire moderne et contemporaine* (Paris, 1900), I, 545-565.

[21] See also his *Projets de gouvernement résolus par M. le duc de Bourgogne, dauphin, après y avoir mûrement pensé* (ed. Paul Mesnard, Paris, 1860); and Henri Sée, "Les idées politique du duc de Saint-Simon," *Revue historique* (Paris, 1900), LXXIII, 1-23.

[22] His principal writings on the nobility and the government were: *Mémoires présentés au duc d'Orléans* (The Hague, 1727), 2 vols.; *Histoire de l'ancien gouvernement de la France, avec XIV lettres historiques sur les Parlements ou États généraux* (The Hague, 1727, also London, 1727, under a slightly different title); *Essais sur la noblesse de France* (Amsterdam, 1732); *État de la France* (London, 1737), 6 vols., especially the author's introduction.

nobility, he argued, could claim descent from the Franks, while roturiers had inherited the Gallo-Romans' liabilities.

Capetian rule, of course, he portrays as having usurped the authority of the noblesse and having done violence to a constitution based on an aristocratic council, which is what Boulainvilliers means when he speaks of the Frankish "parlement." He blames Saint Louis for having bankrupted his vassals with his crusades and Louis XI for having been "the first to draw about himself . . . men of small estate."[23] As for Louis XIV's reign, it had been "despotic, money-minded, very long, and consequently odious."[24] For Boulainvilliers feudalism remained what "we may regard as the masterpiece of the human mind."[25] Small wonder that he could exclaim concerning the monarchy:

> It is astonishing that nowadays it is thought fitting to treat it as founded on the absolute power of the prince, without hearkening to the testimony of thirteen centuries during which we see the kingdom established solely by the blood, the labor, and the expenditures of the old nobility.[26]

Just as in the sixteenth century Hotman and Pasquier had stood for two theories almost as much at odds with each other as with Bodin's indivisible sovereignty, so in the early eighteenth the writings of Boulainvilliers and the claims of the sovereign courts maintained the distinction between feudal and parlementary doctrines. The two were not, of course, mutually exclusive. In both cases the Ludovican experience and the example of revolutionary England had left their marks on the original positions;[27] and both relied heavily on the historical argument from the Franks. The Roman senate had long fascinated the parlementaires—given their Romanist legal background, it could scarcely have been otherwise. But by the eighteenth century, both the robe and the sword were committed to the Germanic theory of French history, to the notion of Frankish innovations

[23] *Essais*, 202-203.

[24] *Mémoires présentés*, 1.

[25] *Lettres sur les anciens parlements de France* (London, 1753), I, 127.

[26] *Essais*, 10-11. Simon, *Henry de Boulainviller*, already cited in several connections, is an encomium which contradicts at almost every point Belliot's sharply critical *Boulainvilliers* (Caen, 1888).

[27] Hazard, *La crise de la conscience*, II, 61; also the first part of Gabriel Bonno, *La constitution britannique devant l'opinion française* (Paris, 1932).

as an element of cleavage with the heritage of Rome, and to the Champ de Mars as a cherished institutional ancestor.[28]

That much the tradition of Hotman, the *Soupirs*, Fénelon, and Boulainvilliers had in common with the tradition of Seyssel, Pasquier, La Roche Flavin, and the *Judicium Francorum*. The differences, however, remained even more important than the similarities. For one succession of theorists the courts still appeared as accomplices of Capetian usurpation. For the other, the feudal interlude and the era of the Estates General had simply interrupted the proper relationship between king and magistracy. Weakened by this lingering division, the theoretical position of the aristocracy had failed to match the resurgence of privileged groups in the sphere of day-to-day political maneuvering. By the 1740's the possibility was growing that this resurgence, born of the peculiar circumstances of a minority and a revulsion of feeling against Louis XIV's rule, might lose its momentum without ever having developed a new set of arguments.

2

Such a possibility was considerably enhanced by the fact that in this same period the *thèse royale* had assumed new vitality. In the seventeenth century it had rested on the principle of absolute sovereignty, whether viewed as a scientific fact[29] or as an expression of the divine will.[30] It was on this basis that the Garde des Sceaux, Voyer d'Argenson, had told the Parlement of Paris in 1718: "Neither the new [laws] nor the old exist save by the will of the sovereign, nor do they need anything except that will in order to be law."[31]

But the phraseology of the sixteenth-century *politiques*, the rationalizations of Richelieu's and Louis XIV's rule no longer sufficed as a defense for royal power. In the very same memorandum of 1718 from which the above quotation is taken, Voyer d'Argenson had himself invoked another, more utilitarian argument:

[28] A. Duméril, *La légende politique de Charlemagne au XVIIIe siècle* (Toulouse, 1879) summarizes the main points in this attitude.

[29] In Bodin, for example, or in Cardin Le Bret's *Souveraineté du Roy* (Paris, 1632).

[30] Especially in Bossuet's *Politique tirée des propres paroles de l'Écriture Sainte* (Printed in 1709). Cf. Georg Lenz, "Staat und Gesellschaft bei Bossuet," *Archiv für Geschichte der Philosophie* (Berlin, 1927), XXXVIII, 129-145.

[31] Flammermont, *Remontrances*, I, 86.

> The king's authority would be insufficient to repress all the abuses . . . caused by the malice of men and the exigencies of the times, if, limiting itself to the maintenance of old laws, it could not establish new ones.[32]

Royal authority is thus no longer simply a power imposed by reason and religion; it is becoming a positive force for good, a center of reform. Without some recognition of this shift of emphasis, it would be impossible to assess correctly the whole theory of enlightened despotism, which made eighteenth-century exponents of social progress, at least prior to Rousseau, predominantly royalist, and left aristocratic defenders of vested privileges free to exploit the appeal of limited monarchy. It was to the royal mandate that Vauban and Boisguillebert had looked for improvement in the tax structure in Louis XIV's last years; and it was to the royal mandate that the Marquis d'Argenson, whom Mathiez calls the "grand seigneur d'esprit moderne,"[33] still looked in the 1730's while writing his *Considérations sur le gouvernement ancien et présent de la France.*[34]

Himself a comfortably situated aristocrat, son of the Garde des Sceaux of 1718, d'Argenson had shared in the general disgust at the vainglory and corruption of Louis XIV's declining years. But the monarchy still seemed to him the only agency for effecting progressive changes, and he consequently distrusted both the sovereign courts and the provincial estates, which he viewed as dangerous obstructions to reform, "whatever Monsieur de Boulainvilliers may say to the greater glory of Charlemagne."[35] He has earlier been seen lashing the heredity and salability of offices.[36] Feudal tenures he viewed as no less dependent on fraud: "Under this bizarre system of government, the greatest authority over the nation was in the hands of certain principal usurpers who had beneath them other, subordinate usurp-

[32] *Ibid.* This change of ground has been clearly pointed out by Bickart, *Les parlements de France*, 71.

[33] "La place de Montesquieu dans l'histoire des doctrines politiques du XVIIIe siècle," *Annales historiques de la Révolution française* (Paris, 1930), VII, 99.

[34] In d'Argenson's *Journal et mémoires* we see the change to an embittered hostility toward the crown after the author's dismissal as secretary of state for foreign affairs in 1747. His earlier period, however, was by far his more important as a theorist, and the d'Argenson of the *Considérations* stands as one of the great champions of strong rule in the interests of the victims of seigneurial abuses. Cf. Jean Lamson, *Les idées politiques du marquis d'Argenson* (Montpellier, 1943).

[35] *Considérations*, 30.

[36] See above, 121.

ers."[37] His central message to his contemporaries was that "democracy is as much the friend of monarchy as aristocracy is its foe."[38]

Only one other theorist on the royalist side had an influence in his own lifetime comparable to that of d'Argenson, and he only because his effort was to meet head-on the historical arguments of both the parlementary and the feudal schools and to refute them by using their own materials. This was the Abbé Du Bos, diplomat, friend of Pierre Bayle, member of the French Academy from 1720,[39] whose huge *Histoire critique de l'establissement de la monarchie française* (1734), embodied a rejection of both Boulainvilliers and the *Judicium Francorum* as sweeping as Bodin's assault on Hotman and Pasquier had been a century-and-a-half before.

The whole Germanist theory, argued Du Bos, rested on a false allegation, namely, that the Franks had entered Gaul as military conquerors. Thus it was nonsense to treat the rise of the French monarchy as a Romanist aberration from sound German beginnings. The Franks, he insisted, had been close allies of the Romans; the pre-eminence of Clovis had rested first and foremost on his rank as a Roman officer; Justinian's cession of the crown had made the Frankish kings direct heirs of the Caesars.[40] The Champ de Mars had been merely a rally of troops for the spring campaign, not a legislative and judicial institution from which either the parlements or the Estates General could claim descent; there had originally been no hereditary fiefs, conquered or otherwise; and when the alliance of king and bourgeoisie had taken form in the later middle ages, it had been for the purpose of combatting noble usurpations.[41] Du Bos' conclusions were frequently over-simplified to serve his thesis, but there can be no question that they have received greater support from the findings of modern scholarship than have the arguments of his opponents.[42]

[37] *Considérations*, 126.

[38] *Ibid.*, 148.

[39] Jean Baptiste, Abbé Du Bos, *Correspondance* (1670-1742) (ed. A. Lombard, Paris, 1913); also A. Lombard, *L'abbé Du Bos, un initiateur de la pensée moderne* (Paris, 1913).

[40] *Histoire critique*, I, 177, 621-622; II, 371-372. These references are to the two-volume edition of 1742, which incorporated numerous additions to and corrections of the text as originally printed eight years earlier. Both were published in Paris.

[41] *Histoire critique*, II, 441-442, 528-529, 598-599.

[42] See, for example, Ferdinand Lot, *Les invasions germaniques* (Paris, 1935), and C. Bayet, in Lavisse, *Histoire de France*, II, part I.

The success of the *Histoire critique* was overwhelming. No fewer than five separate editions appeared between 1734 and 1742. Its influence was apparent in other royalist works, such as the youthful Mably's *Parallèle des romains et des français* (1740)[43] and the later volumes of Richer d'Aube's *Réflexions sur le gouvernement de la France* (1731-1740). Le Gendre de Saint-Aubin might maintain a curious combination of royalism and Germanism, insisting that the kings of France owed their absolute power not to the Caesars but to God and their ancestors' prowess in battle;[44] but in general the Romanists' theory of a continuity transcending the barbarian invasions had become the official line of argument for the monarchist historians.

The debate over constitutional theory had assumed on both sides a rigidly antiquarian character. The frequency with which charges of "usurpation" were levelled at either kings or nobles stemmed from the assumption that somewhere in the past, the very remote past, was to be found the legitimate form of government and that this form must forever be maintained in France. By the time Du Bos and d'Argenson and Mably had finished their major works on the subject (d'Argenson's was widely circulated in manuscript during the late 1730's), the Germanists had clearly had the worst of the argument, posed in those terms. They had failed to construct any comparably plausible theory either of feudal rights originating in conquest and still valid in the eighteenth century or of magistral authority deriving from a Frankish institution. From 1732 to 1748, moreover, France enjoyed a period of prosperity and tranquillity during which the popularity of Louis XV combined with the patent inadequacy of either Boulainvilliers or the *Judicium*, taken alone, to give the royalists a clear margin of predominance in the sphere of political theory.[45] Yet the aristocratic position was about to receive a new and infinitely more persuasive formulation, a formulation which would harness previously conflicting lines of argument, make full use of the English example, and employ the nation's history not simply as a storehouse

[43] Mably's case is in this respect the opposite of d'Argenson's, since the former's pro-royal phase was to prove less important for his work taken as a whole than was his subsequent period of hostility to the crown. Cf. M. W. Guerrier, *L'abbé de Mably, moraliste et politique* (Paris, 1886), and Ernest A. Whitfield, *Gabriel Bonnot de Mably* (London, 1930).

[44] *Antiquités de la monarchie française* (Paris, 1739).

[45] Mathiez, "La place de Montesquieu," 97-105.

of Merovingian and Carolingian precedents, but as a stream of developing human experience too complex and too powerful to be diverted by the brief efforts of monarchist reformers.

3

At this point I must undertake a short digression in order to take account of the social and intellectual milieu which made possible the work of synthesis embodied in Montesquieu's *Spirit of the Laws.* For there is little point in summarizing the previously enunciated doctrines on which the book was based without also recognizing the physical conditions which brought those doctrines into actual contact within the limits of an individual intelligence.

The work of the salons, where the increasingly welcome parlementaires came together with the men for whom Boulainvilliers had spoken, was matched by the upsurge in relevant publications. New medieval histories were crowding one another off the booksellers' shelves; between 1715 and 1748 no fewer than twenty-seven works appeared in France on the Merovingian period alone.[46] The long-delayed printing of the memoirs of Cardinal de Retz in 1718, Ramsay's popularization of Fénelon,[47] and Le Laboureur's *Histoire de la Pairie* (1740) combined with the courts' published remonstrances to keep alive a wide range of anti-absolutist theories, even if none of them could alone match the counter-arguments of Du Bos and his fellow-royalists. The influx of English ideas was maintained either directly through David Mazel's translations of Locke or indirectly through the writings of Voltaire and Prévost and such periodicals as the *Bibliothèque britannique.*[48] The censorship, stringent in principle but ineffectual in practice, did little to prevent the circulation of clandestine publications actually or ostensibly printed in London, The Hague, and Amsterdam. Surely this was a period to be examined in the light of the dictum that the human mind is never so free as in a decaying despotism.

Thoughtful members of the aristocracy enjoyed unprecedented

[46] Lombard, *L'abbé Du Bos*, 580-584.

[47] Andrew Michael Ramsay, *Essai philosophique sur le gouvernement civil* (London, 1721).

[48] On this subject, see Henri Sée, *Les idées politiques en France au XVIIIe siècle* (Paris, 1920), 15.

opportunities for the personal exchange of ideas. About one-half of the members of the Académie Française and the Académie des Inscriptions et Belles-Lettres were noblemen;[49] and in the former's hallowed circle parlementaires such as Novion of Paris, Bouhier of Dijon, and Montesquieu of Bordeaux sat with members of great feudal houses, as well as with such formidable critics of their class as Du Bos and Saint-Pierre.[50] Fréret held meetings at his home for a select discussion group, which prior to 1722 had included Boulainvilliers;[51] and another such assembly met under the aegis of the Comte de Clermont, beginning in 1729.[52] In 1732 the first masonic lodge in France began to meet on the Rue de Bussy, with the Duc d'Antin as its Grand Master, though freemasonry was to count for little until the latter half of the century.[53]

Best known of all such clubs in the capital was the *Entresol*, so-called because it met in the mezzanine apartment of the Abbé d'Alary on the Place Vendôme. For seven years this circle held a three-hour session each Saturday evening. It was composed of a score of members, among whom were ministerial officials (the Marquis d'Argenson and the two Saint-Contests), learned clergymen (d'Alary and Saint-Pierre), robe noblemen (Avocat-Général d'Oby and Councilor Perelle of the Grand Conseil), and nobles d'épée of whom the Duc de Coigny was the highest in rank and the Comte de Plélo ultimately the most famous. D'Argenson has left a charming account of how the meetings were always carefully divided so as to provide one hour for discussion of newspaper items, one hour for criticism of newly published works, and one hour for reports on the members' own research projects. (In good weather a peripatetic note was added in the form of a

[49] Alphonse de Candolle, *Histoire des sciences et des savants depuis deux siècles* (Geneva-Basel, 1885), 505.

[50] In view of his defense of the Polysynodie, Saint-Pierre might appear at first glance to have been a pro-aristocratic theorist. In a sense, he was; but his emphasis on progress and his idealized conception of aristocracy, providing for unrestricted, non-hereditary recruitment, were scarcely an asset to the actual noblesse of his day. See his *Ouvrages politiques*, also Joseph Drouet, *L'abbé de Saint-Pierre* (Paris, 1912).

[51] Simon, *Henry de Boulainviller*, 87.

[52] Jules Cousin, *Le comte de Clermont* (Paris, 1867), I, 108-110.

[53] Albert Lantoine, *Histoire de la franc-maçonnerie française* (Paris, 1925), 54-64. Chérel mentions a masonic meeting at Paris in 1734, presided over by the Duke of Richmond and held in the rented mansion of the Duchess of Portsmouth. Among the few Frenchmen present was Montesquieu. *Fénelon, au XVIIIe siècle*, 64, n. 3.

stroll about the Tuileries.) It was Saint-Pierre whose insistence on debating contemporary issues finally caused Cardinal Fleury to suppress the Entresol in 1731.[54]

But the most important single element required for an understanding of what happened to aristocratic doctrines was the appearance of the provincial academies. This is true not only because the first half of the eighteenth century witnessed the creation of thirteen such assemblies,[55] but also because as a group they were from the beginning the high robe nobility's intellectual arena par excellence. The extent of the magistracy's role in the academy development has to my knowledge never been made clear through comparative analysis.[56]

Consider for a moment the case of Dijon. Here the Académie des Sciences, Arts et Belles-Lettres was born out of the testament of Hector Pouffier, retired dean of councilors in the Parlement of Burgundy, who died in 1736. Under the terms of his will,[57] his town house and the income from his portion of the manor of Aizerey were entrusted to five trustees, who were also to be the first directors of the new academy. These five were Dean of Councilors Lantin, Councilors Vitte and Thomas, Procureur-Général Quarré, and the mayor of Dijon, Burteur (also a councilor in the Parlement). Furthermore, and this was to remain a remarkable feature of the Dijon Academy, their successors in office (i.e., four at the Palais de Justice and one at the Hôtel de Ville) were also to be their successors at the academy! The royal letters patent of 1740 which formally established the society incorporated this provision into its constitution and thus made robe control a certainty for as long as the Parlement itself should last.[58] There is no need here to follow in detail the growth of the Dijon

[54] A.N., M. 781, no. 13; d'Argenson, *Mémoires* (ed. René d'Argenson, Paris, 1825), 247-264, and *Journal*, I, 92-108. See also Drouet, *L'abbé de Saint-Pierre*, 77-81, and Chérel, *Fénelon au XVIIIe siècle*, 63, n., and 64, n.

[55] Lyon (1700), Montpellier (1706), Bordeaux (1712), Pau (1720), Béziers (1723), Marseille (1726), Toulouse (1729), Montauban (1730), La Rochelle (1732), Dijon (1740), Rouen (1744), Clermont-Ferrand (1747), Auxerre (1749).

[56] A valuable discussion of certain other aspects is to be found in Francisque Bouillier, *L'Institut et les académies de province* (Paris, 1879), ch. 1-6.

[57] A.D. Côte d'Or, B. 12208. For a short biography, see Victor Cardot, *Bernard-Hector Pouffier, conseiller doyen au Parlement de Bourgogne* (Dijon, 1876), a *discours de rentrée* originally delivered to the Dijon Court of Appeals.

[58] Bib. Dijon, Ms. 1414 (Baudot 164).

Academy, which was set up with six *académiciens honoraires* (among them Buffon) and a panel of priests, doctors, engineers, and lawyers as *pensionnaires* to do specialized work in science, ethics, and medicine.[59]

It should be noted before leaving the Burgundian case, however, that for a number of years the academy proper had a rival in President Bouhier's (later President de Brosses') Société Littéraire de Dijon, which survived as a separate entity until its absorption into the academy in 1761. One authority has seen in its composition (its sixteen regular members included eight officers of the Parlement or the Chambre des Comptes)[60] a conscious effort to found a more exclusively aristocratic group than the academy, with its roturier specialists, appeared to be.[61] In any case, the eventual amalgamation worked to make even more pronounced the magistral domination of the academy itself.

A glance at several other important academies will show that though none was tied so closely to a parlement as was that of Dijon (and though one must, of course, exclude those in towns such as Béziers and Marseille which had no sovereign courts), robe influence was nonetheless a strikingly consistent feature of the general pattern. At Toulouse in 1746, the six controlling *associés libres* of the academy included President de Nupces, President de Pardauilhan, and Councilor de Saint-Laurens.[62] At mid-century, four of the seventeen members of the Academy of Clermont-Ferrand were members of the Cour des Aides there (a relatively small and unimportant court); eight officers of the Lyon Cour des Monnaies sat among the twenty-five *académiciens ordinaires* in that city; and the thirty-seven members of the Académie des Sciences et Beaux-Arts at Pau included no fewer than twenty parlementaires.[63] It is worth overstepping 1748 as a chronological limit by a few years to note that ten officers of the

[59] Bib. Dijon, Ms. 914 (Baudot 4). These three subjects furnished in rotation the topics for the annual essay contests, including that of 1750, won by a most promising "citoyen de Genève," J.-J. Rousseau.

[60] P. Milsand, *Notes et documents pour servir à l'histoire de l'Académie des Sciences, Arts et Belles-Lettres de Dijon* (Paris, 1871), 7-10.

[61] Bouchard, *De l'humanisme à l'Encyclopédie*, 625-626.

[62] Bib. Toulouse, L^{m}B. 737, 13-16. See also Marie Douais, *L'Académie des Sciences, Inscriptions et Belles-Lettres de Toulouse au dix-huitième siècle* (Toulouse, 1896).

[63] J. de La Porte, *La France littéraire* (Paris, 1757), 43-45, 48-49, 70-72.

Parlement of Franche-Comté took the lead in founding the Academy of Besançon in 1752.[64]

Turning last of all to Montesquieu's own Academy of Bordeaux, one encounters for 1740 a list of twelve permanent academicians of whom *eleven* were either active or retired officers in the Parlement of Guienne or the local Cour des Aides.[65] (Here, as at Dijon, the subordinate members included numerous specialized roturiers, while the honorary academicians included several representatives of the sword.) In the records of the Bordeaux group is to be found convincing evidence of the intensity and variety of intellectual concerns in the academies. Here is Montesquieu, the later student of climatic influences on the nervous system as revealed in the thawing tongue of a sheep,[66] winning the essay prize for 1718 with an analysis of echoes and in 1720 submitting a treatise on transparency.[67] The formal contests sponsored by this academy were, in the period under discussion, always concerned with problems in physical science;[68] but the lending lists of its library reveal the members engaged in reading Thucydides, Caesar, Cicero, Joinville, Guicciardini, Descartes, La Fontaine, Bayle, and a host of other writers on history and philosophy.[69]

The importance of the provincial academies for the development of aristocratic thought, especially that of the high robe, can scarcely be exaggerated. In their libraries and their reading rooms stocked with out-of-town periodicals these societies offered their members access to a wider range of ideas than any individual could have tapped purely on the basis of his private resources. In their meetings the most erudite representatives of the parlementary class benefited from the researches of specialized commoners and exchanged opinions with those noblemen of the sword who, like Boulainvilliers, had acquired some interest in things of the mind. Their existence helps

[64] Auguste Castan, ed., "Neuf lettres du duc de Tallard au conseiller François-Xavier Chiflet sur les origines de l'Académie de Besançon," *Académie de Besançon: Séances publiques* (1882), 91 ff. Also Estignard, *Le Parlement de Franche-Comté*, 261-270.

[65] Bib. Bordeaux, Ms. 828, CV, fol. 49.

[66] *Esprit des lois*, book XIV, ch. 2.

[67] Bib. Bordeaux, Ms. 828, III.

[68] J.-L.-J. de Gères, *Table historique et méthodique des travaux et publications de l'Académie de Bordeaux depuis 1712 jusqu'en 1875* (Bordeaux, 1879).

[69] Bib. Bordeaux, Ms. 833.

to explain, on the one hand, why the French noblesse was not left untouched by the Enlightenment, and, on the other hand, how its background and its contemporary situation conditioned its reception of new, especially English, ideas. Exposure to the centuries of parlementary and feudal theorizing, the chance to consider the implications and possible weaknesses of royalist doctrines, new incentives to buttress the aristocratic defenses, all these elements were necessary to produce a Bouhier, a Lampinet, an Hénault, or, most of all, a Montesquieu.

4

At the head of the *Esprit des lois*, in its original edition, stands the motto: "Prolem sine matre creatam"; and Montesquieu later asserted proudly that "I took no model in composing it."[70] That any theoretical work can be born without parents, however, is doubtful, to say the least. Certainly in the case of the *Spirit of the Laws* the reader is almost as struck by the book's intricate family tree as by its undeniable elements of originality. I have no intention of undertaking a survey of the tremendous range of studies which have dealt with the sources, structure, methodological approach, and subsequent influence of the great treatise,[71] nor even of examining all the ramifications of its sometimes bewilderingly rich contents. I can, however, attempt to make clear its relationship to the debate discussed in the opening sections of the present chapter and its importance in practically bringing back to life the entire aristocratic side of that debate.

Most obvious, of course, is Montesquieu's use of the arguments which have been summarized in Chapter Five and more recently in my references to the parlementary tradition from Seyssel through La Roche Flavin to the *Judicium Francorum* of 1732.[72] It is the former président à mortier who defends venality of offices,[73] condemns either monarchies or democracies when they "despoil the senate, the magistrates, the judges of their functions,"[74] and entitles a chapter "How the Smallest Change of the Constitution Is Attended with the Ruin

[70] *Pensées et fragments* (Bordeaux, 1899-1901), I, 102.

[71] See D. C. Cabeen, *Montesquieu: A Bibliography* (New York, 1947).

[72] See above, 90 ff. and 223 ff.

[73] *Esprit des lois,* book V, ch. 19.

[74] *Ibid.*, book VIII, ch. 6.

of Its Principles."[75] It is the same président à mortier who had many years before written of the sovereign courts:

> These companies are always detested; they approach kings only to tell them strict verities; and while a crowd of courtiers ceaselessly portray a happy people . . . they [the courts] carry to the foot of the throne the laments and the tears of which they are the trustees.[76]

The parlements occupied a special place in Montesquieu's theory of monarchy. They were included, of course, in his concept of "intermediate powers"; but it is well to remember that the latter also comprised the ecclesiastical hierarchy, the nobility, the chartered municipalities, and all the other corporations whose privileges were in any degree beyond the reach of either royal or popular interference. The all-important role of the high robe emerges most clearly in the passage which concedes that the nobility, taken in its entirety, has certain undeniable shortcomings as a check on despotism but goes on to say that:

> It is not enough to have intermediate powers in a monarchy; there must be also a depositary of laws. This depositary can only be the judges of the supreme courts of justice, who promulgate the new laws, and revive the obsolete. . . . The prince's council are not a proper depositary. They are naturally the depositary of the momentary will of the prince, and not of the fundamental laws.[77]

This theme, which echoes the ancient hostility between the courts and the royal ministers, runs throughout the entire book. "Liberty," writes Montesquieu, "often has been weakened in monarchies by a thing of the least use in the world to the prince: this is the naming of commissioners to try a private person."[78] I have already drawn attention to the fact that this denunciation of judgment by ministers or special commissioners, in fact the whole set of strictures on the separation of powers,[79] rested on assumptions which had long been urged in published remonstrances such as those of the Paris Parlement in 1732.[80]

[75] *Ibid.*, book VII, ch. 14.

[76] *Lettres persanes*, no. 140. (I have used the edition of Gonzague Truc, Paris, 1947).

[77] *Esprit des lois*, book II, ch. 4.

[78] *Ibid.*, book XII, ch. 22.

[79] *Ibid.*, book VI, ch. 5 and ch. 6; book XI, ch. 6.

[80] See above, 91.

The contribution of the feudal thesis has not been noted so often as has the parlementary; but if, as Göhring asserts,[81] the *Spirit of the Laws* could not have taken the form it did without La Roche Flavin, it is no less true that without Boulainvilliers the book would have been far different from that which has come down to us. It is an elementary point, no doubt, but an essential one to have clearly in mind, that when Montesquieu talked of the French nobility's proper role he was not applying his definition of aristocracy as a pure form of government. The latter he recognized only in certain isolated historical instances, Sparta, Rome under the Decemvirs, Venice. His own country he saw as a monarchy which could be improved by closer adherence to the ideal principles of that governmental form, including proper utilization of a privileged aristocracy:

> The most natural, intermediate, and subordinate power is the nobility. This in some measure seems to be essential to a monarchy, whose fundamental maxim is, no monarch, no nobility; no nobility, no monarch.[82]

Time after time he returned to the defense of noble privileges and such social boundaries as the rules of dérogeance.[83] As for seigneurial justice and related prerogatives, he conceded that the "privileges annexed to fiefs give a power very burdensome to those governments which tolerate them," then continued:

> These are the inconveniences of nobility—inconveniences, however, that vanish when confronted with its general utility, but when these privileges are communicated to the people, every principle of government is wantonly violated.[84]

And in his discussion of French legal history, he asserted flatly:

> The administration, therefore, of justice, both in the old and new fiefs, was a right inherent in the very fief itself, a lucrative right which constituted a part of it. For this reason it had been considered at all times in this light; whence this maxim arose, that jurisdictions are patrimonial in France.[85]

The full importance of this pronouncement is apparent only if it is recalled that in Montesquieu's lifetime there had been constant debate

[81] *Weg und Sieg*, 74. [82] *Esprit des lois*, book II, ch. 4.

[83] *Ibid.*, book V, ch. 9; book VIII, ch. 9; book XI, ch. 6; book XIII, ch. 20; book XX, ch. 21 and 22.

[84] *Esprit des lois*, book V, ch. 9. [85] *Ibid.*, book XXX, ch. 20.

as to whether seigneurial justice was a royal *concessio* under public law or a total delegation, a cession of property of which it could be said "Fief et juridiction sont tout un."[86]

Montesquieu obviously could not avoid the Romanist-Germanist controversy; but he made a conscious effort to define his own position as somewhere between the extremes: "The Comte de Boulainvilliers and the Abbé Du Bos have formed two different systems, one of which seems to be a conspiracy against the commons, and the other against the nobility."[87] He criticized Boulainvilliers for having based his system on the unproved premise that the Franks had reduced the Gallo-Romans to servitude by formal legislation. There is, nevertheless, no question as to Montesquieu's fundamental preference. Quite aside from his famous characterizations of both the English and French constitutions as having come "from the forests of Germany,"[88] he devoted considerable space to attacking almost every point in the Romanist thesis. "Before I finish this book," he writes, "it will not be improper to write a few strictures on the Abbé Du Bos's performance, because my notions are perpetually contrary to his; and if he has hit on the truth I have missed it."[89] The Romanists are wrong to deny that the Frankish invaders were originally exempt from taxes;[90] they are wrong to charge the medieval noblesse with having usurped authority;[91] they are wrong to de-emphasize the element of military conquest in the coming of the Franks.[92] They are, in effect, guilty of nothing less than lèse-majesté:

> The Abbé Du Bos maintains, that at the commencement of our monarchy there was only one order of citizens among the Franks. This assertion, so injurious to the noble blood of our principal families, is equally affronting to the three great houses which successively governed this realm.[93]

[86] For an excellent discussion of this problem see Giffard, *Les justices seigneuriales*, 32 ff.
[87] *Esprit des lois*, book XXX, ch. 10.
[88] *Ibid.*, book XI, ch. 6; book XXX, ch. 18.
[89] *Ibid.*, book XXX, ch. 23.
[90] *Ibid.*, book XXX, ch. 12-15.
[91] *Ibid.*, book XXX, ch. 20.
[92] *Ibid.*, book XXX, ch. 24.
[93] *Ibid.*, book XXX, ch. 25. As noted above, 232, another parlementaire, Le Gendre de Saint-Aubin, had made this same point just seven years before Montesquieu's work appeared.

No, Montesquieu cannot claim a position midway between Boulainvilliers and Du Bos—the former is his man. His whole conception of feudal law rested heavily on the studious count's investigations,[94] even to the point of repeating Boulainvilliers' expressions of aesthetic admiration for the medieval system:

> The feudal laws [wrote Montesquieu, slipping once more into his sylvan imagery] form a very beautiful prospect. A venerable old oak raises its lofty head to the skies, the eye sees from afar its spreading leaves, upon drawing nearer, it perceives the trunk but does not discern the root; the ground must be dug to discover it.[95]

Although Montesquieu was not intent on writing merely a tract for his times, he could not forego occasional references to contemporary politics, references which take on added meaning against the background of our earlier chapters. In declaring that "a capitation is more natural to slavery; a duty on merchandise more natural to liberty,"[96] he was expressing a view which had led him to write, in a draft memorandum of 1716 to the Regent:

> It is to be hoped that Your Royal Highness can suppress the dixième and capitation; he knows how onerous these imposts are for the people and how injurious to the nobility.[97]

The above-noted opposition to ministerial jurisdiction had an immediate application to the ceaseless disputes over evocation of cases to the royal council.[98] And the cause of regional particularism was not forgotten:

> There are certain ideas of uniformity, which sometimes strike great geniuses (for they even affected Charlemagne), but infallibly make an impression on little souls. . . . If the people observe the laws, what signifies it whether these laws are the same?[99]

[94] This debt, apparent though not clearly acknowledged in the *Esprit des lois*, is made explicit in Montesquieu's notes, for example: *Pensées et fragments*, I, 97, 127-129, 185-187, 318-322; II, 164.

[95] *Esprit des lois*, book XXX, ch. 1.

[96] *Esprit des lois*, book XII, ch. 14.

[97] *Mélanges inédits* (ed. Gaston de Montesquieu, Paris, 1892), 244.

[98] See above, 41.

[99] *Esprit des lois*, book XXIX, ch. 18.

D'Aguesseau's attempts to codify provincial customs in the 1730's had left an abiding mark on the magistral mind; and Montesquieu in the eighteenth century here anticipates Tocqueville in the nineteenth.

5

The preceding selection of quotations from Montesquieu obviously is designed to illustrate only one aspect of his thought. It would be doing him a serious injustice, in examining his work as a synthesis of feudal and parlementary traditions, to forget the incisive social criticism of the *Lettres persanes* or the broad intellectual curiosity which led him to study Roman history, the history of commerce, comparative law, and the physical sciences, and which made him a pioneer in the modern discipline of political sociology. Just as Carcassonne, for whom Montesquieu was the hero of the liberal tradition,[100] and Mathiez, for whom he was nothing but the rationalizer of reaction,[101] selected the particular quotations which best fitted their respective theses, so I have had to limit myself here to passages which exemplify the implications of his message for my specific investigation.

Montesquieu was in some respects, as Voltaire conceded, "le plus modéré et le plus fin des philosophes."[102] In his hatred of religious intolerance, his denunciation of slavery (though it did not apply to Negroes), and his appeal for a humanization of the penal code he deserves a high place among the eighteenth-century reformers. When he wrote that the state owed to each of its citizens "a certain subsistence, a proper nourishment, suitable clothing, and a kind of life not incompatible with health,"[103] he was advancing a theory of social welfare far more modern than were the chilly theories of the bourgeois liberals. Or *was* it more modern? The middle ages had believed in a minimum level of well-being for all, so long as political equality was

[100] *Montesquieu et le problème de la constitution française au XVIIIe siècle* (Paris, 1926).

[101] "La place de Montesquieu." The direct conflict of views is most clearly stated in Mathiez' review of Carcassonne's work, *Annales historiques de la Révolution française* (Paris, 1927), IV, 509-513.

[102] *Lettre sur les français* in *Oeuvres complètes* (ed. Moland, Paris, 1877-1885), XXVI, 509-510.

[103] *Esprit des lois*, book XXIII, ch. 29. I have substituted the word "suitable" for "convenient" in Nugent's translation, since the latter seems to me clearly incorrect as an equivalent for "convenable" in this context.

left out of account. Nothing in the feudal tradition precluded an enlightened paternalism toward "the lower orders."

When called upon to choose between the views of Carcassonne and Mathiez, other commentators[104] have generally tried to avoid the extremes, but have almost invariably ended by describing Montesquieu as either an historically-minded conservative or at most a very aristocratic liberal. This was already the view of eighteenth-century scholars such as Guyot, whose *Répertoire* ranged Boulainvilliers and Montesquieu against Du Bos and Mably.[105] And Voltaire, though on occasion he did the Bordeaux philosopher justice as a man of good sense, nevertheless ripped into the aristocratic message of the *Spirit of the Laws* in his *Siècle de Louis XIV*, in his *Dictionnaire philosophique*, in his *A. B. C.*, and finally, of course, in his *Commentaire sur l'Esprit des lois.*[106]

Voltaire's uneasiness on the subject of passing a definitive judgment on Montesquieu strikes a responsive chord in the modern mind. The Bordeaux president was no toady to the old feudal class, as he showed in ridiculing what seemed to him an arrogant, hollow coterie of courtiers.[107] But in the very same passage, he displayed his even greater scorn for anoblis and bourgeois financiers. "Nothing," he wrote in his personal notes, "struck me in Paris so much as the agreeable indigence of the great lords and the tiresome opulence of the businessmen."[108] In general, his sympathies were unquestionably with the noblesse, as when he opined in a memorandum on church affairs: "We observe . . . that benefices in the king's gift are better in the hands of the nobility than in those of little men."[109] Any reasonably objective student of the period must, it seems to me, distinguish between the urbane and likable man of letters and the political theorist whose views were destined to serve the most reactionary groups in France.

The present context, however, does not demand a general assess-

[104] Notably Sée, *L'évolution de la pensée politique*, 20-50; Göhring, *Weg und Sieg*, 132-141; Neumann, introduction to *The Spirit of the Laws* (New York, 1949).

[105] *Op. cit.*, 65-69.

[106] *Oeuvres complètes* (ed. Moland) XIV, 106-108; XX, 1-13; XXVII, 311-326; XXX, 405-464.

[107] *Lettres persanes*, no. 48.

[108] *Cahiers* (ed. B. Grasset, Paris, 1941), 166.

[109] *Mélanges inédits*, 234.

ment of Montesquieu's qualities as a writer, a person, or, except in a very sharply defined sense, an historian and philosopher. I have sought to present him as the most striking personification at the intellectual level of the phenomenon with which my entire investigation has been concerned. In order to understand the regrouping of the French aristocracy, one must read Montesquieu. Conversely, it would be impossible fully to appreciate the import of his writings except against the background of developments treated earlier in the present chapter. In Montesquieu, the greatest product of the society of courts, academies, and salons, the intellectual heritage of Hotman at last united with that of La Roche Flavin on behalf of the noblesse, both of the sword and of the robe. Thereafter, Mirabeau *père* could resume the languishing defense of decentralization,[110] and La Curne de Sainte Palaye could hold up his portrait of medieval chivalry as an ideal toward which modern society ought still to strive.[111]

[110] *L'ami des hommes* (ed. Rouxel, Paris, 1883), 205-228.

[111] *Mémoires sur l'ancienne chevalerie, considérée comme un établissement politique & militaire* (Paris, 1759), 3 vols.

Conclusion

A BRIEF REVIEW of findings is especially necessary in a study such as this has been. Unilinear, narrative treatment might have required no special conclusion to reassemble its various elements; but the very nature of the phenomenon under examination precluded that approach. Instead, it has been necessary to treat each element of the problem as, on the one hand, a factor which had in itself been operative in French society for generations, and, on the other hand, as a part of the peculiar combination of circumstances which made the early eighteenth century the critical time segment for my subject. As a result, it has frequently been easier to identify the separate threads than to keep track of their relationship to one another within the knot.

The questions with which I introduced the problem I have sought to answer in the intervening chapters as follows: The feudal reaction in eighteenth-century France took the form of a resurgence of power to obstruct the crown—until the very moment when the explosion came from below, the nobility's face was to be turned suspiciously upward toward the king. To explain this resurgence I have had to call attention to a definite regrouping of politically significant elements at court, in the church, and in the army, around the high nobility of the robe. It follows from this interpretation that the term "feudal" is best employed in this connection to indicate not that the original feudal class regenerated itself from within, but that an infinitely more potent group had become in fact a new feudality, which under Louis XV lent its strength to the old. This process was well under way, though obscured, even before 1715, became apparent at the surface of political events in the first years after Louis XIV's death, and was essentially complete by the time Montesquieu published his *Spirit of the Laws* in 1748.

The discussion leading up to these conclusions concentrated successively on three main topics: the situation of the nobility and especially the noblesse de robe in 1715, the elements which underlay the magistracy's rise to power and prestige in the ensuing period, and finally, the overt indications of aristocratic regrouping in the politics, social relationships, and intellectual trends of the years between 1715 and 1748. In purely quantitative terms, the retrospective observations and the consideration of relatively stable conditions unquestionably have outweighed the analysis of identifiable alterations in noble tactics, attitudes, and theories. Yet the core of my presentation has remained the process of change within a privileged class. The statics have been introduced only to the end that the dynamics might become comprehensible.

Just what factors have emerged as the essential agents underlying these dynamics? First was the fluid situation arising out of the end of a long, personalized reign and the accession of a five-year-old child. An important element in this situation was the confusion bequeathed by a king who had stripped the nobility of political power during his lifetime but had not destroyed its ability to rebound after his death. From this in turn followed the need to examine the legal boundaries of a noble order composed of almost two hundred thousand soldiers, churchmen, magistrates, municipal officers, and country gentlemen; and to take note of the variations in wealth, prestige, and influence which further subdivided that class. In order to be prepared for the subsequent progress of events, it was necessary to pause for an institutional analysis of the thirty-one sovereign courts whose officers made up the high noblesse de robe, then concentrate for the space of a chapter on the special legal and social position of the superior magistracy within a nobility of which it constituted scarcely more than one percent. The age-old line between robe and sword proved to be still sharp in 1715.

But the sovereign court officers possessed attributes destined to give them a place of honor within the Second Estate. Associated in the public mind with Jansenist Gallicanism, with opposition to new taxes, and with the defense of regional privileges, they added a growing body of popular support to their newly recovered weapon: the right to remonstrate while delaying the registration of new laws. They owned their public offices outright. They belonged to families many of which had by this time been noble for several generations and most of which were now adding military or ecclesiastical prestige, or both, to their judicial dignities. They were wealthy, for their fortunes included not only their offices, in themselves representing large investments, but also a formidable accumulation of securities, urban property, and rural seigneuries.

Under the Regency the peerage made an abortive bid for leadership within the nobility and lost that leadership to the high robe, which benefited from the violent reaction of all the other nobles against the hauteur of the peers. By their remonstrances and by their active participation in the surviving provincial estates the magistrates proceeded to uphold the aristocracy's opposition to undifferentiated taxation, encroachments on seigneurial autonomy, and ministerial assaults on the fortress of regional particularism. The passing years revealed the nobility coming to recognize more and more clearly the indispensable services of the courts and to accept the primacy of this one remaining institution still under noble control. The social concomitants of this tactical alliance produced, if not the total obliteration of the old robe-épée line, at least its virtual disappearance as a factor in French public life. And the aristocratic spokesmen of the mid-eighteenth century, most of all Montesquieu, represented the amalgamation of feudal and parlementary arguments. In institutional, political, social, or ideological terms, the pattern is the same.

Thus, in place of the seventeenth century's characteristic triangle of tension—the crown, the sword, and the still half-bourgeois robe—there had now appeared a triangle composed of the crown, the middle class reformers, and the noble defenders of existing privileges based on birth and office. The last-mentioned group, speaking through published tracts, through the resolutions of the First and Second Estates in provincial assemblies, through the pastoral letters of bishops and the whispered suggestions of great courtiers, above all, through the remonstrances of the sovereign courts, showed a solidarity which seems to me more important for subsequent history than was the residue of old differences. Not even the Fronde offered a precedent for what was happening under Louis XV; for in 1650 the high robe had still been a narrow professional fraternity with aims distinct from those of the feudal class. Now it emerged as the self-conscious, recognized standard bearer of a nobility which without its institutional strength would have lapsed into atomized, voiceless impotence.

There are several different theoretical systems which can be superimposed on the tightening of the French aristocracy and the emergence of robe leadership. In the course of my investigation it has seemed better to introduce no pre-conceived schema into the work of description and analysis; but at this point I might at least note briefly the application of each of several such systems to the problem at hand. To the corporatist historians, for example, robe power is no mystery since it was based on all three elements in the corporate constitution: (1) the territorial element, that is, fiefs and seigneuries; (2) the official, that is, public functions; and (3) the social, that is, organization by corps and by order.[1] At the same time, the sovereign companies, writes one of the leading corporatists, had begun as early as the mid-seventeenth-century to "deviate" from the proper application of their power. Instead of limiting their use of that power to strictly corporate ends—bargaining with the government for their gages, making group loans to the king, upholding their individual members' interests in private disputes—they had embarked upon a career of wielding it as a public weapon and thus disrupting national life, often for trivial reasons.[2] From this point of view, the record of the courts in the eighteenth century features the still more pronounced misuse of traditional affiliations. Only the most uncritical extremist, I take it, would maintain that this was a case of corporate organization working well.

To the scholar operating on the theory of the circulation of elites, to take another viewpoint, it is not the behavior of the aristocracy, or any subdivision of it, but its composition which is important. For the Paretinist[3] the evolution of the noblesse de robe appears as one phase in the rigidification and attendant degeneration of the prerevolutionary French ruling class. The entry of the robe into the aristocracy was one of those infusions of new personnel from below

[1] Georges Espinas isolates just these categories in his article on the work of Émile Lousse. "La société d'ancien régime: la situation corporative," *Mélanges d'histoire sociale* (Paris, 1944), 94-99.

[2] François Olivier-Martin, "Le déclin et la suppression des corps en France au XVIIIe siècle," in *L'organisation corporative du Moyen Age à la fin de l'Ancien Régime* (Émile Lousse, Louvain, 1937), 149-163.

[3] Pareto's exposition of the circulation of elites is scattered throughout his *Mind and Society*, especially III, 1423 ff., but it is much more clearly presented in his *Systèmes socialistes* (Paris, 1926), I, 25-62. I have several times cited Kolabinska, *La circulation des élites en France.*

without which no privileged class can retain the energy and intelligence to fulfill its social function. But it was the last important infusion of this sort before 1789. The robe's own exclusivism and its insistence on maintaining all the irritating, anachronistic distinctions of the noblesse helps to explain the development of an explosive situation. Wealthy merchants could still buy the first, technical attributes of nobility; but limited accessibility did not prevent the noblesse from becoming odious to a society which was ceasing to value its functions,[4] and in which a steadily growing proportion of the real elite of ability, Pareto's "sujets de choix," remained outside its borders. The signs of a decadent aristocracy posited by Jacob Novikov: exclusivism, a retrogressive philosophy, indolence, and class selfishness, all were discernible in the French nobility, including most of the magistrates, by the middle of the eighteenth century.[5]

In the Marxian view the performance of the aristocracy after Louis XV can, of course, be fully explained by its material interests. This was an old possessing class, left over from an era when control of land had conferred control over the means of production, but now engaged in a losing battle against the new possessing class based on commerce and money power. The political reaction and the internal closing of ranks are nothing but the reflexive acts of just such an endangered class; and the whole intellectual development culminating in Montesquieu is portrayed as simply the ideological smoke screen for a position ultimately determined by economic considerations.

Marxian analysis had made an undeniable contribution to our understanding of the final spasms of the ancien régime. It does not, however, fit all aspects of the situation here examined. The noblesse de robe sprang from the bourgeoisie and never wholly lost its stake in the capitalist development; but over the last century of its existence it identified itself increasingly with the landed aristocracy, so that in the end it was leading the battle of the declining class against the forces of national monarchy and capitalist liberalism. Once it found itself in that situation it acted in a fashion quite in accordance with Marxian laws, but the process of its transformation in the seventeenth and early eighteenth centuries involved prestige values which did not correspond at all to its economic interests.

[4] Carré, *La noblesse de France et l'opinion publique.*

[5] Jacques Nowicow, *Conscience et volonté sociales* (Paris, 1897), 45-50.

To supplement Pareto's theories of circulation and Marx's materialistic determinism, it is useful to turn to distinctions which Max Weber posited between classes in the economic sphere; parties in the political, and status groups in the social.[6] At any rate, the interaction of human groupings thus defined seems to me to explain some historical situations for which no ultimately monocausal system has proven wholly satisfying. What this study has described is the case of a group which in the course of a marked rise in status not only shifted its own economic base, but also abandoned many of the characteristic features of its previous way of life, adopted others from the aristocracy it was invading, and bequeathed its originally bourgeois values to strata of French society which it now considered beneath it. If the argument should be concentrated on strictly intellectual manifestations, if I were to be called upon to compare feudal and parlementary influences on Montesquieu, I should have no hesitation in saying that the former were infinitely the more important for his synthetic formulation. But no such choice is forced upon us, any more than it was forced upon Montesquieu. By the time he wrote, the sovereign courts were pouring scorn upon financiers, defying the royal reformers, and defending the seigneurial rights and fiscal exemptions of the noblesse in general. Landed prestige, military connections, pride in family had come to dominate the political outlook of men whose ancestors had helped Henry of Navarre bring order out of anarchy. In the very process of conquering the feudal nobility, the robe had succumbed to the standards of the older status group.

This, of course, was not a phenomenon peculiar to one nation in one century. Throughout history it lies at the very heart of the problem of special privilege. The evolution of the Roman equestrian class comes readily to mind, as does the change in the Florentine patriciate of the Quattrocento. Fritz Kern might be speaking of eighteenth-century France when he says: "The battle of the officialdom against the feudal aristocracy was seriously hindered by the ever more threatening merger of officeholders and old nobility."[7] Actually, he is referring to nineteenth-century Germany.

The place of the immediate problem in the national history of

[6] *Essays in Sociology* (New York, 1946), 180-195.

[7] "Vom Herrenstaat zum Wohlfahrtsstaat," *Schmollers Jahrbuch für Gesetzgebung* (Berlin, 1928), LII, 398.

France is clear enough, if one avoids the common error of seeing in the record of the late *ancien régime* nothing but a struggle between the crown and the nation. Once free of that unhistorical concept, the student is no longer in danger of hailing every individual or group which opposed the king as automatically the standard-bearer of progress against oppression. The social revolution could have taken place under royal auspices in France, as it did in England; and until almost the last moment there was no certainty that the overthrow of an archaic class structure would also destroy the monarchy.

By the mid-eighteenth century the government was faced with a situation in which high robe power had become the crux of the aristocratic problem. On the crown's response to this challenge would ultimately depend not only the settlement of the question of privilege but its own fate as well. History had a solution to recommend. The age-old technique of the Capetian house when defied by an entrenched class of officials had been to transfer the original delegation of authority to a new and more dependent stratum. But this time there was lacking the firmness which had neutralized provosts in the twelfth century, bailiffs and senechals in the thirteenth, and lordly governors general in the seventeenth. As late as 1771, when Chancellor Maupeou announced the suppression of the parlements and the substitution of appointive judicial boards, it appeared for a moment that the old expedient was being successfully re-applied. Just three years later, however, the new King Louis XVI inaugurated his series of surrenders by reinstating the magistrates. Their return was greeted by joyous public demonstrations; and to many historians of the sovereign courts that fact has sufficed to make the events of 1774 appear as a popular victory over despotism. But the freedom which had conquered was the freedom of the medieval nobleman, clutching his special bundle of prerogatives, crying "Liberty" and meaning only "mon droit." It was to this doomed conception that the crown was henceforth hopelessly committed.

An Essay on Bibliography

Much of the material to be presented here already appears above in footnotes. For some readers, those footnotes, grouping recommended works around specific topics discussed in the text, require no additional comment. Others may desire a still more thorough listing than is to be found anywhere in this book, a formal bibliography, in other words, such as appears in the typescript of my study, originally presented in 1950 for the doctorate and now available in the Widener Library at Harvard under the title, "The High Noblesse de Robe and the Regrouping of the French Aristocracy, 1715-1748." I am assuming, however, that a selective essay has certain aims which neither footnotes nor formal lists can achieve. It should single out readings of interest to other students working in the same general area, at the same time indicating a few which, from the writer's point of view, have contributed less than might have been expected. Above all, its total effect should be to give as honest a picture as possible of the range of materials employed in the study just presented. In seeking to meet these needs, I have had to make some arbitrary choices, so as not to overburden what is at best a confusing agglomeration of sources. This will explain numerous omissions which some authorities may consider unjustified. In addition, since I assuredly do not claim exhaustive knowledge of all the specialized bibliographies involved, I must leave open the possibility of omissions stemming from oversights on my part. All I can certify with confidence is that if the following pages at some points only illustrate important categories of readings, at least they contain no references which have not been significant for me at one stage or another of my research.

I. Unpublished Documents

A. Paris. For the researcher about to begin work in the Archives Nationales, there are several printed aids. One is the *État sommaire par séries des documents conservés aux Archives Nationales* (Paris, 1891). Another is the *Catalogue des manuscrits conservés aux Archives Nationales* (Paris, 1892). These two volumes provide, respectively, a general view of the organization and contents of the various lettered series and a partial listing of descriptive or expository writings, as distinguished from the mass of official records. Both were published by the Ministère de l'Instruction Publique, as was the more specialized *Répertoire numérique des archives du Parlement de Paris* (Paris, 1889). An invaluable guide to important single pieces is Jules Tardif's inventory of *Monuments historiques, Cartons des rois* (Paris, 1866). It must be emphasized, however, that for detailed research in the Archives Nationales, as in all collections of unpublished sources, much depends on judicious use of the hand-written catalogues prepared over the years by devoted archivists and available only on the spot.

I can no more than suggest the immense richness and variety of data to be found in the administrative series (E. 2664, for example, offers records of seventeenth-century inquiries into usurpation of noblesse, and H. 748, 751 and 842, documents concerning the provincial estates). Series K, the "Cartons des rois," contains descriptive and polemical writings of the first importance. Series M and MM should be consulted for pieces dealing with the nobility and questions of rank. For official papers of the sovereign courts, see Series P and PP (Chambre des Comptes), V^5 (Grand Conseil), X (Parlement), Z^{1A} (Cour des Aides), and Z^{1B} (Cour des Monnaies). Remonstrances, memoranda and other discursive writings will be found in Series U, on the judiciary in general.

In turning to the Bibliothèque Nationale, one must again begin with printed aids. The *Catalogue général des manuscrits français*, published in 13 volumes under the editorship of Henri Omont (Paris, 1895-1918), does not detail every item in the mammoth collection, which practically defies full analysis. It does, however, represent an impressive work on archival scholarship, made the more manageable by A. Vidier and P. Perrier, whose *Table générale alphabétique* of Omont's catalogue had itself reached five volumes (Paris, 1931-1939) and was up to the letter "R" at the time I was using it.

As in the case of the Archives Nationales, so in that of the Bibliothèque I can only illustrate the types of material available. Mss. fr.

7013-7014, for example, are two volumes of "Pièces concernant les Princes légitimés, les Parlements, etc." for the years 1716-1718. Ms. fr. 7547 is a collection of memoranda, lists, and notes dealing with the parlements, as are Mss. fr. 10893-10894, 11427, 16581 and 16819, to cite only a few. There are specific manuscripts of great interest, such as "Du rang de la robe chez les Romains et en France" (Ms. fr. 10789, pp. 381-412) or "De le vénalité des charges" (Ms. fr. 10791, pp. 411-445). There are the 6,780 volumes of the Cabinet des Titres, which include pieces on sovereign court officers (Mss. fr. 32985-32990), as well as d'Hozier's original "Armorial général de France" of 1697-1709, in 34 volumes (Mss. fr. 32194-32227). There are other special collections, that of the successive Presidents de Lamoignon (Mss. fr. nouv. acq. 7979-8500), for example, or that of the antiquarian, Antoine Lancelot (Mss. fr. nouv. acq. 9632-9826). Finally, in the Cabinet des Estampes, there are priceless pictorial records, including the Fevret de Fontette collection on the history of France (Qb. I and II for the early eighteenth century), "Caricatures politiques du dix-huitième siècle," Volume I (Tf. 17), and the "Galeries historiques," Volume IV (Aa. 31.g.).

Elsewhere in Paris are smaller documentary centers, less inexhaustible for purposes of my study but valuable nonetheless. The Departmental Archives (Seine) yielded notarial records (Series DC^6) covering testaments and various types of contracts bearing on both economic and genealogical aspects of the nobility's situation. The Bibliothèque Mazarine, which may be approached through Auguste Molinier's four-volume *Catalogue* (Paris, 1885-1892), contains several useful items, including the correspondence of the Sieur de Fumeron, 1716 to 1733, and letters to the Marquise de Lacour-Balleroy, 1704 to 1723 (Mss. 2316 and 2334-2341, respectively), as well as the Abbé Lallemant's later "Prérogatives et dignité du clergé, de la noblesse et de la magistrature" (Ms. 3073). At the Bibliothèque Sainte-Geneviève, catalogued in two volumes by Charles Kohler (Paris, 1893-1896), are to be found "Pièces touchant le Grand Conseil" (Ms. 492) which deserve special notice.

B. Other centers. Outside of Paris there are important documentary sources for the history of the French nobility in all the former provincial capitals, especially in those which had parlements prior to 1789.

I have not worked in certain of those cities, notably Rouen and Rennes, which would have been well worth exploring; but in allocating my time I took account of the great quantity of material on Normandy and Brittany that has found its way into the Parisian collections just discussed, as well as the relatively large proportion of Norman and Breton documentation already published.

With respect to departmental archives, the student has at his disposal several works published by direction of the Ministère de l'Instruction Publique. Of a general nature are the *État sommaire par fonds des archives départementales* (Paris, 1903) and the *État des inventaires des Archives nationales, départementales, communales et hospitalières au ler Janvier, 1937* (Paris, 1938). For more detailed listings he can turn to the appropriate volumes of the huge *Inventaire-sommaire des archives départementales antérieures à 1790*, printed in various departmental capitals from 1863 to the present. The unpublished sources in municipal libraries he will find listed, with differing degrees of completeness, in the *Catalogue général des manuscrits des bibliothèques publiques des départements*, 7 vol. (Paris, 1849-1885) and the *Catalogue général des manuscrits des bibliothèques publiques de France*, 48 vols. (Paris, 1886-1933). In addition, there are special publications such as the *Catalogue des fonds particuliers de la Bibliothèque Publique de Dijon* (Dijon, 1909) and Edmond Maignien's two-volume *Catalogue des livres et manuscrits du Fonds dauphinois de la Bibliothèque de Grenoble* (Grenoble, 1908). The above must be supplemented, of course, by the unprinted inventories at the archives and libraries themselves.

The Bibliothèque Publique at Toulouse offers a variety of manuscripts, among which I would call attention particularly to the first volume of "Les heures perdues" in Pierre Barthès' own hand (Ms. 699), an eighteenth-century collection concerning the Parlement of Languedoc (Ms. 692), and the treatise on academies attributed to Councilor de Ruffy of Dijon (Ms. 864). The Departmental Archives (Haute-Garonne) contain not only secret minutes of the local parlement's deliberations (B. 1355 ff.) but also indispensable sources of economic data in the form of *testaments séparés* and registers of *insinuations*, showing deeds of gifts-in-life and other contracts for the *sénéchaussée* of Toulouse. Remonstrances and records of receptions of sovereign court members also are to be found in Series B.

At Bordeaux, as at Toulouse, the testaments in notarial files and the insinuation registers lend value to the Departmental Archives, in this case those of the Gironde. Aside from the standard judicial records, the fine collection of letters between the central government and successive intendants of the place, in Series C, should be noted. In Series C too are capitation rolls for Louis XV's reign (C. 2694 ff.). The Bibliothèque Municipale de Bordeaux has secret registers kept by members of the Parlement of Guienne (Mss. 369, XXII-XXVII, and 383), Fontainemarie's two-volume "Recueil sur la Cour des Aides" (Ms. 380), the Abbé de Bellet's history of the parlement (Ms. 828, V), letters of President de Lacaze (Ms. 1010) and of other nobles de robe (Ms. 828, XXV), as well as an abundance of material on the Academy of Bordeaux (Mss. 828, CV, and 833). These are only a few of the items in this massive accumulation of documents.

Equally impressive for its resources is the Bibliothèque Publique de Dijon, which offers not only a wealth of data on the Parlement of Burgundy and its companion Chambre des Comptes, as well as some interesting private letters, but also P. L. Baudot's collections of pieces relating to the Burgundian nobility, the parlement, and the Dijon Academy (Mss. 912, 914, 919, 925, 1059 and 1159, for example). There is also the Juigné collection (Mss. 1304 ff.) covering the judiciary and the provincial estates. In the same city, the Departmental Archives (Côte-d'Or) have the usual Series B for the courts, and Series C, for the intendancy and the estates. Instead of notarial archives, at Dijon I consulted the family papers in Series E for a number of important houses, including Berbisey, Bouhier, Jehannin, Mairetet, etc. (E. 81, 104-105, 1001, and 1244 *bis*). Among the judicial records, furthermore, are to be found some interesting testaments, such as those of First President de Berbisey (B. 12176) and Councilor Pouffier (B. 12208). In the Bibliothèque Publique of nearby Besançon are a variety of sources touching on the nobility of Franche-Comté, as well as useful collections dealing with its parlement (Ms. 913 and 1203).

At Grenoble the Departmental Archives (Isère) contain several series of interest here: records of receptions of members into the Parlement of Dauphiné (B. 2271-2277) and miscellaneous letters, remonstrances and memoranda of that court (B. 2322-2323); family papers in Series II.E; notarial files in Series III.E; and lists of donors to the Hôpital Général de Grenoble (H [Supplément] B. 5 and 7), useful for the economic data they provide. The Bibliothèque Municipale de Grenoble has manuscripts paralleling in range of subject matter those of Bordeaux and Dijon. Of special importance are the rough notes on family histories, compiled in 34 volumes by Edmond Maignien (no catalogue manuscript number, R. 9011 by the local system).

Lastly, I have had access to the superb Bibliothèque Méjanes at Aix-en-Provence, notable not only for its manuscript histories of and documents originating with the sovereign courts of Provence, its sources on the Provençal nobility, and its special items, including Jacques Cundier's portraits of successive first presidents of the parlement (Ms. 951 [963]), but also for certain materials on the magistracy and the rest of the nobility elsewhere in France, such as the "Notices sur les membres du Parlement de Paris, Grenoble, Toulouse" (Ms. 565 [39]). It would be difficult, if not actually gratuitous, to make comparisons among different French libraries; but certainly the Bibliothèque Méjanes is one of the most rewarding for any student of the ancien régime.

II. Printed Primary Sources

Among the published collections of legal or governmental documents on which I have relied, several deserve mention for their general utility. Of central importance as background in the Louis XIV period are G. B. Depping's edition of *Correspondance administrative sous le règne de Louis XIV*, 4 vols. (Paris, 1850-1855) and A. M. Boislisle's and P. de Brotonne's of *Correspondance des contrôleurs généraux des finances, avec les intendants des provinces, 1683-1715*, 3 vols. (Paris, 1874-1897). The *Ordonnances des roys de France de la troisième race*, 23 vols., E.-J. de Laurière *et al.*, eds. (Paris, 1723-1849) and the *Recueil des anciennes lois françaises*, 29 vols., F. A. Isambert *et al.*, eds. (Paris, 1823-1829), though old and marked by numerous omissions, are still indispensable for the legislative texts they supply. Jules Flammermont's edition of *Remontrances du Parlement de Paris au XVIIIe siècle*, 3 vols. (Paris, 1888-1898) is invaluable both for the documents themselves and for the editor's informed analysis. The same is true of A. Le Moy, *Remontrances du Parlement de Bretagne au XVIIIe siècle* (Angers, 1909), but not of François Prost's and P.-A. Robert's similarly entitled works covering Franche-Comté (Lyon, 1936) and Provence (Paris, 1912), respectively; since the latter are descriptive essays rather than collections of full texts. One other compilation should be included here: *Documents relatifs aux rapports du clergé avec la Royauté de 1705 à 1789*, 2 vols., Léon Mention, ed. (Paris, 1893-1903).

Only about a dozen of the literally countless editions of memoirs of the early eighteenth century can be singled out for special notice. It is necessary to subdivide even these selected few in accordance with their authors' differing vantage points. Thus, the approach of the lawyer is represented by E.-J.-F. Barbier, *Journal historique et anecdotique du règne de Louis XV, 1718-1763*, 4 vols., A. de La Villegille, ed. (Paris, 1847-1856), and by Mathieu Marais, *Journal et mémoires sur la Régence et le règne de Louis XV*, 4 vols., M. de Lescure, ed. (Paris, 1863-1868). Jean Buvat, a *petit fonctionnaire* in the royal library, supplies the gossip of Paris to supplement that of the Palais. His *Journal de la Régence*, 2 vols., Émile Campardon, ed. (Paris, 1865), is of infinitely greater value than his less informative *Mémoires-Journal* (Paris, 1900), which deals almost exclusively with his professional duties at the Bibliothèque from 1697 to 1729. For a high robe version of events, see C.-J.-F. Hénault, *Mémoires*, François Rousseau, ed. (Paris, 1911); and for the ministerial viewpoint, the *Journal et mémoires* of the Marquis d'Argenson, 9 vols., E. J. B. Rathery, ed. (Paris, 1859-1867).

The court aristocracy has left numerous journals, most famous of which, of course, are the *Mémoires* of the Duc de Saint-Simon. These I have used in A. de Boislisle's 41-volume edition (Paris, 1879-1928), with the *Table* of 1918 and the *Table générale* of 1930, two volumes each. Less readable but more reliable on many points of fact is the *Journal* of the Marquis de Dangeau, 19 vols., E. Soulié, L. Dussieux *et al.*, eds. (Paris, 1854-1860), which includes Saint-Simon's annotations. Other chronicles by courtiers are the Duc de Luynes' *Mémoires*, 17 vols., same editors as for Dangeau (Paris, 1860-1865); the Duc de Villars' *Mémoires*, 6 vols., the Marquis de Vogüé, ed. (Paris, 1884-1904); and the Duc de Richelieu's *Mémoires authentiques*, A. de

Boislisle *et al.*, eds. (Paris, 1918), which should not be confused with the *Mémoires* published in nine volumes (Paris, 1792-1793) under Richelieu's name but actually composed by the Abbé Jean Soulavie.

Two less exalted noblemen left records of interest. One was the Chevalier de Piossens, whose *Mémoires de la Régence*, 3 vols. (The Hague, 1729) offer a contemporary account marked by both unreliable gossip and some useful details. The other was the southern French Marquis de Franclieu, who has bequeathed a picture of country and city life in Languedoc and Navarre, *Mémoires*, Louis de Germon, ed. (Paris-Auch, 1896). Finally, for the reactions of a foreign noble who traveled much in France, see the *Mémoires* of Karl-Ludwig, Freiherr von Pöllnitz, 4 vols. (London, 1755).

The profusion of collections of correspondence is comparable to that of published journals. Of the former, I would cite the 14-volume edition of the Marquise de Sévigné's letters, Louis Monmerqué, ed. (Paris, 1862-1866), in the series, *Les grands écrivains de France*. The voluble and witty lady is a priceless source of background information on the reign of Louis XIV. In no sense an adequate continuation, but nonetheless welcome, is *Les correspondants de la Marquise de Balleroy, 1706-1725*, 2 vols., E. de Barthélemy, ed. (Paris, 1883). Two collections of special relevance to the robe nobility are Chancellor d'Aguesseau's *Lettres inédites*, D. B. Rives, ed. (Paris, 1823) and Montesquieu's *Correspondance*, 2 vols., F. Gebelin and A. Morize, eds. (Paris, 1914). Of considerable importance for both social and intellectual history is the *Correspondance, littéraire et anecdotique, entre M. Saint-Fonds et le président Dugas, membres de l'Académie de Lyon, 1711-1739*, 2 vols., William Poidebard, ed. (Lyon, 1900).

There is little to be said in an essay of this type concerning contemporary newspapers and pamphlets, which are discussed in various works on eighteenth-century bibliography. It should be stated, however, that for the preparation of this book, the *Nouvelles ecclésiastiques*, printed beginning in 1728, and the *Journal historique sur les matières du tems*, better known as the "*Journal de Verdun*," after its principal place of publication, proved much more valuable than apparent alternatives, such as the *Journal des sçavans*, the *Mercure de France*, or the early eighteenth-century version of the *Gazette de France*. Pamphlets are to be found in every major French library, catalogued both among manuscripts and among regular *imprimés*. In the Bibliothèque Nationale, for example, one may examine the huge *Recueil général des pièces touchant l'affaire des princes légitimes et légitimés, mises en ordre*, 4 vols. (Rotterdam, 1717); in the Bibliothèque Publique de Toulouse, *Lettres d'establissement, statuts de l'Académie des Sciences, Inscriptions et Belles-lettres à Toulouse*, as well as a list of academicians for 1746; in the Bibliothèque Municipale de Grenoble, a *Rôle de Nosseigneurs les présidents, conseillers et gens du Roy de la Cour de parlement, aydes et finances de Dauphiné* (Grenoble, 1734). The preceding may at least suggest the range of items at the student's command.

A major category of printed sources is the body of theoretical and historical writings published before or during the early eighteenth century. Obviously the most important of all, for present purposes, are those of Montesquieu. Two newly published editions of his *Oeuvres complètes* have only appeared in time to be mentioned here: that of Roger Caillois, 2 vols. (Paris, 1949-1951) is popular but reliable within its avowed limits. That of André Masson, the first volume of which appeared in Paris in 1950, promises to become the authoritative collection. The older seven-volume edition of E. Laboulaye (Paris, 1875-1879), though available when I was doing my initial research, is neither complete nor sufficiently critical to warrant using it alone. I relied, therefore, on separate printings of Montesquieu's principal works, particularly his *Cahiers*, B. Grasset, ed. (Paris, 1941); his *Lettres persanes*, G. Truc, ed. (Paris, 1946); his *Considérations sur les causes de la grandeur des Romains et de leur décadence*, Gabriel Compayré, ed. (Paris, 1911); his *Mélanges inédits* (Paris, 1892) and *Pensées et fragments inédits*, 2 vols. (Bordeaux, 1899-1901), both edited by Baron Gaston de Montesquieu. *L'esprit des lois* is available in numerous editions, of course, including that of G. Truc in two volumes (Paris, 1944-1945). For an English version, I recommend Franz Neumann's edition of the Thomas Nugent translation (New York, 1949).

In dealing with this general category of sources, it seems best to direct the reader to the bibliographical footnotes grouped at various points in the preceding text. For writers on the law of nobility—Bacquet, Tiraqueau, Loyseau, La Roque, Belleguise, Bertaut—see Chapter Two, Part I, and Chapter Four, Part I. For theorists of government and aristocracy, whether earlier figures like Girard du

Haillan, Hotman, Pasquier, Seyssel, and La Roche Flavin, or men of the Louis XIV-Louis XV era, like Fénelon, Boulainvilliers, Saint-Simon, d'Argenson, Du Bos, and Mably, see Chapter Twelve, Parts I and II. I would only add that the *Oeuvres* of Chancellor d'Aguesseau, 13 vols. (Paris, 1754-1789) deserve to be included with the above as political documents.

Works of fiction should not be overlooked. Used with caution, the early eighteenth-century novel or play can contribute sound descriptive passages, interspersed among gilded fantasies. Furthermore, in this respect like the American movie, it can serve as indirect evidence, giving the student a feel for the conditions of life and thought which lent currency to the particular illusions of the age. The following are examples of what I have in mind: Prévost's famous *Histoire du chevalier des Grieux et de Manon Lescaut*, Gilbert Lely, ed. (Paris, 1946); Campan's *Le mot et la chose* (s. l., 1752); Gimat de Bonneval's *Voyage de Mantes* ("Amsterdam," 1753); the anonymous *Mémoires et aventures du baron de Puineuf* ("The Hague," 1737); and Marivaux' *Le prince travesti* (Paris, 1727), as well as Marcel Arland's edition of the same writer's *La vie de Marianne* (Paris, 1947). Practically all of Marivaux' plays, in fact, are useful, if somewhat repetitious.

III. Secondary Works

The student faced with the problem of finding his way through the staggering number of books and articles on France under the ancien régime must ultimately make his selections for intensive study after having handled the volumes themselves. He can, however, block out the boundaries of his task by taking advantage of certain lists which group available items by subject. One such, valuable both for printed primary sources and for older secondary works, is the official *Catalogue de l'histoire de France* of the Département des Imprimés, Bibliothèque Impériale (later Nationale), 11 vols. plus tables (Paris, 1855-1879). Another only partially outdated compilation is Gabriel Monod's *Bibliographie de l'histoire de France* (Paris, 1888). More recent is Charles Du Peloux' full, though uncritical *Répertoire général des ouvrages modernes relatifs au XVIIIe siècle français* (Paris, 1926), with its *Supplément* of 1927. Especially valuable for finding articles in periodicals appearing during the last third of the nineteenth century is the two-volume *Bibliographie des travaux publiés de 1866 à 1897 sur l'histoire de France de 1500 à 1789*, E. Saulnier and A. Martin (Paris, 1932-1938). The same function is served for portions of the twentieth century by three publications: the *Répertoire méthodique de l'histoire moderne et contemporaine de la France*, 9 vols., G. Brière, P. Caron *et al.*, eds. (Paris, 1899-1932); the *Répertoire bibliographique de l'histoire de France*, 6 vols., P. Caron and H. Stein, eds. (Paris, 1923-1938); and the *Bibliographie critique des principaux travaux parus sur l'histoire de 1600 à 1914*, 3 vols., published by the Société d'Histoire Moderne (Paris, 1935-1937). The above cover, respectively, works published in the years 1898-1913, 1920-1931, and 1932-1935. It should also be pointed out that most large libraries, both in France and in the United States, have the *Catalogue général des livres imprimés de la Bibliothèque Nationale* (Paris, 1897-present).

It is difficult to choose the general or monographic works on French narrative history calling for inclusion in this summary. A few, however, clearly demand notice. Henri Carré's volume on *Le règne de Louis XV* (Paris, 1909), which is Volume VIII, Part Two, of Lavisse' great *Histoire de France*, though less distinguished than its immediate predecessors in that collection, is nonetheless basic. For the first years after 1715 it may be supplemented by Dom H. Leclercq's painstaking *Histoire de la Régence*, 3 vols. (Paris, 1921-1922). Book Six, "Die Regentenschaft und Kardinal Fleury," in Leopold von Ranke's *Französische Geschichte*, Volume VI (Stuttgart, 1879) may still be read with profit for its judicious, if cold, presentation of political events.

Certain books designed to supply background for the French Revolution have much to offer the student of the late seventeenth and early eighteenth centuries. Two which are normally mentioned in the same breath, despite their very different theses, are Alexis de Tocqueville's *L'ancien régime et la Révolution* (Paris, 1856) and Hyppolyte Taine's *L'ancien régime* (Paris, 1876), the latter representing Volume I of its author's *Origines de la France contemporaine*. Albert Mathiez' *La chute de la royauté* (Paris, 1922), the first volume of his history of the Revolution, is especially valuable for its chapter on "La révolte nobiliaire." Similarly worthwhile for its retrospective comments is Georges

Lefebvre's *The Coming of the French Revolution*, R. R. Palmer, tr. (Princeton, 1947). Félix Rocquain, *L'esprit révolutionnaire avant la Révolution* (Paris, 1878) is in part misnamed, since it concentrates almost wholly on religious unrest; but it is for that reason all the more interesting to a researcher concerned in any way with Jansenist and Gallican themes.

Numerous sociological treatises touching in one way or another on aristocracies have supplied helpful suggestions. Vilfredo Pareto, even at his most rancorous, is stimulating, both in *The Mind and Society*, 4 vols., Andrew Bongiorno and Arthur Livingston, trs. (New York, 1935) and in *Les systèmes socialistes*, 2 vols., G.-H. Bousquet, tr. (Paris, 1926). So are Max Weber, *Essays in Sociology*, H. H. Gerth and C. Wright Mills, eds. and trs. (New York, 1946); Thorstein Veblen, *The Theory of the Leisure Class* (New York, 1899); and Jacob Novikov, *Conscience et volonté sociales* (Paris, 1897). The section on "Aristokratische Lebensformung und Barock" in Alfred Weber's *Kulturgeschichte als Kultursoziologie* (Leyden, 1935) and J. Schumpeter, "Zur Soziologie der Imperialismen—Der Imperialismus im absoluten Fürstenstaat," *Archiv für Sozialwissenschaft*, XLVI (1918), especially pp. 277 ff., should also be noted. Aside from the "pre-sociological" works of Granier de Cassagnac and Hyppolyte Passy in the nineteenth century, there are two more recent instances of authors who have dealt with the question of aristocracies in specifically French terms. One is Édouard de Naurois, *Les classes dirigeantes* (Paris, 1910). The other is Marie Kolabinska, *La circulation des élites en France* (Lausanne, 1912). Both are disappointing in their tendency to superficial generalization, though Naurois did some extremely close research on certain points.

Concerning the history of the French nobility, there is a pair of articles to which I am deeply indebted: Marc Bloch, "Sur le passé de la noblesse française: Quelques jalons de recherche," *Annales d'histoire économique et sociale*, VIII (1936), 366-378, and Henri Carré, "La noblesse de robe au temps de Louis XV," *Bulletin de la Faculté des Lettres de Poitiers* (1890), 344-355 and 385-394. There are countless histories of the noblesse which cannot be listed here. Some, like Édouard de Barthélemy's of 1858 and the Comte de Sémainville's of 1860, are more important as documents of their own times—when

Napoleon III had restored noble self-consciousness to full vigor—than as analytical studies. One of these older works, however, may still be read with some confidence: Charles Louandre, *La noblesse française sous l'ancienne monarchie* (Paris, 1880), though Louandre felt himself drawn in one direction, the republican, almost as strongly as Sémainville did in the other.

A rewarding introduction to the period treated in my study is the Vicomte d'Avenel, *La noblesse française sous Richelieu* (Paris, 1901), while Henri Carré, *La noblesse de France et l'opinion publique au XVIIIe siècle* (Paris, 1920) is obviously fundamental for the Louis XV period itself. So, with regard to the gentry, is Pierre de Vaissière's *Gentilshommes campagnards de l'ancienne France* (Paris, 1903, 2nd edition, 1925). The detailed *Abrégé chronologique d'édits, règlements, etc., concernant le fait de noblesse* of L.-N.-R. Chérin (Paris, 1788) has proved invaluable. The variety of more localized studies may be sufficiently indicated if I cite two books, quite different one from the other in scope and subject matter: Paul de Rousier's own family history, *Une famille de hobereaux pendant six siècles* (Paris, 1935) and Henri Frotier de La Messelière, *La noblesse en Bretagne avant 1789* (Rennes, 1902). The latter is sketchy in parts and is not uniformly well-documented, but it contains some informative passages both on the Estates and the Parlement of Brittany and on the economic status of nobles in that province.

As for the sovereign courts, it must be said at once that practically every parlement has had its historian, and in some cases two or three: Glasson for Paris; Communay, as well as Boscheron des Portes, for Guienne; Cabasse and, much later, Boisgelin, Clapiers-Collongues and Wolff for Provence; Delmas for Navarre; Dubédat for Languedoc; Michel for Metz; Truchis de Varennes and Estignard for Franche-Comté; La Cuisine, Des Marches and others for Burgundy; Pillot for Flanders; and so on. Certain of the Chambres des Comptes have also received separate treatment: that of Dijon by d'Arbaumont, for example, and that of Paris by Denys, Coral, Coustant d'Yanville, and Boislisle, over a period of nearly a century. A few such works, however, stand out from the others. A. Floquet, in his seven-volume *Histoire du Parlement de Normandie* (Rouen, 1840-1842) did not succeed in avoiding the adulatory note which mars so many of the works cited above, but he far surpassed them in the richness of his documentation and has left a veritable monument of institutional history. A. Le Moy, *Le Parlement de Bretagne et le pouvoir royal au XVIIIe siècle* (Angers, 1909), and Jean Egret, *Le Parlement de Dauphiné et les affaires publiques*, 2 vol. (Grenoble-Paris, 1942), are brilliant studies by any standard and deserve a place by themselves in this generally uninspiring literature. An old work of synthesis, uncritical but nonetheless full of interesting details, is the Vicomte de Bastard d'Estang, *Les parlements de France* (Paris, 1857). A twentieth-century analysis which, despite its title, includes a good deal on the seventeenth and early eighteenth centuries is Henri Carré, *La fin des parlements* (Paris, 1912). An intelligent short discussion by Alfred Cobban, "The *Parlements* of France in the 18th Century," appeared in *History* (February-June, 1950). Finally, there are two important monographs on special problems: Gustave Saulnier de La Pinelais, *Les Gens du roi au Parlement de Bretagne* (Rennes-Paris, 1902) and Gustave Carrelet, *Les avocats du Parlement de Franche-Comté* (Besançon, 1913). I have already inserted, at the end of Chapter Seven, a note on Jean Egret's article, "L'aristocratie parlementaire française à la fin de l'Ancien Régime," *Revue historique*, July-September, 1952, 1-15.

Questions concerning numerous other institutions inevitably arise in any study of the aristocracy and the sovereign courts. With regard to administration, one must take account of a voluminous literature going back at least as far as Tocqueville's provocative thesis attacking the notion that centralization had been a new departure brought only by the Revolution. Relatively early monographs on the subject include H. de Luçay, "Des origines du pouvoir ministériel en France: Les secrétaires d'État et les conseils, 1715-1718," *Revue historique de droit français et étranger* (May-June 1868), and Boyer de Sainte-Suzanne, *Le personnel administratif sous l'ancien régime* (Paris, 1868). Among the more important twentieth-century books in this category, I would cite four to illustrate the range of problems discussed. Gustave Dupont-Ferrier concentrated on the lower echelons in *Les officiers royaux des bailliages et sénéchaussées et les institutions monarchiques locales* (Paris, 1902). Paul Ardascheff, on the other hand, turned to the intermediate level with *Les intendants de province sous Louis XVI*, L. Jousserandot, tr. (Paris, 1909), which is useful for Louis XV's reign as well, provided eighteenth-century changes are borne in mind. Paul Viollet sought out the king in council: *Le roi et ses ministres pendant les trois derniers siècles de la monarchie* (Paris, 1912). Finally, Georges Pagès has done much to encourage more analysis at all levels, through writing *La monarchie d'ancien régime en France* (Paris, 1928) and through editing *Études sur l'histoire administrative et sociale de l'ancienne France* (Paris, 1938). Despite all, however, Professor Edmond Esmonin's long-awaited study of the royal administration is sorely missed.

Aside from the books on *vénalité des offices* discussed above, page 106, there are several others on special institutional aspects of my problem. With regard to the provincial estates, for example, see Armand Rebillon's *Les états de Bretagne, de 1661 à 1789* (Paris, 1932) with its accompanying volume of sources, and the chapter by Émile Appolis, "Les états de Languedoc au XVIIIe siècle: Comparaison avec les états de Bretagne," in *L'organisation corporative du moyen âge à la fin de l'ancien régime*, Émile Lousse, ed. (Louvain, 1937). On seigneurial justice there are valuable passages in such major legal histories as Joseph Declareuil, *Histoire générale du droit français des origines à 1789* (Paris, 1925), in addition to more specific works, including A. Combier, *Les justices seigneuriales du bailliage de Vermandois sous l'ancien régime* (Paris, 1897), and A. E. Giffard, *Les justices seigneuriales en Bretagne aux XVIIe et XVIIIe siècles* (Paris, 1903). Léon Mention, *L'armée sous l'ancien régime* (Paris, 1900), and Louis Tuetey, *Les officiers de l'ancien régime: Nobles et roturiers* (Paris, 1908), are important references in matters of military personnel.

A special aspect of institutional history demanding separate mention here is that of corporate organization. In this connection, see Georges Espinas, "La société d'ancien régime: La situation corporative," *Mélanges d'histoire sociale*, V (1944), 94-99, and F. Olivier-Martin, "Le déclin et la suppression des corps en France au XVIIIe siècle," in *L'organisation corporative du moyen âge à la fin de l'ancien régime*, Émile Lousse, ed. (Louvain, 1937). Important longer studies include Émile Lousse, *La société d'ancien régime: Organisation et représentation corporatives* (Louvain, 1943), and Émile Coornaert, *Les corporations en France avant 1789* (Paris, 1941). There are certain unpleasant undertones in the writings of the "corporatists," not the least of which is the recurrent theme of interest shading into sympathy for fascist experiments, especially in Italy. They are, nevertheless, products of extensive scholarship; and if it is fair to read them with caution, it would be unfair to deny their contribution to the history of the old monarchy.

A few writers on French religious history have emphasized the rôle of the high magistracy. One such is L. Bassieux, *Théorie des libertés gallicanes du Parlement de Paris au XVIIIe siècle* (Paris, 1906). Others are Léon Cahen, *Les querelles religieuses et parlementaires sous Louis XV* (Paris, 1913); Jules Flammermont, *Les jésuites et les parlements au XVIIIe siècle* (Paris, 1885); Jean Egret, "Le procés des Jésuites devant les parlements de France," *Revue historique* (July-September 1950). Bernard de Lacombe, *La résistance janséniste et parlementaire au temps de Louis XV* (Paris, 1948); J. Carreyre, *Le Jansénisme durant la Régence*, 2 vols. (Louvain, 1932-1933). For the more remote background of the problem, see G. Mollat, "Les origines du gallicanisme parlementaire aux XIVe et XVe siècles," *Revue d'histoire ecclésiastique*, XLIII (1948), 90-147. An institutional study essential to any analysis of the French aristocracy is Augustin Sicard, *L'ancien clergé de France*, Volume I: *Les évêques avant la Révolution* (Paris, 1893). Even the most summary bibliography in this field must include Saint-Beuve's great history of *Port-Royal*, which I have used in the seven-volume 4th edition (Paris, 1878).

Apart from numerous monographs on specific topics, such as John Law's *Système*, economic history has some general works to offer the student of a problem such as mine. The Vicomte d'Avenel has contributed both a six-volume *Histoire économique de la propriété, des salaires, des denrées et de tous les prix en général depuis l'an 1200 jusqu'en l'an 1800* (Paris, 1894-1912) and a more concise *Histoire de la fortune française* (Paris, 1927). Similarly broad in scope are E. Levasseur, *Histoire du commerce de la France*, Volume I: *Avant 1789* (Paris, 1911); Marcel Marion, *Histoire financière de la France depuis 1715*, Volume I (Paris, 1914); and a combination of books by Henri Sée, including his *La France économique et sociale au XVIIIe siècle* (Paris, 1925). Invaluable for the backward look it takes from the threshold of the Revolution is *La crise de l'économie française à la fin de l'ancien régime*, Volume I: *Aperçus généraux* (Paris, 1943), by C.-E. Labrousse.

For a matchless study of agrarian history, see Marc Bloch, *Les caractères originaux de l'histoire rurale française* (Paris, 1931). Arthur Young's famous *Travels in France*, Matilda Betham-Edwards, ed. (London, 1889) relates specifically to the years 1787-1789; but it is of interest to anyone seeking to understand the gentry of even the first half of the century.

In the sprawling field of French social history, certain general analyses will help the student to get his bearings. One is E. Levasseur, *La population française*, 3 vols. (Paris, 1889-1892). Another is Philippe Sagnac, *La formation de la société française moderne, 1661-1789*, 2 vols. (Paris, 1945-1946). At least three books treating the seventeenth century must be viewed as indispensable for any approach to the eighteenth: the ubiquitous Comte d'Avenel, *Prêtres, soldats et juges sous Richelieu* (Paris, 1907); Charles Normand, *La bourgeoisie française au XVIIe siècle* (Paris, 1908); and the brilliant essay by Gaston Roupnel, deserving of a place beside Bloch's *Caractères originaux*, *La ville et la campagne au XVIIe siècle* (Paris, 1922).

For pictures of life in a pair of large cities, see E.-F. de La Cuisine, *Esquisses dijonnaises* (Dijon, 1850), and Alfred Franklin, *La vie privée d'autrefois: La vie de Paris sous la Régence* (Paris, 1897), *La vie de Paris sous Louis XV* (Paris, 1899). Two often underrated types of source material for social history, the novel and the street song, are involved in F. C. Green's analysis of *La peinture des moeurs de la bonne société dans le roman français de 1715 à 1761* (Paris, 1924) and in Émile Raunié's ten-volume *Chansonnier historique du XVIIIe siècle* (Paris, 1879-1884), which might with equal justice have been placed in the section on primary sources, above. The student particularly interested in manners and dress should include in his reading Henri Brocher, *Le rang et l'étiquette sous l'ancien régime* (Paris, 1934); André Blum, *Les modes au XVIIe et au XVIIIe siècles* (Paris, 1928); and Joseph Boulaud, "Vêtements, bijoux et parures de la noblesse au XVIIe et au XVIIIe siècles," *La science historique*, XIX (1930), 57-68, 131-136, XX (1931), 5-14, 43-54, 145-152.

Turning to the subject of political and social ideas, the researcher would do well to begin by seeking a background in earlier history from such books as *Constitutional Thought in Sixteenth-Century France*, by W. F. Church (Cambridge, Mass., 1941); the less searching but chronologically more extensive *Weg und Sieg der modernen Staatsidee in Frankreich*, by Martin Göhring (Tübingen, 1946); and *Les idées politiques en France au XVIIe siècle*, by Henri Sée (Paris, 1923). Still another valuable piece of background reading is Paul Hazard's brilliant *La crise de la conscience européenne, 1680-1715*, 3 vols. (Paris, 1934-1935). For an aspect of late medieval and early modern thought of special significance for the high robe, see Myron P. Gilmore, *Argument from Roman Law in Political Thought, 1200-1600* (Cambridge, 1941). Without leaving two of these authors, one may then move into the age of Louis XV with Sée, *Les idées politiques en France au XVIIIe siècle* (Paris, 1920); the same writer's *L'évolution de la pensée politique en France au XVIIIe siècle* (Paris, 1925); and Hazard, *La pensée européenne au XVIIIe siècle*, 3 vols. (Paris, 1946). The last is unquestionably less striking in terms of freshness of interpretation than is its author's earlier book; but it provides, nonetheless, a welcome survey of dominant trends. Other notable works on eighteenth-century thought include Gustave Lanson, "Questions diverses sur l'histoire de l'esprit philosophique en France avant 1750," *Revue d'histoire littéraire de la France*, XIX (1912), 1-29, 293-317; Daniel Mornet, *Les origines intellectuelles de la Révolution française, 1715-1787* (Paris, 1933); F. Piétri, *La réforme de l'état au XVIIIe siècle* (Paris, 1935); and the first hundred pages of Hedwig Hintze's *Staatseinheit und Föderalismus im alten Frankreich* (Stuttgart, 1928). Two interesting views of more specialized aspects appear in *La légende politique de Charlemagne au XVIIIe siècle*, by A. Duméric (Toulouse, 1879), and *La constitution britannique devant l'opinion française, de Montesquieu à Bonaparte*, by Gabriel Bonno (Paris, 1932).

On the important topic of the provincial academies, Francisque Boullier, *L'Institut et les académies de province* (Paris, 1879), supplies a general introduction. In addition, there are numerous individual studies, such as *L'Académie des Sciences, Inscriptions et Belles-Lettres de Toulouse au dix-huitième siècle*, by Célestin Douais (Toulouse, 1896). The academy development at Dijon has had unusually close attention from Philippe Milsand, *Notes et documents pour servir à l'histoire de l'Académie des Sciences, Arts et Belles-Lettres de Dijon* (Paris, 1871); from Victor Cardot, *Bernard-Hector Pouffier* (Dijon, 1876); from Marcel Bouchard, *De l'humanisme à l'Encyclopédie;*

L'esprit public en Bourgogne sous l'ancien régime (Paris, 1930); and from Roger Tisserand, *Au temps de l'Encyclopédie: L'Académie de Dijon de 1740 à 1793* (Paris, 1936).

Books and articles on individual figures obviously occupy a major place in the bibliography for my research, though only a few can be noted here. For Fénelon, see Albert Chérel, *Fénelon au XVIIIe siècle en France (1715-1820): Son prestige, son influence* (Paris, 1917), and Élie Carcassonne, *Fénelon, l'homme et l'oeuvre* (Paris, 1946). For Saint-Simon, Henri Sée, "Les idées politiques du duc de Saint-Simon," *Revue historique*, LXXIII (1900), 1-23, and André Liard, "Saint-Simon et les états généraux," *Revue historique*, LXXV (1901), 319-331. For Boulainvilliers, Renée Simon, *Henry de Boulainviller* (Gap, 1940), her bibliographical treatise, *A la recherche d'un homme et d'un auteur* (Paris, 1941), and her *Un révolté du Grand siècle: Henry de Boulainviller* (Garches, 1948), which together completely supersede the older biography by M. Belliot (Caen, 1888). On the ministerial or royalist side, one should include Jean Lamson, *Les idées politiques du marquis d'Argenson* (Montpellier, 1943); A. Lombard, *L'abbé Du Bos, un initiateur de la pensée moderne* (Paris, 1913); and Ernest A. Whitfield, *Gabriel Bonnot de Mably* (London, 1930). F. Monnier, *Le chancelier Daguesseau* (Paris, 1859); Henri Mamet, *Le président de Brosses* (Lille, 1874); Yvonne Bezard, *Le président de Brosses et ses amis de Genève* (Paris, 1939); and Alan C. Taylor, *Le président de Brosses et l'Australie* (Paris, 1937), though of incidental interest, are less important. For a study of a seventeenth-century theorist and magistrate, demanding attention by students of the ensuing period as well, see Gilbert Picot, *Cardin Le Bret (1558-1655) et la doctrine de la souveraineté* (Nancy, 1948).

So far as secondary works on Montesquieu are concerned, I must content myself with referring to D. C. Cabeen's *Montesquieu: A Bibliography* (New York, 1947), since the publication of which any ambitious listing by me would be clearly supererogatory. One study, worth noting for its emphasis on non-Germanic themes, is L. M. Levin, *The Political Doctrine of Montesquieu's Esprit des Lois: Its Classical Background* (New York, 1936). Although my own inclination is to stress the Frankish tradition in the great treatise, I should like to acknowledge the value of Levin's book as an antidote to oversimplification. In addition, I must cite the importance for my purposes of the collision between Élie Carcassonne's laudatory *Montesquieu et le problème de la constitution française au XVIIIe siècle* (Paris, 1926) and Albert Mathiez' vehement attack on that work in "La place de Montesquieu dans l'histoire des doctrines politiques du XVIIIe siècle," *Annales historiques de la Révolution française*, VII (1930), 97-112.

Index

NOTE. The present index combines personal, geographical, and topical references. For obvious reasons, however, no attempt has been made to list all the names appearing in the body of the book, many of them solely for purposes of illustration, and possessing no great intrinsic importance in themselves.

Académie Française, 106, 216, 231, 234
Academies, provincial, 235-238, 270-271
Aguesseau, Henri-François d', 18-19, 34, 57, 85, 87, 91, 97, 139, 149, 174, 189, 193, 215, 221, 243, 260, 262, 271
Aix-en-Provence, x, 129, 132, 136, 156, 162-163, 213, 220, 258; Parlement of Provence, 38, 42, 44, 92, 103-104, 119, 125, 126, 130, 134, 157, 195, 204, 213, 220, 258, 259, 265; Chambre des Comptes, 39, 119, 153, 195, 258
Alsace, 36, 38, 112, 165. *See also* Colmar, Strasbourg.
Anne of Austria, 63
Argenson, Marc-René de Voyer d', 34, 95, 229-230
Argenson, René-Louis, marquis d', 86, 102-103, 121-122, 174, 230-231, 232, 234, 259, 262, 271
Armorial général, 26, 30-31, 67, 125, 255
Army, vii, 11-12, 17-18, 28, 34, 120, 137-139, 219, 267
Arras, Conseil Provincial of Artois, 38, 46
Arrière-ban. *See* Ban et arrière-ban.
Artois, 38, 46, 112, 194. *See also* Arras.
Auvergne, 10, 30, 128, 143, 165, 167, 203. *See also* Clermont-Ferrand.
Avocats, 47, 55, 118-119
Avocats-généraux. *See* Gens du roi.

Bacquet, Jean, 61, 62, 64, 261
Baillis and sénéchaux. *See* Lower courts.
Ban et arrière-ban, 11-12, 28
Barbier, Edmond-Jean-François, 55, 88, 97, 98, 100, 119, 142, 145, 158, 178, 211, 213, 259
Barcelonnette, 38, 42
Belleguise, A., 23-26, 261
Belle-Isle, Charles-Louis-Auguste Fouquet, duc de, 18
Besançon, 129, 136, 214, 220, 237, 257; Parlement of Franche-Comté, 38, 44, 50, 51, 64, 97, 101, 104, 153, 193, 199, 220, 237, 257, 259, 265, 266
Bishops. *See* Prelates.
Blois, 84; Chambre des Comptes, 39, 53
Bodin, Jean, 228, 229, 231
Boileau, Nicolas, 8, 30
Boisguillebert, Pierre Le Pesant, sieur de, 230
"Bonnet, Affaire du," 177-178, 181
Bordeaux, viii, x, 71, 127, 131, 134-136, 140, 141, 150, 156, 158, 161, 162, 165, 166, 198, 208, 212, 217, 220, 223, 234, 235, 237, 244, 257, 258; Parlement of Guienne, 37, 38, 42, 43, 53, 56, 57, 89, 96, 102-103, 105, 129, 131, 135-136, 137, 141, 147-148, 150, 157, 161, 162, 189, 198, 217, 220, 237, 257, 265; Cour des Aides, 39, 42, 44, 53, 129, 131, 135, 137, 157, 217, 237
Bossuet, Jacques-Bénigne, 18, 229
Boulainvilliers, Henri de, 19, 22, 27, 30, 69, 120, 145, 184-185, 190, 191, 203, 218, 219, 226-229, 230, 232, 233, 234, 237, 240, 241-242, 244, 262, 271

Bourbon, duc de, 86
Bourgogne, duc de, 30, 226
Brittany, ix, 30, 32, 36, 38, 46, 48, 50, 53, 73-75, 86, 90, 110, 113, 126, 130, 131, 137, 146, 149, 153, 164, 165, 167, 168, 192, 194-197, 204, 210, 220, 224, 256, 259, 265, 266, 267. *See also* Nantes, Rennes.
Brosses, Charles de, president, 116, 216, 220, 236, 271
Buffon, George-Louis Leclerc, comte de, 216, 236
Bureaux des finances, 54, 63, 65, 140
Burgundy, 36, 38, 41, 45, 48, 49-50, 63, 116, 124, 126, 132, 140, 143, 147, 157, 159, 161, 162, 164, 165, 166, 169, 189, 194, 195, 196, 216, 217, 220, 235, 236, 257, 265. *See also* Dijon.

Capitation. *See* Taxation.
Cellamare, Antonio del Giudice, duke of, 86, 177
Cenitème. *See* Taxation.
Ceremonies and etiquette, 7, 8, 16, 28-29, 41-42, 50, 55-57, 73, 141, 177-178, 183, 210, 215, 227, 269
Chambres des comptes, 37, 39, 41, 46, 50, 53, 64, 67, 151, 265. *See also* names of cities where located, e.g., Dijon, Montpellier, Paris.
Champ de Mars, 93, 180, 223, 225, 229, 231
Champagne, 11, 38, 165, 194
Chancellery officers, 49, 50
Charles V, king of France, 39, 45, 94
Charles VII, king of France, 11, 94
Charles VIII, king of France, 65
"Chasot de Nantigny, Louis" (pseud.), 51, 52, 140
Châteaux. *See* Seigneuries and châteaux.
Châtelet. *See* Lower courts.
Chauvelin, Germain-Louis de, 97, 139, 150, 204, 215
Chevaliers d'honneur, 50, 57
Chevigny, sieur de, 9-10, 71
Cinquantième. *See* Taxation.
Clermont-Ferrand, 57, 235, 236; Cour des Aides, 39, 53, 143, 205, 236
Colbert, Jean Baptiste, 4, 7, 8, 10, 13, 18, 23, 110, 111, 114, 154, 162, 194
Colmar, 136, 141; Conseil Supérieur of Alsace, 38, 141, 153
Commerce, 14, 75, 137, 144-145, 148, 161-162, 166, 208, 250
Condé, Louis II de Bourbon, prince de, 17, 94
Conseil and conseillers d'État, 41, 62, 66, 109, 140, 181
Conseil privé. *See* Conseil d'État.
Contrôleur-général, 15, 39, 258
Costumes and styles of dress, 55-57, 67-68, 70, 72, 216, 269
Councilors (sovereign courts), 49, 50, 53, 56, 63, 69, 112, 113, 134, 147-148, 150, 152, 153-154, 155, 158, 216
Cours des aides, 37, 39-40, 41, 50, 53, 64, 67, 151. *See also* names of cities where located: Bordeaux, Clermont-Ferrand, Montauban, Paris.
Cours des monnaies, 37, 40, 46, 50, 53, 64, 67, 151. *See also* names of cities where located: Lyon, Paris.
Court and courtiers, vii, 9-10, 71, 143, 186, 188, 205, 215, 239, 248

Dauphiné, ix, 27, 38, 42, 48, 63, 75, 84, 113, 118-119, 130, 138, 139, 142, 143, 146, 165, 193, 198, 216, 220, 261, 266. *See also* Grenoble.
Dijon, x, 45, 49, 129, 131-132, 136-137, 138, 139, 140, 141, 156, 161, 162, 163, 165, 194, 210, 217, 220, 221, 234, 235, 236, 237, 256, 257, 258, 269, 270-271; Parlement of Burgundy, 38, 41-42, 43, 48, 49-50, 53, 56, 63, 116, 124, 126, 132, 135-137, 140, 141, 143, 147, 150, 153, 157, 159, 162, 166, 169, 189, 194-195, 212, 216, 220, 235, 236, 257, 265; Chambre des Comptes, 39, 41-42, 64, 125, 132, 136-137, 140, 141, 147, 154, 217, 236, 257, 265
Dixième. *See* Taxation.
Dôle, Chambre des Comptes, 39, 44, 51
Douai, 150, 220; Parlement of Flanders, 38, 46, 64, 86, 96, 97, 220, 265

Dubois, Guillaume, cardinal, 84, 86, 87, 99, 205
Du Bos, Jean-Baptiste, abbé, 231-233, 234, 241-242, 244, 262, 271
Dueling, 69, 75, 76, 180
Du Haillan, Bernard de Girard, 223, 225, 261-262

Education, 87, 188-189, 218-221, 227
Élections. *See* Lower courts.
England. *See* Great Britain.
Enquêtes, chambres des, 47, 48, 85, 128, 135, 143
Entresol, Club de l', 234-235
Épices, 151-152, 154-155, 166
Estates General, 10, 59, 73, 94, 184, 185, 190-192, 223, 225, 226, 229
Estates, provincial, 10, 36, 45, 74, 159, 163, 169, 193-197, 201, 230, 248, 265, 267
Estienne, Henri, 225
Etiquette. *See* Ceremonies and etiquette.
Evocations, 40-41, 181, 200, 242
Exclusivism, 16, 73-74, 113, 116-118, 137, 145-146, 149, 152, 208, 249-250, 264

Families, 124-146, 178, 186, 188, 247, 248, 255, 256, 257
Fénelon, François de Salignac de La Mothe-, 19, 120, 226, 227, 229, 233, 262, 271
Fevret de Fontette, Charles-Marie, 216, 217, 255
Fiefs, feudalism and feudal law, viii, 24, 28, 33, 39, 43, 66, 115, 121, 162-169, 174-175, 222, 224-229, 230-232, 240-242, 244, 246, 248, 249, 251
Flanders, 32, 36, 38, 64, 86, 110, 112, 114, 165, 220, 265. *See also* Douai.
Fleury, André-Hercule de, cardinal, 85, 86, 87, 92, 94, 97, 100, 235, 263
Franche-Comté, 36, 38, 51, 64, 97, 104, 129, 193, 199, 220, 237, 257, 259, 265, 266. *See also* Besançon, Dôle.
Francis I, king of France, 108, 121, 122
Franclieu, Jacques Laurent Pierre Charles Pasquier, marquis de, 199, 204, 205-206, 219, 260
Fronde, 5, 6, 7, 10, 63, 93, 191, 223, 226, 248

Gabelle. *See* Taxation.
Gages, 97, 111, 152-154, 166, 196, 249
Gallicanism, 4, 6, 85, 87, 88, 99, 100, 102, 247, 264, 268
Gascony, 36, 38
Gens du roi, 48-49, 50, 53, 56, 63, 69, 80, 97, 112, 118, 119, 147, 150, 153, 266
Germanist-Romanist controversy, 184-185, 223, 225, 227, 228, 231, 232, 241-242
Grand' chambre, 44, 46-47, 56, 81, 85, 90, 96, 155, 177, 181, 210
Grand Conseil, 37, 40-41, 43, 44, 45, 46, 50, 51, 52, 53, 63, 67, 94, 96, 114, 126, 137, 143, 151, 153, 159, 215, 234, 254, 255
Grande Recherche, 13-14, 23-26, 65, 209
Great Britain, 22, 36, 86, 91, 94, 102, 131, 173, 175, 180, 181, 182, 222, 224, 228, 232, 233, 238, 241, 252, 270
Great Officers of the Crown, 32, 62, 73, 183
Greffiers-en-chef, 49, 50, 56, 63, 147
Greniers à sel. *See* Lower courts.
Grenoble, x, 46, 127, 129, 132, 136, 138, 158, 159, 160, 165, 166, 217, 220, 256, 257-258, 261; Parlement of Dauphiné, 37, 38, 42, 44, 48, 63, 75, 84, 101, 113, 118-119, 130, 131, 134, 136, 139, 142, 146, 153, 159, 193, 198, 220, 257, 258, 266; Chambre des Comptes, 39, 42, 63, 126, 131, 136, 159, 216
Guienne, 38, 42, 106, 127, 129, 131, 141, 157, 161, 189, 198, 217, 220, 237, 257, 265. *See also* Bordeaux.

Hénault, Charles-Jean François, president, 55, 84, 98, 100, 121, 150, 204, 212, 238, 259
Henry II, king of France, 60
Henry IV, king of France, 17, 60, 61, 107, 109, 251

Hobereaux. *See* Rural gentry.
Honorary councilors, 49, 110
Hotman, François, 225, 226, 227, 228, 229, 231, 245, 262
Hozier, Charles d', 26, 30-31, 125, 127, 128, 132, 255
Huissiers, premiers, 49, 50, 56

Île de France, 38, 165, 224
Intendants, 7, 15, 30, 32, 36, 39, 71, 139-140, 189, 197, 198, 209, 258, 266

Jansenism, 4, 69-70, 75, 84, 87, 88, 99, 100, 101, 103, 211, 220, 247, 264, 268
Jesuits, 6, 70, 86, 87, 100, 103, 219, 220, 268
"Joyeux avènement." *See* Taxation.
Judicium Francorum, 93-95, 180, 223, 229, 232, 238
Jurieu, Pierre, 226
Jussion, lettres de, 81, 193

La Bruyère, Jean de, vii, 8, 14, 22, 70-71, 188
La Force case, 91, 180, 181, 200
Langùedoc, 27, 36, 38, 47, 48, 49, 71, 90, 127, 129, 130, 139, 141, 143, 150, 178, 194-196, 205, 210, 216, 220, 256, 260, 265, 267. *See also* Montauban, Montpellier, Toulouse.
La Roche Flavin, Bernard de, 223, 224, 229, 238, 240, 245, 262
La Vrillière, Louis Phélypeaux, marquis de, 8, 91
Law, John, and the "Système," 84, 87, 90, 91, 98, 99, 121, 150, 159-161, 170, 191, 268
Le Gendre de Saint-Aubin, Gilbert Charles, 232, 241
Légitimés, 62, 176-177, 178, 179, 182, 183, 184, 185, 190, 191, 255, 261
Le Tellier, Michel, 7, 8
Lionne, Hugues de, 7
Lit de justice, 56, 82, 84, 90, 95, 96, 98, 135, 177, 178, 229
Locke, John, 102, 224, 233
Lorraine, 53
Louis IX (Saint), king of France, 224, 228
Louis XI, king of France, 94, 132
Louis XIV, king of France, vii, viii, 3-21, 23, 30, 31, 34, 36, 50, 55, 58, 59, 64, 65, 68, 69, 70, 74, 82, 83, 87, 88, 92, 95, 110, 111, 112, 113, 114, 117, 132, 138, 147, 148, 175, 176, 177, 178, 179, 182, 186, 190, 191, 197, 209, 210, 213, 226, 229, 230, 246, 258, 260, 262
Louis XV, king of France, x, 6, 31, 34, 35, 39, 40, 45, 73, 81, 83, 85, 88, 92, 96, 97, 98, 106, 112, 113, 114, 115, 124, 127, 136, 142, 148, 151, 154, 156, 158, 162, 167, 183, 191, 198, 201, 205, 213, 214, 217, 223, 232, 246, 247, 248, 259, 262, 263, 264, 268, 269, 270
Louis XVI, king of France, viii, 34, 252
Louvois, François-Michel Le Tellier, marquis de, 4, 8, 12, 17
Lower courts, 39-40, 114, 149; baillis and sénéchaux, 7, 28, 54, 107, 111, 112, 128, 149, 162, 252, 256, 266; Châtelet, 54, 65, 128, 140; élections, 40, 112, 149; greniers à sel, 35, 40, 111, 112; présidiaux, 28, 54, 111, 128, 149; prévôtés, 54, 112
Loyseau, Charles, 61-62, 64, 107, 108, 128, 225, 261
Lyon, 65, 161, 205, 235, 236, 260; Cour des Monnaies, 40, 44, 46, 53, 127, 140, 205, 236

Mably, Gabriel Bonnot de, 232, 244, 262, 271
Maine, duc du. *See* Légitimés.
Maîtres des requêtes, 65, 139-140
Marais, Mathieu, 55, 103, 119, 218, 259
Marc d'or, 108, 110, 116, 151
Marivaux, Pierre Carlet de Chamblain de, 207, 209, 262
Marriages, 44, 142-145
Marseille, 79, 235, 236
Maupeou, René-Charles de, 97, 128
Maupeou, René-Nicolas-Charles-Augustin de, vii, 34, 53, 139, 150, 252
Maurepas, Jean-Frédéric Phélypeaux, comte de, 8, 85, 100

Mazarin, Jules, cardinal, 9, 19, 63, 175, 208, 226
Mercurials, 18-19, 57
Mesmes, Jean-Antoine de, president, 83, 90, 97, 144, 152, 158, 181, 185, 191, 211
Metz, 129, 136-137, 150, 163; Parlement of, 38, 46, 48, 51, 53, 64, 89, 116, 125, 152, 163, 220, 265
Minorité and parenté rules, 111, 113, 116, 117
Mirabeau, Victor-Riqueti, marquis de, 133, 203, 245
Molière, Jean-Baptiste Poquelin, 207
Molinism, 92, 100
Montauban, 235; Cour des Aides, 39, 44, 53, 57, 65, 96, 132, 194
Montesquieu, Charles de Secondat, baron de La Brède et de, viii, 57, 91, 95, 102, 106, 123, 129, 134-135, 138, 141, 150, 165, 213, 216, 217, 222, 232, 233, 234, 237, 238-245, 246, 248, 250, 251, 260, 261, 270, 271-272
Montpellier, 220, 235; Chambre des Comptes, 39, 44, 53, 64, 65, 194

Names. *See* Titles and names.
Nancy, Parlement of Lorraine, 53
Nantes, 50, 65, 75, 205, 220; Chambre des Comptes, 39, 44, 64, 73-75, 130
Navarre, 32, 38, 44, 51, 150, 152, 205-206, 220, 260, 265. *See also* Pau.
Nicolay family, 118, 137, 142, 156, 200, 213
Noailles, Adrien-Maurice, duc de, 175, 179, 182, 190, 191, 198, 205
Nobility, 264-265 and *passim;* ennoblement, 12-14, 24-25, 32, 40, 61-62, 206, 207, 208, 221; proofs, 23-26; usurpation, 24-25, 206, 208-209; dérogeance and déchéance, 25-26, 240; number, 29-31; internal diversity, 32-34, 147; under Louis XIV, 6-21; opposition to peers, 182-187, 198; Noblesse de cloche, 32, 65, 71, 140-141; noblesse d'épée, 17-18, 50, 68-73, 130, 132-133, 137-139, 143-144, 202-221, 225-226, 234, 237, 248; noblesse de race (immemorial possession), 24-25, 32, 71, 143, 206; noblesse des hautes fonctions gouvernementales, 19, 24, 34, 137, 200; noblesse de robe, viii, 16-17, 20-21, 24, 32, 37, 50, 51, 53-58, 76, 132-133, 202-221, 234, 248, 255, 264. *For other material on* Noblesse de robe, *see* Sovereign courts.
Normandy, 36, 38, 50, 64, 90, 116, 150, 165, 193, 220, 256, 265-266. *See also* Rouen.
Nouvelles ecclésiastiques, 100, 101, 260

Orange, 38, 42
Orléans, Philippe, duc d'. *See* Regent and Regency.

Paris, x, 3, 33, 44-45, 71, 79, 99, 100, 101, 102, 121, 131, 132, 136-137, 139, 140, 150, 156, 157, 159, 165, 204, 206, 214, 219, 234, 244, 253-255, 269; Parlement, 18, 32, 33, 38, 40, 41, 42-43, 44, 47, 48, 49, 50, 51, 52, 53, 56-57, 60, 63, 66, 72, 73, 79, 82-84, 85, 86, 88, 89, 90, 92, 93, 94, 95, 96, 98, 99, 101, 103, 104, 114, 117, 118, 119, 120, 125, 127-129, 134, 135, 137, 140, 142, 144, 149, 150, 152, 153, 158, 159, 174-186, 189, 190, 191, 192, 198, 200, 210, 212, 214, 220, 224, 229, 239, 254, 258, 265; Chambre des Comptes, 39, 42-43, 44, 48, 51, 52, 53, 63, 90, 111, 112, 117, 118, 125, 129, 134, 137, 142, 150, 153, 155, 200, 254, 265; Cour des Aides, 13, 39, 42, 44, 46, 52, 53, 60-61, 90, 125, 126, 128, 129, 137, 143, 150, 153, 200, 208, 209, 215, 254; Cour des Monnaies, 40, 44, 46, 51, 52, 53, 90, 137, 142, 153, 254
Parlements, 6, 11, 37, 38, 46-48, 50, 53, 67, 95, 112, 151, 199-200, 220, 222, 265-266. *See also* names of cities where located, e.g., Dijon, Paris, Rouen, Toulouse.
Parquet. *See* Gens du roi.
Particularism, 87, 89, 192-193, 242-243, 247, 248, 270
Parties casuelles, 109-110, 113, 151

Pasquier, Étienne, 223, 228, 229, 231, 262
"Patro et avo consulibus," 60, 61, 62, 63, 64, 113
Pau, 57, 132, 220, 235, 236; Parlement of Navarre-Béarn, 38, 44, 46, 51, 89, 150, 152, 220, 236, 265
Paulet, Charles, and the "Paulette," 109-110, 112, 113, 128, 151
Peers and the peerage, 20, 47, 49, 56, 57, 68, 72, 91, 132, 173-187, 189, 191, 192, 198, 201, 215, 233, 248
Pensions, 16, 96, 152, 188
Perpignan, 220; Conseil Supérieur of Roussillon, 38, 46, 53, 89, 220
Philanthropies, 158-159, 167-168
Philip II (Augustus), king of France, 93
Philip IV (the Fair), king of France, 14, 39, 45
Philip V, king of Spain, 83, 86, 190
Philip VI, king of France, 94
Pöllnitz, Karl Ludwig, Freiherr von, 45, 102, 103, 212, 260
Polysynodie, 176, 177, 180, 186, 234
Pontchartrain, Louis Phélypeaux, comte de, 8, 36
Pontoise exile(1720), 84, 98, 99, 135, 158, 211
Portraiture, 138, 213-214
Potier de Novion, André, president, 97, 118, 127-128, 165, 178, 189, 234
Pouffier, Hector, councilor, 235, 257
Prelates, vii, 34, 40, 49-50, 68, 73, 88, 92, 137, 139, 163, 174, 194, 199, 205, 239, 248, 268
Préséance. *See* Ceremonies and etiquette.
Presidents (sovereign courts), 48, 50, 53, 56, 63, 69, 97, 112, 118, 119, 134, 137, 147-150, 152, 153, 154, 155, 200, 216
Présidiaux. *See* Lower courts.
Prévost, Antoine-François, abbé, 233, 262
Prévôtés. *See* Lower courts.
Privileges and immunities, 14-15, 17, 27-29, 66-67, 87, 103, 112-113, 147, 170, 193, 201, 227, 240, 248, 251-252
Procureurs-généraux. *See* Gens du roi.
Protestants, 220, 224, 225, 226
Provence, 27, 36, 38, 42, 103-104, 119, 125, 126, 129, 130, 133, 134, 157, 164, 165, 194, 195, 196, 203, 204, 213-214, 220, 259, 265. *See also* Aix-en-Provence, Marseille.
Public sentiment, 3, 9, 43, 98-104, 183-184, 189, 206-207, 269
Pucelle, René, abbé, 85, 101, 139

Regent and Regency, ix, 5, 6, 41, 72, 83, 84, 90, 91, 97, 98, 103, 114, 121, 162, 174-187, 190-192, 193, 195, 197, 199, 200, 210, 213, 226, 242, 248, 259, 263, 268, 269
Reims, archbishop, 174, 179, 181; university, 220
Remonstrances and registration, 11, 79-104, 120, 161-162, 163, 189, 192, 194, 196, 197, 198, 199, 223, 224, 239, 247, 248, 256, 257, 258-259
Rennes, 50, 75, 92, 136, 205, 256; Parlement of Brittany, 38, 43, 46, 48, 53, 56, 73-75, 86, 90, 110, 113, 130, 153, 154-155, 192, 193, 196, 220, 224, 259, 265, 266
Requêtes, chambres des, 47, 48, 85, 140
"Resignatio in favorem," 107-109, 116, 149
Retz, Jean-François-Paul de Gondi, cardinal de, 226, 233
Richelieu, Armand-Jean du Plessis, cardinal, duc de, vii, 7, 9, 10, 19, 62, 110, 175, 213, 229, 265, 269
Richelieu, Louis-François-Armand de Vignerot du Plessis, duc de, 84, 180-181, 186, 207, 259-260
Richer d'Aube, François, 232
Rome, 61, 63, 72, 89, 117, 121, 218, 223, 228, 229, 231, 240, 243, 251, 270. *See also* Germanist-Romanist controversy.
Rouen, 46, 129, 132, 136-137, 235, 256; Parlement of Normandy, 38, 43, 51, 52, 53, 64, 90, 116, 150, 193, 220, 265-266; Chambre des Comptes, 39, 52
Rousseau, Jean-Jacques, 230, 236
Roussillon, 38, 46, 89, 220. *See also* Perpignan.

Rural gentry, vii, 28, 33, 144, 206, 207, 214, 215, 221, 265, 269

Saint-Palaye, Jean-Baptiste de La Curne de, 245
Saint-Esprit, Ordre du, 33, 215
Saint-Louis, Ordre de, 18, 143, 204
Saint-Pierre, Charles-Irénée Castel, abbé de, 120, 176, 209, 234, 235
Saint-Simon, Louis de Rouvroy, duc de, 3, 5, 19, 55, 69, 72-73, 76, 83, 84, 86, 100, 120, 121, 122, 132, 144, 175-183, 186, 190, 191, 200, 207, 214, 226, 227, 259, 262, 271
Salons, 204-206, 233, 245
Secrétaires du roi, 65, 128
Seigneurial justice, 85, 168-169, 227, 240-241, 248, 267
Seigneuries and châteaux, 69, 131, 148, 162-169, 201, 235, 248
Sénéchaux. *See* Lower courts.
Serres, Olivier de, 225
Sévigné, Marie de Rabutin-Chantal, marquise de, 9, 110, 199, 204, 260
Seyssel, Claude de, 223, 229, 238, 262
Sieyès, Emmanuel-Joseph, abbé, 29-30
Soupirs de la France esclave, 226, 229
Sovereign courts, viii, 11, 16-17, 28, 35-58, 66, 130, 230, 239; types and distribution, 37-41; rivalries, 41-44; palais de justice, 44-46, 85; subdivisions and grades of members, 46-51; number and special position of parlementaires, 51-55; costumes and ceremonies, 55-57; political power, 79-104, 188-201, 247-249; venality of offices as applied to, 111-115, 149; hold of robe dynasties, 133-137; relation to provincial estates, 193-197. *See also* various types of courts, e.g., parlements, chambres des comptes.
Strasbourg, 141, 220
Swedish nobility, 133
"Système." *See* John Law.

Taille. *See* Taxation.
Taxation, 6, 14-15, 17, 27-29, 32-33, 35, 36, 39-40, 60-61, 66-67, 87, 100, 103, 230, 241, 247, 248; capitation, 14-15, 17, 32-33, 147-148, 190, 197, 198, 242; centième, 197, 199; cinquantième, 84, 87, 90, 100, 197, 199; dixième, 15, 17, 84, 87, 104, 162, 190, 197, 198, 242; gabelle, 28, 35, 39, 103; "joyeux avènement," 40, 66-67; taille, 17, 27-28, 39, 60, 63, 196; vingtième, 102
Tiraqueau, André, 60, 62, 261
Titles and names, 68-69, 70, 129-130, 131, 134, 162
Toulouse, x, 49, 65, 71, 79, 127, 129, 131-132, 136, 141, 150, 156, 157, 158, 159, 164, 165, 205, 213, 220, 223, 235, 236, 256, 261, 270; Parlement of Languedoc, 37, 38, 43, 46, 47, 48, 49, 53, 56, 65, 90, 129, 130, 141, 143, 150, 178, 194, 210, 216, 220, 236, 256, 258, 265
Toulouse, Comte de. *See* Légitimés.
Tournelle, 47, 48
Town houses, 131, 148, 155-158, 169, 205-206, 211, 235, 248
Trésoriers de France, 54, 65, 140
Turgot, Anne-Robert-Jacques, baron de l'Aulne, vii, 34, 137, 139

Unigenitus, 4, 85, 87, 88, 100

Vacations, chambres des, 47, 48
Valbonnais, Jean Pierre Moret de Bourchenu, marquis de, 158, 216, 217, 218, 220
Vauban, Sébastien Le Prestre, marquis de, 29, 230
Venality of offices, ix, 35-36, 50, 105-123, 148-155, 200, 226, 230, 238, 247, 255, 267
Villars, Claude-Louis-Hector, duc de, 42, 199, 207, 259
Vincennes, Declaration of, 83
Vindiciae contra tyrannos, 225
Vingtième. *See* Taxation.
Visconti, Primi, 70-71
Voltaire, François-Marie Arouet, 102, 123, 168-169, 174, 210, 216, 233, 243, 244

Walpole, Horace, earl of Orford, 200-201
Walpole, Sir Robert, 173, 182
Wealth and private fortunes, 32-33, 144-145, 147-170, 188, 203, 207-208, 248, 268

Harvard Historical Studies

(*Out of print titles are omitted.*)

23. *Robert Howard Lord.* The Second Partition of Poland: A Study in Diplomatic History. 1915.
32. *Lawrence D. Steefel.* The Schleswig-Holstein Question. 1932.
33. *Lewis George Vander Velde.* The Presbyterian Churches and the Federal Union, 1861–1869. 1932.
34. *Howard Levi Gray.* The Influence of the Commons on Early Legislation. 1932.
35. *Donald Cope McKay.* The National Workshops: A Study in the French Revolution of 1848. 1933.
36. *Chester Wells Clark.* Franz Joseph and Bismarck: The Diplomacy of Austria before the War of 1866. 1934.
37. *Roland Dennis Hussey.* The Caracas Company, 1728–1784: A Study in the History of Spanish Monopolistic Trade. 1934.
38. *Dwight Erwin Lee.* Great Britain and the Cyprus Convention Policy of 1878. 1934.
39. *Paul Rice Doolin.* The Fronde. 1935.
40. *Arthur McCandless Wilson.* French Foreign Policy during the Administration of Cardinal Fleury, 1726–1743. 1936.
41. *Harold Charles Deutsch.* The Genesis of Napoleonic Imperialism. 1938.
42. *Ernst Christian Helmreich.* The Diplomacy of the Balkan Wars, 1912–1913. 1938.
43. *Albert Henry Imlah.* Lord Ellenborough: A Biography of Edward Law, Earl of Ellenborough, Governor-General of India. 1939.
44. *Vincent Mary Scramuzza.* The Emperor Claudius. 1940.
48. *Jack H. Hexter.* The Reign of King Pym. 1941.
49. *George Hoover Rupp.* A Wavering Friendship: Russia and Austria, 1876–1878. 1941.
52. *John Black Sirich.* The Revolutionary Committees in the Departments of France. 1943.
53. *Henry Frederick Schwarz.* The Imperial Privy Council in the Seventeenth Century. 1943.
55. *Holden Furber.* John Company at Work. 1948.
57. *John Howes Gleason.* The Genesis of Russophobia in Great Britain. 1950.
58. *Charles Coulston Gillispie.* Genesis and Geology: A Study in the Relations of Scientific Thought, Natural Theology, and Social Opinion in Great Britain, 1790–1850. 1951.
59. *Richard Humphrey.* Georges Sorel, Prophet without Honor: A Study in Anti-Intellectualism. 1951.

60. *Robert G. L. Waite.* Vanguard of Nazism: The Free Corps Movement in Postwar Germany 1918–1923. 1952.
62. *John King Fairbank.* Trade and Diplomacy on the China Coast: The Opening of the Treaty Ports, 1842–1854. Vol. I. Text. 1953.
63. *John King Fairbank.* Trade and Diplomacy on the China Coast . . . 1842–1854. Vol. II. Reference Notes, Appendices, Bibliography, Glossary. 1953.
64. *Franklin L. Ford.* Robe and Sword: The Regrouping of the French Aristocracy after Louis XIV. 1953.
65. *Carl E. Schorske.* German Social Democracy, 1905–1917. The Development of the Great Schism. 1955.
66. *Wallace Evan Davies.* Patriotism on Parade: The Story of Veterans' and Hereditary Organizations in America, 1783–1900. 1955.
67. *Harold Schwartz.* Samuel Gridley Howe: Social Reformer, 1801–1876. 1956.
68. *Bryce D. Lyon.* From Fief to Indenture: The Transition from Feudal to Non-Feudal Contract in Western Europe. 1957.
69. *Stanley J. Stein.* Vassouras: A Brazilian Coffee Country, 1850–1900. 1957.
70. *Thomas F. McGann.* Argentina, the United States, and the Inter-American System, 1880–1914. 1957.
71. *Ernest R. May.* The World War and American Isolation, 1914–1917. 1958.
72. *John B. Blake.* Public Health in the Town of Boston, 1630–1822. 1959.